TEACHING SYSTEMATIC SYNTHETIC PHONICS
IN PRIMARY SCHOOLS

Sara Miller McCune founded SAGE Publishing in 1965 to support the dissemination of usable knowledge and educate a global community. SAGE publishes more than 1000 journals and over 800 new books each year, spanning a wide range of subject areas. Our growing selection of library products includes archives, data, case studies and video. SAGE remains majority owned by our founder and after her lifetime will become owned by a charitable trust that secures the company's continued independence.

Los Angeles | London | New Delhi | Singapore | Washington DC | Melbourne

TEACHING SYSTEMATIC SYNTHETIC PHONICS
IN PRIMARY SCHOOLS

3RD EDITION

WENDY JOLLIFFE,
DAVID WAUGH and
ANGELA GILL

Learning Matters
An imprint of SAGE Publications Ltd
1 Oliver's Yard
55 City Road
London EC1Y 1SP

SAGE Publications Inc.
2455 Teller Road
Thousand Oaks, California 91320

SAGE Publications India Pvt Ltd
B 1/I 1 Mohan Cooperative Industrial Area
Mathura Road
New Delhi 110 044

SAGE Publications Asia-Pacific Pte Ltd
3 Church Street
#10-04 Samsung Hub
Singapore 049483

First published in 2013
Second Edition published in 2015
Third Edition published in 2019

Library of Congress Control Number: 2018961091

British Library Cataloguing in Publication data

A catalogue record for this book is available from the British Library.

Editor: Amy Thornton
Senior project editor: Chris Marke
Project Management: Deer Park Productions, Tavistock
Marketing Manager: Lorna Patkai
Cover Design: Wendy Scott
Typeset by: C&M Digitals (P) Ltd, Chennai, India
Printed in the UK

ISBN: 978 1 5264 3639 9
ISBN: 978 1 5264 3640 5 (pbk)

At SAGE we take sustainability seriously. Most of our products are printed in the UK using responsibly sourced papers and boards. When we print overseas we ensure sustainable papers are used as measured by the Egmont grading system. We undertake an annual audit to monitor our sustainability.

Contents

Acknowledgements

With thanks to Rebecca Chester for contributions to planning and tracking children's learning and to students from Durham University for their contributions to research for this book. Thanks also to Busy Bears Children's Day Nursery, Durham, and Wingate Primary School, County Durham.

About the authors

Wendy Jolliffe is Professor of Education and worked in Initial Teacher Education (ITE) for 14 years, latterly as Head of Teacher Education at the University of Hull. She worked previously as a Regional Adviser for the National Strategies and advised ITE providers on effective provision for literacy. She has published extensively in Primary English and Cooperative Learning.

David Waugh is a former deputy headteacher who worked in ITE from 1990 at the University of Hull, where he led the PGCE course and became Head of Department. In 2008 he was appointed as one of two (the other being Wendy) National Strategies Regional Advisers for ITE. He currently lectures at Durham University. He has published extensively in primary English, as well as developing e-learning resources for National Strategies for English, mathematics and mentoring and coaching. David also writes children's stories, including *The Wishroom*, which was written with 45 children from 15 East Durham primary schools and published in 2017.

Angela Gill (formerly Carss) is a former primary school teacher and English subject leader. She taught in schools in County Durham and Bath and North East Somerset for more than 20 years. She is the Primary English Subject Lead at Durham University, where she teaches both undergraduates and postgraduates. She has written books, articles and chapters on many aspects of Primary English for ITE students and primary practitioners.

Introduction

Background

The teaching of reading has been the subject of extensive research and polarised views. As Chall set out in a seminal study in 1967, it has become known as the 'great debate' and described by Goodman (1967) as the 'reading wars'. Such a debate has led to diametrically opposed views: either promoting 'whole language' or learning with what is often called 'real books', or the teaching of specific skills to enable children to decode texts – in particular phonics. It is not only among academics and educationalists that such a debate has raged, however; it has become an area of political interest, particularly in the UK. Since 2006, there has been increased emphasis on the teaching of phonics, and in 2010 the Government intensified the scrutiny this received and set out requirements for schools and those training to teach to become proficient in systematic synthetic phonics.

The evidence upon which such requirements are based draws on a range of research. It was a study in Clackmannanshire in Scotland that triggered much of the focus on phonics. This study, carried out by Professor Rhona Johnston and Dr Joyce Watson (2005), looked at 300 children in the first year of the Scottish primary school system. It compared three different teaching methods: synthetic phonics; analytic phonics; and an analytic phonics method that included systematic phonemic awareness teaching. At the end of the programme, those children who had been taught by synthetic phonics were found to be on average seven months ahead of the other two groups in reading.

Previously, during the 1990s, a wealth of research on the effective teaching of reading, most notably Adams' seminal work (1990), indicated the clear need for explicit teaching of phonics within a meaningful context of texts. Other key findings from Bryant (1993) and Goswami (1995) highlighted the need for developing phonological awareness. The work carried out by Clay (1979), through Reading Recovery to support pupils in need of additional support, emphasised the need to make explicit how print works, how to successfully link reading and writing, and to ensure swift intervention when children begin to exhibit a lack of effective progress.

More recently, a great deal of progress has been made in understanding the development of reading, not least through advances in neuroscience: as Frith (1998: 1051) states: 'reading literally changes the brain' and does so differently in different languages, which is an important consideration in teaching and learning phonics.

A key milestone in the adoption of synthetic phonics was the *Independent Review of the Teaching of Early Reading* produced in 2006 by Sir Jim Rose (The Rose Review), which drew on research findings, consultation with practitioners, teachers, trainers, resource and policy makers, and visits to schools and training events. The recommendations of the review set out best practice in the teaching of early reading and phonics including:

- clear guidance on developing children's speaking and listening skills;

- high-quality, systematic phonic work as defined by the review should be taught;

- the knowledge, skills and understanding that constitute high-quality work should be taught as the prime approach in learning to decode print (to read) and encode (to write/spell);

- phonic work should be set within a broad and rich language curriculum that takes full account of developing the four interdependent strands of language: speaking, listening, reading and writing, and enlarging children's stock of words.

The recommendations of The Rose Review have since been widely adopted. Measures to monitor the adoption have included a specific focus by Ofsted for the inspection of schools and teacher training providers, and in the Teachers' Standards in 2012, a specific statement that to gain qualified teacher status trainees should,

> *if teaching early reading, demonstrate a clear understanding of systematic synthetic phonics.*

> *(DfE, 2011, para. 3)*

It is important to remember that The Rose Review highlighted that the teaching of reading requires two main components. First, being able to decode the letters on the page and map these to the sounds of the language and then pronounce these to make words, building up a store of known words: called word recognition. The second key component is being able to comprehend what has been read: called language comprehension. These are integrated processes and both are equally important. Learning phonics supports the decoding element and helps unlock what is often termed the 'alphabetic code'. While this book focuses on the effective teaching of systematic synthetic phonics, teaching phonics alone will not produce good readers – children also need to develop the skills of language comprehension.

It is not just in the UK that the focus on teaching reading and the use of phonics has received government focus, however. In the US, the National Reading Panel (NRP) report by the National Institute of Child Health and Human Development (NICHD) provided a meta-analysis of research into the teaching of reading and concluded that

> *systematic phonics instruction proved to be universally effective, it should be implemented as part of literacy programs to teach beginning reading, as well as to prevent and remediate reading difficulties.*

> *(NICHD, 2000, p.2–89)*

The NRP found that for beginning reading, findings from a meta-analysis of evidence-based research consistently indicated that direct, systematic instruction in phonics makes a significantly greater contribution to children's development in reading, writing, spelling and comprehension than alternative approaches involving unsystematic or no phonics instruction. The NRP also emphasised that 'systematic phonics instruction should be integrated with other reading instruction to create a balanced reading program' (NICHD, p.2–136) and that it should not dominate the teaching of reading.

In Australia, a review of research into the teaching of reading also concluded:

> {T}he incontrovertible finding from the extensive body of local and international evidence-based reading research is that for children during the early years of schooling, they must first master the alphabetic code via systematic, explicit, and intensive instruction in: phonemic awareness, phonics, reading fluency, vocabulary, and reading comprehension strategies. Because these are foundational and essential skills for the development of competence in reading, writing and spelling, they must be taught early, explicitly, and taught well.
>
> (Australian Government, DoEST, 2005, p.25)

However, even although there have been substantial studies reviewing the research literature, the debate still continues and critics of a focus on systematic phonics argue that there is

> no reliable empirical evidence that synthetic phonics offers the vast majority of beginners the best route to becoming skilled readers.
>
> (Wyse and Goswami, 2008, p.691)

Wyse and Goswami argue that greater and more extensive research is required to warrant such a universal introduction of a specific teaching method. They further state that while evidence supports approaches based on systematic tuition in phonics, greater research is needed to determine the effectiveness of discrete systematic phonics compared with contextualised systematic phonics. The latter refers to phonics instruction contextualised with sentence-level and/or text-level work such as reading of connected text.

One of the most vocal opponents of the teaching of synthetic phonics is Andrew Davis (2012), who argues that in England there is 'A monstrous regimen of synthetic phonics' (p.560). He argues that the research base for this is shaky and he is: 'opposing the universal imposition of text decoding outside "real" reading contexts' (p.562), and that decisions about methods of teaching reading should be left to teachers.

As Hattie (2003) notes, one element is paramount in success in teaching reading and every aspect of learning: the expertise of the teacher. Hattie asserts that governments and educationalists seek solutions to low standards of pupil attainment in a number of ways:

> *Interventions at the structural, home, policy, or school level is like searching for your wallet which you lost in the bushes, under the lamp post because that is where there is light. The answer lies elsewhere – it lies in the person who gently closes the classroom door and performs the teaching act – the person who puts into place the end effects of so many policies, who interprets these policies, and who is alone with students during their 15,000 hours of schooling.*

(2003, pp.2–3)

This book focuses on the teacher, and specifically support for the trainee teacher, in order to deepen understanding to enable effective practice.

About the book

This third edition explores a range of aspects of systematic synthetic phonics teaching and includes references to current research findings in the teaching of early reading and phonics. It provides the trainee teacher and experienced teacher alike with a balance of research and practice to ensure an in-depth understanding of what works in the effective teaching of phonics. It starts with the clear aim to support subject knowledge in Section 1. It will help in ensuring understanding of the four key elements in teaching phonics:

1. *grapheme–phoneme correspondences (that is, the alphabetic code) in a clearly defined, incremental sequence*
2. *to synthesise (blend) phonemes (sounds) in order all through a word to read it*
3. *to segment words into their constituent phonemes for spelling*
4. *that blending and segmenting are reversible processes.*

(Ofsted, 2014, p.17)

Section 1 provides a detailed review of the key aspects of the alphabetic code, from discriminating sounds and phonemes to teaching long vowel phonemes and their different spellings and pronunciations, as well as common challenges.

In Section 2, the book looks at effective pedagogy, ranging from the early years and the need to set phonics teaching within a broad and rich language curriculum, to Key Stage 2 where phonics is often ignored to the detriment of developing spelling skills. Aspects such as ensuring a systematic progression are dealt with in depth, together with how to plan for teaching phonics. Methods of assessing pupils' progress, including the statutory phonics screening check introduced in 2012, are discussed, together with information on tracking and intervention programmes to support children who are in danger of falling behind. Multi-sensory and interactive methods are stressed, together with a review of different phonics programmes, set against the DfE (2011) criteria for high-quality phonics teaching. This third edition also includes a chapter that looks at the contribution of technology to the teaching of phonics and, particularly, the use of tablets and apps to support children.

National Curriculum links

The 2013 National Curriculum sets out two dimensions in the programmes of study to develop pupils' competence in reading: word recognition and comprehension. It emphasises the importance of developing skills in both dimensions and that 'phonics should be emphasised in the early teaching of reading to beginners (i.e. unskilled readers) when they start school' (DfE, 2013, p.15).

Each chapter provides case studies and activities directly related to the experiences of trainees and beginner teachers, to exemplify what works. Self-assessment questions at the end of each chapter are provided to enhance and consolidate understanding. Answers to these questions can be found at the end of the book. In addition, all chapters, with the exception of chapters 10 and 14, include a more detailed audit and test section with answers, so that readers can check their knowledge and understanding. Chapters also provide references to further reading and an extensive range of research into the teaching and learning of reading.

References

Adams, M.J. (1990) *Beginning to Read: Thinking and Learning about Print*. Cambridge, MA: MIT Press.

Australian Government, Department of Education, Science and Training (2005) *Teaching Reading: Report and Recommendations. National enquiry into the teaching of literacy*. Barton: Department of Education, Science and Training.

Bryant, P. (1993) 'Phonological aspects of learning to read', in R. Beard (ed.), *Teaching Literacy: Balancing Perspectives*. London: Hodder & Stoughton.

Chall, J.S. (1967) *Learning to Read: The Great Debate*. New York: McGraw-Hill.

Clay, M. (1979) *The Early Detection of Reading Difficulties: A Diagnostic Survey with Reading Recovery Procedures*, 2nd edn. London: Heinemann.

Davis, A. (2012) 'A monstrous regimen of synthetic phonics: Fantasies of research-based teaching 'methods' versus real teaching', *Journal of Philosophy of Education*, 46 (4): 560–73.

DfE (2011) *Teachers' Standards in England from September 2012*. London: Department for Education.

DfE (2013) *The National Curriculum in England*. Available from: www.gov.uk/dfe/ nationalcurriculum (accessed 1/3/15).

Frith, U. (1998) 'Editorial: Literally changing the brain', *Brain*, *121*: 1051–2.

Goodman, K.S. (1967) 'Reading: A psycholinguistic guessing game', *Journal of the Reading Specialist*, *4*: 126–35.

Goswami, U. (1995) 'Phonological development and reading by analogy: What is analogy and what is not', *Journal of Research in Reading*, *18* (2).

Hattie, J. (2003) *Teachers Make a Difference: What is the Research Evidence?* Paper presented at the Australian Council for Educational Research (ACER) Annual Conference on Building Teacher Quality, Melbourne, 19–21 October. Available at www.acer.edu.au (accessed 29/01/12).

Johnston, R. and Watson, J. (2005) *The Effects of Synthetic Phonics Teaching on Reading and Spelling Attainment: A Seven Year Longitudinal Study*. Edinburgh: Scottish Executive.

National Institute of Child Health and Human Development (2000). *Report of the National Reading Panel*. 'Teaching children to read: An evidence-based assessment of the scientific research literature on reading and its implications for reading instruction' (NIH Publication No. 00-4769). Washington, DC: US Government Printing Office.

Ofsted (2014) Getting them reading early. Distance learning materials for inspecting reading. Reference 110122. Available at https://www.gov.uk/government/publications/getting-them-reading-early (accessed 13/4/18).

Rose, J. (2006) *Independent Review of the Teaching of Early Reading, Final Report, March 2006* (The Rose Review – Ref: 0201-2006DOC-EN). Nottingham: DfES.

Wyse, D. and Goswami, U. (2008) 'Synthetic phonics and the teaching of reading', *British Educational Research Journal*, *34* (6): 691–710.

SECTION 1 SUBJECT KNOWLEDGE FOR TEACHERS

1. Discriminating sounds and phonemes

Learning Outcomes

By the end of this chapter, you will have:

- an understanding of the importance of being able to correctly discrimate individual phonemes in words;
- an understanding of key terminology;
- an understanding of the debate concerning the role of phonological awareness training;
- an overview of the difficulties faced by adults in being able to discriminate phonemes and ways of overcoming them;
- an understanding of different methods of teaching phonemic awareness;
- an understanding of the importance of developing children's vocabulary alongside phonological awareness.

Teachers' Standards

3. Demonstrate good subject and curriculum knowledge:

- demonstrate a critical understanding of developments in the subject and curriculum areas, and promote the value of scholarship;
- if teaching early reading, demonstrate a clear understanding of systematic synthetic phonics.

Criteria for assuring high-quality phonic work (DfE, 2011)

Enable children to start learning phonic knowledge and skills using a systematic, synthetic programme by the age of five, with the expectation that they will be

(Continued)

(Continued)

fluent readers having secured word recognition skills by the end of Key Stage 1 (see note 2).

Note 2: Teachers will make principled, professional judgements about when to start on a systematic, synthetic programme of phonic work but it is reasonable to expect that the great majority of children will be capable of, and benefit from doing so by the age of five. It is equally important for the programme to be designed so that children become fluent readers having secured word recognition skills by the end of Key Stage 1.

Introduction

This chapter will enable you to understand the importance of developing phonological awareness and the key differences between phonological awareness and phonemic awareness. Having a clear understanding of such underlying concepts will support effective phonics teaching. The chapter will also explore the common and surprising issue that discriminating phonemes in words can be difficult for literate adults. This is because once we have a thorough knowledge of the spelling system of our language, we focus on the written representation of a word even when a word is said and do not think of the individual sounds that make up the words. Ways of supporting this for adults, or those new to learning phonics, will be reviewed. The chapter will also provide an overview of ways of teaching phonemic awareness and demonstrate how developing a teaching programme involves commencing the teaching of phonics early, alongside phonemic awareness training. To support this, you will be provided with an overview of children's development of the ability to perceive and pronounce sounds. This knowledge of development patterns will enable you to identify when children may need additional help. A further area addressed is the need to focus on individual phonemes, and the issues around letter names, which can cause confusion. A review of the importance of developing vocabulary alongside phonological awareness concludes the chapter. You will find the glossary on page 311 will help with any unfamiliar terminology related to phonics.

Theoretical perspectives/subject knowledge

It is first important to have a clear understanding of the difference between phonological awareness and phonemic awareness.

Phonological awareness

Phonological awareness is the understanding of different ways that oral language can be divided into smaller components and manipulated. Phonological awareness is defined by Torgensen et al. (1994, p.276) as 'sensitivity to, or explicit awareness of, the phonological structure of the words in language'. Phonological awareness is a broad term that encompasses levels of manipulation of sounds in language. It is a skill which enables a child to analyse the sound structure of a language (Schuele and Boudreau, 2008), and includes dividing words into syllables, identifying and generating rhymes and matching words with the same initial sound. Phonological awareness therefore is the ability to perceive, recall and manipulate sounds and specifically within language. Phonological awareness is often confused with phonics, but a child can demonstrate such ability orally without any understanding of the correspondence between letters and the sounds they make. In phonics, children are working with print symbols or letters that represent the sounds of oral language.

Phonemic awareness

Phonemic awareness is a subset of the broader term, phonological awareness, and relates to the ability to perceive and manipulate phonemes in spoken words. Examples of phonemic awareness skills includes:

Blending sounds, e.g. /h/o/t/ = *hot*.

Identifying individual sounds and segmenting words into their constituent phonemes, e.g. the first sound in *hot* = /h/, the final sound (/t/ in *hot*) and the medial sound (/o/ in *hot*).

Substituting sounds, e.g. substituting the initial sound /l/ to make *lot*.

Ofsted (2014) emphasises the importance of being able to hear individual phonemes in words and provides guidance for inspectors for this. This highlights that this skill needs developing in adults as well as children, but for adults it is usually a case of making explicit what they may know implicitly.

Activity

Checking your understanding of terminology

Read the following transcripts between two trainees and their class teachers and decide whether the issue they are discussing relates to phonological or phonemic awareness.

(Continued)

(Continued)

Trainee 1: I have been assessing the pupils' phonic knowledge and realise that several of them are struggling to hear sounds correctly. I have tried getting these pupils to say words that rhyme, so when I say *cat* the children have to say *sat* or something similar.

Teacher 1: You could try checking if they can distinguish rhyme by asking them for the odd one out if you give them a number of words that rhyme and one that doesn't. If they can't then we need to look at being able to discriminate sounds in the environment, you will find Letters and Sounds Phase 1 is helpful for this.

Trainee 2: I have been assessing the pupils' phonic knowledge and realise that several of them are unable to give me all the phonemes in a CVC word I have said. How can I support them?

Teacher 2: I would suggest you assess whether it is only, say, the middle sound they are struggling with, and if so work on that. They can usually hear the initial and final sounds more easily.

Trainee and Teacher 1 were discussing phonological awareness and specifically difficulties with the skill of rhyming. Trainee and Teacher 2 were discussing phonemic awareness and the ability to discriminate phonemes in consonant-vowel-consonant (CVC) words.

Phonological awareness training

The importance of phonological awareness training has dominated the research literature in this field and the National Reading Panel (NICHD, 2000) identified over 2,000 studies in the area. Harrison reiterated the general view of its importance: 'Unless you have phonemic awareness ... it is impossible to gain much from instruction in phonics' (2004, p.41). A previous commonly held theory maintained that phonological awareness gradually develops in children, and this development is a lengthy process with explicit awareness of phonemes only developing in children at around six or seven years (Adams, 1990). This had a profound impact on teaching phonics and can be likened to other developmental theories, for example, in teaching mathematics where a once held belief that young children should only be expected to work with small numbers, such as one to ten, has been dispelled, as long as teaching is rooted in meaningful contexts. The contribution of phonemic awareness to children's reading has, in the USA, led to calls for systematic instruction in linking letters and sounds (NICHD, 2000). Such curricula, however, have led, in some cases, to the idea that phonemic awareness is an end in itself rather than a stepping-stone to improved literacy.

With regard to phonological awareness, language development studies demonstrate that awareness of phonemes is present at birth, and by about six months children begin to extract words from the stream of speech they hear. Babies' early babbling demonstrates this too, with babies around the world all saying consonant/vowel sounds, e.g. *ba*, *da*. By three years of age, children are generally capable of demonstrating what they know, and one study (Chaney, 1992) found that 93 per cent of three-year-olds could listen to a sequence of phonemes and blend them into a word. Of particular interest in this study is that children of the same age had enormous difficulty with what has been regarded as the more simple tasks – rhyming and alliteration.

A further misconception is that phonemic awareness is difficult to teach as phonemes are difficult to separate in words and consonants cannot be pronounced without a vowel (in fact, this only applies to the voiced consonants – b, d, g, j, l). If it is accepted that young children are able to discriminate and manipulate phonemes at the age of three, researchers have questioned whether all children need a specific programme to teach this in readiness for learning grapheme–phoneme correspondences. McGuinness (2004) provides a detailed review of 72 studies and the meta-analysis revealed that such training had moderate impact on reading but, when the training is merely auditory, the impact on reading and spelling is substantially reduced. She concludes that 'being phonemically aware has little functional utility' (2004, p.157).

Research does, however, indicate that children who show a lack of progress in early phonics teaching benefit from specific phonological awareness training (Hatcher et al., 2004). This reinforces the need for early identification of difficulties, which will be reviewed in detail in Chapter 11.

For a more detailed discussion of the research in this area, see pages 10–12.

Adult phonemic awareness

For adults, the issues are different. They are not explicitly aware of individual phonemes in words as their attention is drawn to the meaning, unless the word is unfamiliar and then phonic strategies may be applied, as in unusual technical words. Generally, once the alphabetic code is mastered, the phonemes are at a subconscious level. In contrast, children are able to discern phonemes aurally as they begin the process of learning phonics, but adults are immersed in visual print-borne information and it is difficult to hear the sounds rather than focus on the letters. One common mistake in teaching phonics is that adults use their knowledge of the letters in the written word, as this overrides the number of phonemes in the word. This is clearly demonstrated by asking adults to say how many sounds are in a word such as *stretch* – and an assorted number will be given. The common use of consonant clusters at the beginning of words in English adds to the confusion, so that *str* is sometimes perceived to be one phoneme, when in fact it is a blend of three different phonemes, so that /s/ /t/ /r/ /e/ /tch/ has five phonemes: the *tch* is a trigraph – three letters making one phoneme. The list below contains other examples of common blends. The slashes indicate the division between phonemes:

sp, as in *spoon* /s/p/oo/n/

st as in *star* /s/t/ar/

sc as in *scarf* /s/c/ar/f/

sm, as in *smug* /s/m/u/g/

sn, as in *snack* /s/n/a/ck/

sl as in *slip* /s/l/i/p/

sw as in *swan* /s/w/a/n/

tw as in *twin* /t/w/i/n/

dw as in *dwarf* /d/w/ar/f/

cr as in *crab* /c/r/a/b/

gr as in *grain* /g/r/ai/n/

fr as in *frog* /f/r/o/g/

bl as in *blot* /b/l/o/t/

cl as in *clock* /c/l/o/ck/

fl as in *fly* /f/l/y/

pr as in *pram* /p/r/a/m/

br as in *brush* /b/r/u/sh/

dr as in *drag* /d/r/a/g/

pl as in *plum* /p/l/u/m/

spl as in *splash* /s/p/l/a/sh/

str as in *string* /s/t/r/i/ng/

When you are learning to teach phonics, a key aspect is the need to be able to differentiate or segment the phonemes in words. Ways to support this include:

- making use of a phoneme chart (for example, the chart contained in *Letters and Sounds*, 'Notes of Guidance for Practitioners and Teachers' (DfES, 2007, p.16) or the chart contained in Jolliffe (2007, p.58);

- ensuring the words are said clearly and slowly. Each distinctive sound represents an individual phoneme, for example *brick* = /b/r/i/ck/;

- awareness of consonant blends where consonant letters placed at the beginning and end of words are blended together, but they consist of separate phonemes. For example, in the word *strap* we hear five phonemes: /s/t/r/a/p/;

- focusing on the sounds and not the spelling when counting phonemes or segmenting words into phonemes;

- referring to the international phonetic alphabet, which is included in the National Curriculum (DfE, 2013, p.73) or at the front of dictionaries; for example, the *Oxford English Dictionary* and can be a very useful tool when there is any confusion identifying individual phonemes (for a reference chart, see www.antimoon.com/how/pronunc-soundsipa.htm).

Blending

Alongside being able to segment words into their constituent phonemes, it is also useful to practise the reversible skill of 'blending'. Try this with the activity below.

Activity

Blending unfamiliar words

Read the following unfamiliar words:

> phalanstery
> doronicium
> palmaceous

You will probably have started at the left, converted the letters into sounds, blended them, and arrived at a pronunciation of the word. This is known as 'blending'. It is a sophisticated skill that literate adults have acquired over many years. Blending individual phonemes is only needed for words that have never been read before, such as the words above. Literate people try to work out new words by blending the sounds. They rarely ask others, or guess at words, but poor readers do. It is, therefore, very important to teach and provide opportunities for children to practise blending phonemes into words. One way of doing this with young children is to use 'robot talk': to segment words into phonemes and then practise blending the phonemes into words. This is discussed in greater length in Chapter 8.

Strategies for teaching phonemic awareness

The following are suggested strategies for teaching phonemic awareness, which you may like to use when you are teaching the correspondence between graphemes and phonemes.

The use of phoneme frames can both support practitioners' knowledge and be an effective teaching tool. Using this method, children segment written words into the corresponding phonemes by placing the graphemes in separate boxes. You may like to provide boxes of three, four, five or more sections on a laminated sheet which children can write on with a dry-wipe pen and then erase for future use. For example, *splash*:

s	p	l	a	sh

'Phoneme fingers' is another method of supporting children in practising segmenting words into phonemes. Here you say a word, ask the children to repeat it and then to count individually the number of phonemes as they say it. They then show you how many 'phoneme fingers' are in a word. You may also like them to pretend to write the letters on each finger for each phoneme.

Phoneme 'buttons' are used to present a written version of the word on an easel or interactive whiteboard, then place 'buttons' or dots underneath each phoneme, using longer dashes for digraphs or trigraphs, for example:

b r igh t

· · __.

Development of phonology

Children's ability to talk is well developed before beginning to learn to read and write. This means they have shown that they are able to segment the stream of speech into words and are able to pronounce them. As the skills of talking, reading and writing are linked, it is important to have an understanding of the normal development of children's ability to perceive and pronounce the speech sounds of their language. Children from an early age develop the ability to perceive sounds, and from around 12 months are tuned in to phonetic patterns in their own language. Learning to say the sounds is dependent on the development of motor skills. Vowel sounds appear early, as do consonants made at the front of the mouth (in English *b*, *p* and later *t* and *d*). Single consonants are heard before clusters, so that *stop* becomes *sop*, while unstressed syllables and final consonants are often omitted – with *banana* becoming *nana*. For a more detailed table showing this acquisition, see Dodd et al. (2005). It is worth realising that some children may be five years old before being able to correctly pronounce the range of phonemes in English. In general, children's early speech problems are often remedied and this does not impact on their ability to read and spell correctly. However, where concerns persist, it is always worth checking with a special needs coordinator in a school and, following discussions with parents or carers, a referral may be made to a speech therapist.

Teaching phonological awareness

As discussed above, it is not necessary for most children to spend a lengthy time on developing their ability to discriminate sounds in the environment generally, and then to progress from larger units of sounds (syllables) to smaller units (onsets and rimes, alliteration and rhymes), and finally to phonemes as a specific teaching programme. Phase 1 of *Letters and Sounds* (DfES, 2007) centres on providing a broad and rich language experience for children, and this should be happening alongside any teaching of phonics. As the guidance to *Letters and Sounds* states:

> *Key features of a rich curriculum which are essential to Phase One and beyond are the range and depth of language experienced by the children. Good teaching will exploit, for example, the power of story, rhyme, drama and song to fire children's imagination and interest, thus encouraging them to use language copiously.*

(DfES, 2007, p.6)

A study by Kempert et al. (2016) looked at the effects of an early musical training, in combination with conventional phonological training, for children with weak phonological awareness skills and found a positive relationship between them. These, as well as the use of story, rhyme and drama are all key parts of a good Early Years curriculum. However, an assumption that specific teaching of awareness of sounds in the environment will progress to voiced sounds as a precursor to teaching grapheme–phoneme correspondences has led, in some cases, to a delay in teaching phonics. It is only for those children who demonstrate difficulties in discriminating and manipulating sounds that such intervention is necessary. As the research has shown, phonological awareness is developed alongside effective teaching of phonemes and their corresponding graphemes, and most effectively within a broad and rich language curriculum (see Chapter 7 for more detail of this).

Teaching letter names

Teaching letter names alongside the sounds has been another ongoing debate. However, teaching children that letters have a name and that this letter also makes a sound, generally does not confuse children. A significant problem, however, is that the complex orthography (or spelling patterns) in English mean that letters do not consistently make the same sound; for example, the letter 'c' commonly makes the sound /c/ as in cat but can also make the sound /s/ as in *ceiling*. The most common practice is to teach the alphabet and letter names very early and this knowledge acts as a basis for new knowledge, particularly when children learn that letters can make different sounds.

However, McGuinness (2004) argues that using letter names is detrimental to children's progress in learning phonics. Treiman and Tincoff (1997) found that learning letter names focuses children's attention on the syllable instead of the phoneme and blocks their conceptual understanding of how the alphabet works. An example to demonstrate this is writing words using letter–name sequences on paper and then asking someone what they spell:

Sea-oh-double-you,

aitch-ee-ay-tee,

ef-are-oh-gee

(McGuinness, 2004, p.117)

Nevertheless, while this highlights possible confusion, letter names are not written phonetically in this way. The Rose Review states that it is

sensible to teach both names and sounds of letters. Names may be easier to learn because, being syllables rather than phonemes, they are more perceptible, and also because children expect things to have names.

(Rose, 2006, para.81)

In summary, the key point to be aware of in this debate is the need to differentiate clearly between letter names and sounds so as to not confuse the two with young children. One of the benefits of the use of letter names is that the complex orthography of English means that letters do not consistently make the same sound (as, for example, the *c* in *cat* and in *circus*). Some phonics schemes delay teaching letter names and begin with the sounds; however, many children come to school knowing letter names from alphabet songs, friezes or from popular children's television programmes. As Farmer et al. (2006) state, if they already know these, it seems sensible to use them as an 'anchor' for new knowledge about sounds.

Research Focus: Combining phonological awareness training with teaching grapheme–phoneme correspondences

A large number of studies have combined training in phonological awareness with the teaching of reading-related skills such as grapheme–phoneme correspondences, and have shown increases in reading attainment (Share, 1995; Castles and Coltheart, 2004). The key is teaching both together as phonological awareness and alphabetic knowledge have a reciprocal relationship. Adams (1990) showed that phoneme awareness ability develops alongside learning to read words; that is, children who read well also have good phoneme awareness. Johnston et al. (1996) found in work with non-readers that some four-year-olds were able to recognise initial sounds in words and every phoneme in CVC words, and the ability to articulate phonemes all through a word was found in non-readers who knew the letters of the alphabet: 'This gives us an indication that becoming aware of phonemes is not just a natural skill that children acquire through learning to speak, as it is closely related to learning the alphabet and learning to recognise the printed word' (Johnston and Watson, 2007, p.17). Reading, therefore,

→

tunes children into phonemes. Even the ability to read the product names on packets and sweet wrappers has been shown to be associated with phoneme awareness ability in pre-school children (Johnston et al., 1996).

There is a danger, particularly when reviewing Phase 1 of *Letters and Sounds* (DfES, 2007), that the development of phonological awareness ability is a goal in itself, and it needs explicit training not linked to letters. It is the combination of the equally important pho-neme awareness and letter knowledge that matters. Teaching synthetic phonics, where children blend and segment phonemes using letters and words, is particularly effective in developing phonemic awareness. The key to this discussion is that lengthy periods train-ing children to hear sounds first in the environment and then gradually moving from larger units of sounds, for example syllables, to smaller parts such as onsets and rimes, and then to phonemes, is an unnecessary process. A major review of the literature by Castles and Coltheart (2004) concluded that no study has established that phoneme awareness train-ing on its own assists reading development, but there is overwhelming evidence that when phoneme awareness is taught in the context of letters it has a positive effect on learning to read. In addition, Ehri et al. (2001), in a meta-analysis of 52 studies for the US National Reading Panel, showed that when phoneme awareness was taught using letters this was statistically more effective in developing reading skill.

A further study undertaken by Hatcher et al. clarified that phonological training is not nec-essary for most children, although it is useful for those children who demonstrate delay in learning to read:

> A reading programme that contains a highly structured phonic component is sufficient for most 4 to 5-year-old children to master the alphabetic principle and to learn to read effec-tively, without additional explicit phonological training. In contrast, for young children at risk of reading delay, additional training in phoneme awareness and linking phonemes with letters is beneficial.

> (2004, p.338)

Snow also indicates some of the issues of an undue emphasis on phonological awareness training:

> The helpfulness of phonemic awareness to children exposed to initial literacy instruction has led to calls for universal instruction in phonological awareness and considerable attention to phonological awareness within early reading curricula (National Institute of Child Health and Human Development, 2000). Unfortunately, such curricula have led in some cases to the notion that phonological awareness is an end in itself, rather than a stepping-stone to better literacy learning. There is no evidence that learners need or benefit from phonological awareness curricula after Grade 2; there is evidence that a total of about 20 hours of explicit attention to phonological awareness is sufficient to produce the desired effect in almost all children (Ehri et al., 2001); and there is evidence that supporting children to write

⟶

with invented or estimated spelling generates phonological awareness as effectively as explicit curricula.

(*Snow, 2005, p.282*)

The above survey of a range of research studies indicates that an emphasis on phonological awareness training is not necessary except for children who have difficulties in discriminating sounds and thus may experience delay in learning to read.

Vocabulary and phonological awareness

There is a clear association between the development of vocabulary and phonological awareness in children. This is because if a word is not in a child's vocabulary it is likely that in decoding he or she may distort it, or even it is decoded, the meaning is not understood. For example, a child may be able to read the word *decade* using their phonic knowledge but, without understanding the word, will struggle with understanding a sentence containing it. While accurate decoding is crucial, as comprehension is the goal of reading, it requires a good vocabulary as well as good oral comprehension skills for success. Nation and Snowling's study (1977) reinforces this.

The link between vocabulary and phonological awareness is also demonstrated because, as vocabulary grows, there is pressure on the memory to store a greater number of phonological representations of words to allow discrimination between an increasing number of sounds. Walley (1993) suggests that gradually there is a restructuring of phonological representations of words from *holistic* to *segmental* representations, or phonemes, which serves to differentiate between word meanings. In other words, there is a developing ability to store and recall first the sounds of words and then smaller units or phonemes, and that this is linked to making meaning and distinguishing between words.

The impact of this is demonstrated by children who struggle from the start with learning to read, particularly if they have limited opportunities to engage with print. This is often termed the 'Matthew effect' (Stanovich, 1986), implying a biblical reference to the notion that 'the rich get richer and the poor get poorer'. If children come from disadvantaged backgrounds with limited opportunities to discover books, they may have poorer phonological awareness, poorer letter knowledge and poorer oral language skills than those who succeed easily with reading (Duff et al., 2008). Early interventions have therefore attempted to develop children's abilities in these three areas.

However, we cannot rely on vocabulary development as the main method for the development of phonological awareness, as children from socially deprived backgrounds may come to school with low levels of vocabulary. Nor can we rely solely on children being taught to read in an alphabetic language for its development, as children with reading difficulties who are able to read to some degree often continue to experience difficulties with phoneme awareness tasks.

As demonstrated in Hatcher et al.'s study (2004), for 'at risk' children there is clear benefit from explicit teaching of phonological awareness alongside reading instruction. Hence the current emphasis on the importance of systematic phonics teaching, which includes teaching phoneme segmentation and blending skills alongside the teaching of grapheme–phoneme correspondences.

Activity

The case study below provides two examples of two children's early reading development. List the key factors that support Lucy's growing success and some of the potential factors that have led to Sean's limited progress in reading.

Case Study: Lucy's and Sean's early reading development

Read the examples below of two children's early reading development.

Lucy is five and has made a good start at learning systematic phonics. She comes from a home where she has been read to frequently, and from 18 months showed a strong liking for rhyming books. Her favourite story, which she insisted on being read at around two years, was *Brown Bear, Brown Bear, What Do You See?* by Bill Martin Jr. and Eric Carle (1995). At nursery she learned an alphabet song and loved to look at a pop-up alphabet book at home with mum. She enjoyed magnetic letters and soon learned the letter names and had an alphabet puzzle and frieze she liked to look at in her bedroom. She had a circle of young friends and with constant conversations with parents and other family members she had developed a wide vocabulary. Lucy applies her knowledge to beginning to read and write. She can write her name and makes phonically plausible attempts at spelling words, for example, 'pla wiv me'.

Sean is five and attended nursery school sporadically from five years old. He lives with his mum and has had a series of different childminders from a young age. There are no books at home and Sean's frequent illnesses and ear infections have led to hearing problems. He likes to watch TV and shows little interest in books at nursery. His knowledge of stories and nursery rhymes is very limited and he prefers to be active, finding little enjoyment in listening to stories. Sean's vocabulary is largely restricted to common nouns, and he answers questions with 'yes' or 'no' and finds constructing whole sentences difficult. He enjoys anything to do with cars, and his teacher tries to engage his interest in books by sharing books and pictures about cars. She shares this with his mum and a spark of interest in books has begun. Sean writes the first letter of his name but struggles to write the rest, and his attempts at writing reflect little phonic knowledge.

The examples in this case study demonstrate the importance of the home background and developing language skills, and in particular how vocabulary development in rich spoken and literary contexts form the basis of reading development. This forms the foundation on which systematic teaching of phonics can be built.

National Curriculum links

The 2013 National Curriculum sets out two dimensions in the programmes of study to develop pupils' competence in reading: word recognition and comprehension. It emphasises the importance of developing skills in both dimensions. 'Skilled word reading involves both the speedy working out of the pronunciation of unfamiliar printed words (decoding) and the speedy recognition of familiar printed words. Underpinning both is the understanding that the letters on the page represent the sounds in spoken words. This is why phonics should be emphasised in the early teaching of reading to beginners (i.e. unskilled readers) when they start school' (DfE, 2013, p.15).

Learning Outcomes Review

In this chapter you have reviewed some of the keys to effective phonics teaching, including differences between more generic phonological awareness and phonemic awareness that distinguishes phonemes in words. You will have become aware that phonological awareness training delivered on its own and not accompanied by teaching of grapheme–phonemes correspondences has limited impact, although such training is beneficial to children experiencing difficulties in reading. Some adults may experience difficulties in segmenting words into phonemes as this skill is carried out at an unconscious level and adults focus on the meaning and the written representation of the word. An understanding of children's language development in perceiving and pronouncing sounds helps in identifying possible language delay which may impact on learning phonics. Both letter names and sounds are important for children but we need to differentiate clearly between the two when teaching. There is a clear link between developing vocabulary and phonological awareness, and it is important to increase children's vocabulary alongside their growing knowledge of grapheme–phoneme correspondences and to apply this in reading words. Phonological awareness develops within a rich language curriculum and the important influence of the home background needs to be considered.

Self-assessment questions

1. Phonological awareness often embraces the term 'phonemic awareness' – why is this, and what is the difference between phonological and phonemic awareness?
2. Name some ways in which adults can improve their ability to segment words into the constituent phonemes.
3. How can phonological awareness be effectively developed in children?
4. How can any confusion between letter names and sounds be avoided?
5. State some reasons for the link between vocabulary and phonological awareness.

Further Reading

For a useful chapter on speaking and phonological awareness by Elspeth McCartney, see:

Lewis, M. and Ellis, S. (eds) (2006) *Phonics, Practice, Research and Policy.* London: Paul Chapman.

References

Adams, M.J. (1990) *Beginning to Read: Thinking and Learning about Print.* Cambridge, MA: MIT Press.

Castles, A. and Coltheart, M. (2004) 'Is there a causal link from phonological awareness to success in learning to read?', *Cognition*, 9 (1): 77–111.

Chaney, C. (1992) 'Language development, metalinguistic skills, and print awareness in 3-year-old children', *Applied Psycholinguistics*, *13*: 485–514.

DfE (2011) *Teachers' Standards in England from September 2012.* London: Department for Education.

DfE (2013) The National Curriculum in England. Available from: www.gov.uk/dfe/nationalcurriculum (accessed 2/1/14).

DfES (2007) *Letters and Sounds: Principles and Practice of High Quality Phonics.* London: DfES.

Dodd, B., Holm, A., Crosbie, S. and McCormack, P. (2005) 'Differential diagnosis of phonological disorders', in B. Dodd (ed.), *Differential Diagnosis and Treatment of Children with Speech Disorder*, 2nd edn. London: Whurr. pp.44–70.

Duff, F.J., Fieldsend, E., Bowyer-Crane, C., Hulme, C., Smith, G., Giffs, S. and Snowling, M.J. (2008) 'Reading with vocabulary intervention: Evaluation of an instruction for children with poor response to reading intervention', *Journal of Research in Reading*, *31* (3): 319–36.

Ehri, L.C., Nunes, S.R., Willows, D.M., Schuster, B.V., Yaghoub-Zadeh, Z. and Shanahan, T. (2001) 'Phonemic awareness instruction helps children learn to read: Evidence from the National Reading Panel's meta-analysis', *Reading Research Quarterly*, 36: 250–87.

Farmer, S., Ellis, S. and Smith, V. (2006) 'Teaching phonics: The basics', in M. Lewis and S. Ellis (eds), *Phonics, Practice, Research and Policy*. London: Paul Chapman. pp.34–44.

Harrison, C. (2004) *Understanding Reading Development*. London: SAGE.

Hatcher, P.J., Hulme, C. and Snowling, M.J. (2004) 'Explicit phoneme training combined with phonic reading instruction helps young children at risk of reading failure', *Journal of Child Psychology and Psychiatry*, 45: 338–58.

Johnston, S., Anderson, M. and Holligan, C. (1996) 'Knowledge of the alphabet and explicit awareness of phonemes in pre-readers: The nature of the relationship', *Reading and Writing*, 8: 217–34.

Johnston, R. and Watson, J. (2007) *Teaching Synthetic Phonics*. Exeter: Learning Matters.

Jolliffe, W. (2007) *You Can Teach Phonics*. Leamington Spa: Scholastic.

Kempert, S., Gotz, R., Blatter, K., Tibken, C., Artlelt, C., Schnieder, W. and Stanat, P. (2016) 'Training early literacy related skills: To which degree does a musical training contribute to phonological awareness development?', *Frontiers in Psychology*, 7: 1–16.

Martin, B. Jr. and Carle, E. (1995) *Brown Bear, Brown Bear, What Do You See?* London: Puffin.

McGuinness, D. (2004) *Early Reading Instruction: What Science Really Tells Us about How to Teach Reading*. Cambridge, MA: MIT Press.

Nation, K. and Snowling, M. (1977) 'Assessing reading difficulties: The validity and utility of current measures of reading skill', *British Journal of Educational Psychology*, 67: 359–70.

National Institute of Child Health and Human Development (NICHD) (2000) *Report of the National Reading Panel*. 'Teaching children to read: An evidence-based assessment of the scientific research literature on reading and its implications for reading instruction: Reports of the subgroups', NIH publication no. 00-4754. Washington, DC: US Government Printing Office.

Ofsted (2014) *Getting them reading early. Distance learning materials for inspecting reading*. Reference 110122. https://www.gov.uk/government/publications/getting-them-reading-early (accessed 13/4/18).

Rose, J. (2006) *Independent Review of the Teaching of Early Reading, Final Report, March 2006* (The Rose Review – Ref: 0201-2006DOC-EN). Nottingham: DfES.

Schuele, C.M. and Boudreau, D. (2008) 'Phonological awareness intervention: Beyond the basics', *Language, Speech and Hearing Services in Schools*, 39 (1): 3–20.

Share, D. (1995) 'Phonological recoding and self-teaching: Sine qua non of reading acquisition', *Cognition*, 55: 151–218.

Snow, C.E. (2005) 'What counts as literacy development', in K. McCartney and D. Phillips (eds), *Blackwell Handbook of Early Child Development*. Oxford: Blackwell. pp.274–95.

Stanovich, K.E. (1986) 'Matthew effects in reading: Some consequences of individual differences in the acquisition of literacy', *Reading Research Quarterly*, 22: 360–407.

Torgensen, J.K., Wagner, R.K. and Rashotte, C.A. (1994) 'Longitudinal studies of phonological processing and reading', *Journal of Learning Disabilities*, 27 (5): 276–86.

Treiman, R. and Tincoff, R. (1997) 'The fragility of the alphabetic principle: Children's knowledge of letter names can cause them to spell syllabically rather than alphabetically', *Journal of Experimental Child Psychology*, 64: 425–51.

Walley, A.C. (1993) 'The role of vocabulary development in children's spoken word recognition and segmentation ability', *Developmental Review*, 13: 286–350.

Chapter 1 Audit and Test

Work through each section below, responding to each question or task. When you have completed each section, you can read the answers at the end of the chapter.

Section 1: Key terminology for discriminating sounds and phonemes

It is important that you understand the terms below before you move on to the next activity. Provide a definition of each and check your definitions against those at the end of the chapter:

Phonemes

Graphemes

Phonological awareness

Phonemic awareness

Segmentation and blending

Adjacent consonants

Section 2: Segmenting words

Test your knowledge by trying to work out the number of phonemes in the words below. Remember that there are always the same number of phonemes as graphemes, as a grapheme can be any number of letters that represent that phoneme.

Remember:

in 'bat' we can hear 3 phonemes b/ a/ t/

in 'ship' we can hear 3 phonemes sh/ i/ p/

in 'night' we can hear 3 phonemes n/ igh/ t/

Word	Number of phonemes	Split the word into phonemes	Word	Number of phonemes	Split the word into phonemes
then	3	/th/e/n/	stress		
chip			strap		
bring			flow		
crash			brand		
way			bake		

Section 3: Phoneme frames

In schools, many teachers use phoneme frames to help children to segment words into phonemes and graphemes. For example:

sh	a	n	d	y	
b	r	igh	t		
f	l	a	sh	i	ng

Use the frame below to segment the following words: blow, shortly, blast, window, draining

ANSWERS

Section 1: Key terminology for discriminating sounds and phonemes

Phonemes

Phonemes are individual sounds. In English, there are around 44 phonemes (the number varies slightly according to accent and which phonics programme you look at).

Graphemes

Graphemes are phonemes written down, so in the word cat there are three phonemes and they are represented by three graphemes /c/a/t/. In the word shop there are three phonemes but the first is represented by two letters making one sound (a digraph): /sh/o/p/

Phonological awareness

Phonological awareness involves being able to hear, recall and manipulate sounds.

Phonemic awareness

Phonemic awareness is the ability to hear and manipulate the phonemes in spoken words and to remember the order of phonemes in words. For example, the phonemes in the word 'big' can be segmented as /b/ /i/ /g/.

Segmentation and blending

Oral blending and segmentation, which are the reverse of each other, help children to blend and segment for reading and spelling when they learn letters and sounds.

Adjacent consonants

Consonants which are side by side but have separate phonemes, for example: s/t in stop, c/l in club and s/t/r in strip. Although we blend these sounds together, it is important to emphasise that the letters each have individual sounds.

Section 2: Segmenting words

Word	Number of phonemes	Split the word into phonemes	Word	Number of phonemes	Split the word into phonemes
then	3	/th/e/n/	stress	4	/s/t/r/e/ss/
chip	3	/ch/i/p/	strap	5	/s/t/r/a/p/
bring	4	/b/r/i/ng/	flow	3	/f/l/ow/
crash	4	/c/r/a/sh/	brand	5	/b/r/a/n/d/
way	2	/w/ay/	bake	3	/b/a/k/e

21

If you managed to segment all of the words correctly, well done! If you didn't you may have struggled because you are already a sophisticated reader who doesn't always pay attention to every sound in a word. For example, you may have segmented 'stress' as str/e/ss/ because you are used to seeing *str* in words and assume that this is a single sound. In fact, *str* is three sounds. Try saying the letter sounds slowly and notice what happens in your mouth: you make three different shapes – one for each letter sound or phoneme.

You may similarly have decided that 'crash' should be segmented as cr/a/sh/ because you are familiar with words which begin with *cr* (crack, crumb, cricket). Again, try sounding the phonemes slowly and you will notice that your mouth makes two shapes as you do so. These groups of letters which occur frequently in words are called consonant clusters or consonant blends and, more recently, adjacent consonants. It is very useful for readers to be aware of them as their reading develops, but beginner readers need to be able to identify every sound in new words if they are to be able to say them correctly and then spell them accurately.

Section 3: Phoneme frames

b	l	ow			
sh	or	t	l	y	
b	l	a	s	t	
w	i	n	d	ow	
d	r	ai	n	i	ng

How did you manage this time? In the first word, 'blow', there are three phonemes and you needed not only to realise that *bl* represents two sounds, but also that *ow* represents a single sound which is signified by two letters: a digraph. Try saying 'ow', making the same sound as in blow. Notice that your mouth stays open throughout, which is a feature of vowel phonemes.

In *shortly*, *sh* represents a single sound and both letters are consonants, so *sh* is a **consonant digraph**. The *or* part of the word is a single sound and even though *r* is a consonant the sound is a vowel sound, so *or* is referred to as a **vowel digraph**.

Blast has five sounds; although the *bl* at the beginning and *st* at the end are consonant clusters, each represents two sounds.

Window has a vowel digraph at the end (*ow*) – notice that your mouth remains open as you make the sound.

Draining includes the vowel digraph *ai*, which you probably spotted, but did you decide that the *ng* at the end was one sound or two? For most English-speakers *ng* is a single sound, but for some, particularly in parts of the English Midlands and some areas in Yorkshire *ng* can be sounded as two sounds. Phonics programmes tend to regard *ng* as a single sound.

The split vowel digraph

In Chapter 5 you will look at words in which the vowel sound is made by two letters which are not immediately adjacent to each other (as in *make, safe, bite* etc.).

What to do next?

Reinforce your knowledge and understanding of segmenting by doing as many as possible of the following:

1. Observe teachers working with children and note how they model segmenting. How do they show children how to count phonemes?

2. Re-read Chapter 1 to clarify any queries you may have.

3. Practise with a colleague segmenting the following words. The number of phonemes for each is given in brackets. Decide between you how to segment each word into its individual sounds: smash (4), dart (3), grab (4), chocolate (7), bean (3), Sunday (5).

2. Challenges

Learning Outcomes

By the end of this chapter you will:

- understand the importance of correct enunciation of phonemes;
- understand issues related to accent;
- be able to discriminate between phonemes in consonant clusters;
- have considered strategies to help parents to support their children's reading effectively.

Teachers' Standards

3. Demonstrate good subject and curriculum knowledge:
   - if teaching early reading, demonstrate a clear understanding of systematic synthetic phonics.

Criteria for assuring high-quality phonic work (DfE, 2011)

Enable children to start learning phonic knowledge and skills using a systematic, synthetic programme by the age of five, with the expectation that they will be fluent readers having secured word recognition skills by the end of Key Stage 1 (see note 2).

Note 2: Teachers will make principled, professional judgements about when to start on a systematic, synthetic programme of phonic work but it is reasonable to expect that the great majority of children will be capable of, and benefit from doing so by the age of five. It is equally important for the programme to be designed so that children become fluent readers having secured word recognition skills by the end of Key Stage 1.

Introduction

As you have seen in Chapter 1, teaching systematic synthetic phonics gives rise to debate and discussion even between those who are committed to this approach. The controversy over the use of letter names discussed in Chapter 1 is just one area in which some teachers disagree. In this chapter, we will look at ways in which this and other challenges might be met. In particular, we will focus on accents, enunciation, variations in grapheme–phoneme correspondences, and ways of helping parents to support their children's reading development.

Because English has developed from different languages, it has a complex and varied matching of phonemes to graphemes. This is an issue even at the earliest stages of learning to read since, as we will see in Chapter 3, many of the most common words in the language include phonic irregularities. In Chapter 7 we will look at how this impinges upon the teaching and learning of spelling.

Additional challenges arise because not only do we pronounce many phonemes in ways which deviate from what might be seen as a norm, but we also pronounce many phonemes in different ways in different regions.

A further challenge is presented by the fact that many adults who help children to learn to read were taught synthetic phonics poorly or not at all. This can lead to confusion for children and even for trainee teachers, as can be seen in the case study below.

Case Study: Confusion over letter names and sounds

Rachel, a bright final-year trainee with excellent grades both for teaching and academic work, attended a revision session on systematic synthetic phonics at her university. After a session in which the trainees practised sounding common phonemes for individual letters with an emphasis upon avoiding adding a *schwa* sound (an unstressed vowel sound), Rachel suggested that it must be confusing for children that there were 'three names for each letter'. Her tutor asked her to explain what she meant and Rachel told him that children learned, for example, the letter name 's', the sound *sss* (as in a hissing noise), and the name *suh*.

The tutor explained that the letters only have one name each and that for 's', *sss* was its sound. *Suh* was a poorly enunciated representation of the sound, which would be unhelpful to children when blending letters to make words. However, Rachel's experience in schools had been that teachers often referred to letters by their poorly enunciated sound when talking with children. The tutor asked about children's spelling errors, which Rachel had noticed in her last Year 1 class and was not surprised to find that these included *cl* for *colour* and *bt* for *butter*.

Enunciation

The spelling errors Rachel's Year 1 class made are almost certainly a direct result of their teacher's incorrect enunciation. Those who are not phonics specialists often find it difficult initially to enunciate each phoneme in the correct way, and indeed are unsure what the correct enunciation sounds like. It is important that each phoneme is pronounced without the *schwa*, an unstressed vowel or extra sound added to some phonemes. In the Ofsted publication *Getting Them Reading Early* it is stated that

> *correct articulation is vital in helping children to learn to blend sounds together. This means making sure that the sound produced (each individual phoneme) is as precise and accurate as possible and that no additional sounds are added. For instance, the sound /m/ that starts 'mother' or is embedded in 'impress' needs to sound /mmmm/ and not /muh/. The clearer the sound, the easier it is for a child to blend together (synthesise) the individual sounds to read a word because there are no unnecessary sounds getting in the way.*

(Ofsted, 2014, p.22)

It is important that all adults involved in phonics teaching familiarise themselves with the correct enunciation of phonemes in order to teach phonics correctly and effectively. *Sonic Phonics* (2011) materials and other high-quality resources found online, including at www.getreadingright. co.uk can be used to hear how phonemes are pronounced.

Activity

Visit www.getreadingright.co.uk and listen to the correct pronunciation of each phoneme. Practise articulating all 44 phonemes, in order to familiarise yourself with how they sound and how they should be correctly enunciated. You could also use the DVD provided with *Letters and Sounds* (DfES, 2007), which not only plays correct enunciations, but also shows the mouth shapes made when they are pronounced. Another good source is *Mr Thorne Does Phonics* (www.mrthorne.com/ or/), where you will find a teacher demonstrating a range of phoneme–grapheme correspondences.

Accents

One of the challenges related to the teaching of phonics is regional pronunciations – particularly where a teacher's accent is different from that of the children in the class. In fact, Crystal maintains that 'Probably no two people are identical in the way they use language' and that the dialect we call Standard English may be 'spoken in a vast range of regional accents' (2005, p.290). However, Miskin asserts that 'all but four or five of the 44 sounds are pronounced consistently across all accents' (2006, p.10). You might like to reflect upon the regional accents you know well and consider what these sounds might be.

Letters and Sounds (DfES, 2007) provides scant guidance on the effect of regional accents on the teaching of phonics, limiting its comments to the example of the lack of an /u/ phoneme as in southern pronunciations of *up, cup* and *butter* for many people from the north of England, and concluding: 'While practitioners will need to be sensitive to these and other occurrences most find that these differences can be dealt with on a common sense basis' (DfES, 2007, p.17). The National Curriculum's (DfE, 2013) attention to accents is also limited. An entry in the glossary states:

> *Some words are exceptions in some accents but not in others – e.g. past, last, fast, path and bath are not exceptions in accents where the **a** in these words is pronounced / æ (ae dipthong) as in cat.*

> *(DfE, 2013, p.58)*

The Ofsted publication *Getting Them Reading Early* states that

> *{t}eachers need to be alert and sensitive to the differences. However, the key point is that teaching starts with sounds and not with letters. The teacher will know what letter(s) to teach to represent the sound the children say, even if it is not what she says.*

> *(Ofsted, 2014, p. 19)*

So although for many trainee teachers accent is a major concern when teaching phonics, the subject received little attention in many key documents. Anyone involved in teaching phonics needs to be familiar with the way the children they are teaching pronounce each phoneme, and should take this into account when delivering phonics sessions. However, this can present both a challenge and a dilemma. Should teachers, or indeed children, have to modify their accents for the purposes of teaching and learning reading?

Research Focus: What is an accent?

Crystal and Crystal (2014) explain that differences between accents are mainly found in the way we sound vowels. They describe three main types:

- *Pure vowels* have a single auditory quality. Say *ah* (as at the doctor's) and keep it going. It has the same quality throughout.

⟶

- *Diphthongs* have two auditory qualities. The tongue starts with one position in the mouth and quickly moves to another. Say *my* slowly, and you'll feel (and hear) the tongue start in a mouth-open position and move up towards the roof of the mouth.
- *Triphthongs* have three auditory qualities. Say *fire* as 'fie-yuh' and you'll sense the first part doing the same as in *my* above, but followed by an 'uh' ending in the centre of the mouth. (If you normally say *fire* as 'fah', you'll have to work on this one.)

Crystal and Crystal, 2014, p.27

Activity

To see how much we rely on differences in vowel sounds to identify different accents, try saying the words below with a range of accents: *bath, grass, my, might, aim, coat, no, hope, now, but, bought, caught, nose, house, allowed, boil, wire, loan, mouth, don't.*

Our accent is part of our heritage and provides a means of identifying with our family and friends. Nevertheless, we do tend to modify our accents according to whom we are talking with. Think about the ways in which people change their voices when they take or make a phone call. We can often tell who our friends and family are speaking to by their voices. We also speak differently when we are with friends from the way we talk in a classroom or at an interview, and this is often not limited to the vocabulary and phrasing we use; it can also involve a modification of our accents. Is it unreasonable, then, that we should modify our accents when teaching phonics? The case studies below include potential solutions that you might discuss.

Activity

As you read the case studies below, consider what you would do if you found yourself in a similar situation to Anna, Claire or Simon. Talk with experienced teachers about their strategies when children's accents differ markedly from their own.

Case Studies: Challenges presented by accents

The Queen's hat

Anna, a final-year trainee teacher from Northern Ireland, had discovered that children in the north-east of England often found it difficult to understand her because her accent was

→

markedly different from those they were used to hearing. She cited, in particular, the *ow* sound as in *now*, *out* and *town* which she pronounced *nie*, *ite* and *tine*. She went back to her old primary school in Belfast during student holidays and asked her former teachers for advice. One invited her to observe a phonics lesson with a class which included children with different accents. The teacher talked with the children in her normal accent, but when it came to learning the phoneme /ow/ she asked the children to put on their 'Queen's hat'. The children put on imaginary hats and then sounded /ow/ in the way they thought the Queen might say it. The teacher talked with Anna about the importance of children understanding that people spoke in different ways in different places, and said that while she was not trying to change their accents, she wanted them to be able to understand and be understood by people from other regions.

A wardrobe of accents

Claire, a second-year student from Hull, asked her tutor for advice because children in her school placement made some odd attempts at spelling some of the words she had given them in an informal spelling test that was designed to assess their knowledge of grapheme-phoneme correspondences prior to a unit of work. Some children had written *hurp* or *herp* for *hope* and *slurp* for *slope*. Claire recognised that her Hull accent, which involved making the *oa* sound long and more like *er*, was having an effect upon the children's spellings. Her tutor spoke to colleagues at a literacy conference and one suggested he talk to Claire about the idea of 'a wardrobe of accents'. Thus, just as we often consciously or even subconsciously modify our accents according to our audiences, we might choose from a range of accents when teaching on some occasions.

North and South

Simon, a PGCE (Postgraduate Certificate in Education) student from South London, was told by his school mentor that children were confused by the way he pronounced words such as *laugh* (*larf* rather than *laff* as people in the region pronounced it) and *bath* (*barf*). Simon was upset that the way he spoke was being criticised and sought advice from his English tutor who discussed, in particular, the longer *a* sound associated with southern accents. The tutor told Simon that he should not worry about his accent and that people could speak Standard English with any accent. He might consider modifying his pronunciation of some words in some situations if it would avoid confusion for the children, but he might also talk with the children about the ways in which people pronounced words and could show them some clips from TV programmes to illustrate the point. However, the tutor did suggest that Simon's pronunciation of *th* as *ff* could be unhelpful in any region and that he should try to avoid this.

Accents can be an emotive issue. Within every class there will be a range of different accents, even if all children grew up in the same area. However, in many classes there will be considerable differences between accents, since children will have English as an additional language or may simply have moved from another area of the country. Teachers need to tread a fine line between helping children to enunciate clearly and avoiding appearing critical of children's speech. For a fascinating insight into accents and the way they have changed over time, see Chapter 6 of Bryson (1990), as well as Chapter 3 of this book in which accents are discussed further.

Grapheme variations

A further challenge for the teacher of phonics is the fact that there are so many different ways in which to give a written representation of English phonemes.

The number of phonemes in English is generally said to be 44, although it has been estimated at 43, and totals 42 in the Jolly Phonics programme. However, most phonemes can be represented by more than one grapheme. A simple representation of the grapheme possibilities for 44 phonemes can be found on a Teaching Handwriting Reading and Spelling Skills (THRASS) chart (Davies and Ritchie, 1998), where 120 possible graphemes are shown, including, for example, *k*, *ck*, *q*, *ch* and *c* for the *c* sound in *cat*, and *er*, *ar*, *or*, *ure*, *a*, *e*, *i*, *o* and *u* for the *schwa* sound in *teacher, collar, doctor, measure, zebra, garden, fossil, lion, circus*. The THRASS chart also includes an asterisk next to each group of graphemes to indicate that there may be more possibilities. For the '*c*' sound in cat this could include, for example, *cq* as in *acquire* and *cc* as in *account* (note the added complication that *cc* in *accent* makes two phonemes and a similar sound to the *x* in *box*!). For more information about THRASS, see Chapter 13.

Some of the most common examples that children will encounter early in their reading development include *ee/ea, ie/igh, f/ff* and *ai/ay* as in *see* and *sea*, *if* and *off*, *rain* and *day*. It is important that teachers of phonics are aware of grapheme variations, which can be a challenge for children – how do they know which is the correct grapheme to choose and how can we teach them this?

Teachers can support children in their selection of the correct grapheme by:

- Teaching common rules for graphemes. If we take *ai/ay* as a common example, the general rule is that the *ai* grapheme appears in the middle of a word (as in *snail, paint, raid*), while the *ay* grapheme is used at the end (as in *play, Saturday, away*). There are, of course, exceptions to these rules and it is important that children are made aware of this.

- Grouping words by grapheme type (as in *night, light, sight, fright*) to enable children to learn several words by association and to understand common rules and spelling patterns.

- Ensuring that the meaning of the word in question is clearly understood. A simple example of this is when asking children to spell or read the words *see/sea*. If children understand whether they are being asked about the word that is associated with sight or the word which means 'similar to the ocean' they may have an improved chance of selecting the correct grapheme.

- Reviewing and revisiting common groups of words with grapheme variations to ensure that children have regular and consistent reminders through a variety of games and activities.

Activity

How many different phonemes can you list in ten minutes that can be represented by more than one grapheme? For example, the /e/ sound in feet could also be made by *ea* in *meat, ei* in *receipt;* the /k/ sound in *cat* could be represented by *k* in *king, ck* in *sick, ch* in *school, cc* in *account, que* in *oblique.*

Look at your list. Are there any common rules associated with these graphemes that will help you to teach pupils about phoneme variations?

Phoneme variations

Similarly, there are many graphemes that are represented by more than one phoneme. It is important that teachers are also aware of these phoneme variations. Common examples include *oo* (as in *good* or *moon*), *y* (as in *happy* or *by*) and *ch* (as in *chief, school* or *chef*). This can, of course, also challenge children – how can we teach them which phoneme is the correct one?

Teachers can support children in their selection of the correct phoneme in similar ways to those when choosing the correct grapheme. These may include:

- Teaching common rules for phoneme variations. For example, if *y* is the final grapheme in a word, it usually represents the /i:/ phoneme (happy, baby, hurry etc). Again, there are exceptions to these rules (usually short words such as *my, by, try*) and it is important that children are taught these.

- Grouping words by phoneme type (as in *moon, soon, loom, spoon*) to enable children to learn several words by association and to understand common rules and spelling patterns.

- Ensuring that the meaning of the word in question is clearly understood. If children understand whether they are being asked about the word that means to have already read something (I read a book) as opposed to reading it now or in the future (I am going to read a book), they may have an improved chance of selecting the correct phoneme.

- Reviewing and revisiting common groups of words with phoneme variations to ensure children have regular and consistent reminders through a variety of games and activities.

Activity

Many people who are new to teaching phonics can find answering the questions below challenging. The teaching of phonics can be daunting for non-phonics specialists because of the amount of precise terminology and specific subject knowledge. It is important that correct terminology and accurate enunciation is learned by the teacher before being modelled for children.

- How many phonemes does the word *scrum* have?
- What is a split digraph? Which of these words include a split vowel digraph? *good, these, time, back, rode*

Let's take a look at the first question above and explore a little further. There are five phonemes in *scrum*: /s/c/r/u/m/. One of the most frequently encountered challenges for trainee teachers is counting phonemes, particularly in words which include consonant clusters, such as in *splash*, *sprint* and *string* (see also Chapter 1). Because they are already sophisticated readers, they often naturally run the consonant clusters together so that when they encounter a new or invented word they read it quickly. For example, read and say the invented words below:

splink, strimble, sprerd

You probably did this very quickly and accurately. Now say the words again and decide how many phonemes there are in each.

If you decided there were six in *splink*, seven in *strimble* and five in *sprerd*, you were correct. However, you may have looked at some of the common consonant clusters *spl-*, *-nk*, *str-* and *spr-* and decided that these comprised one sound each. If you did, try saying each word slowly while thinking carefully about the movements your mouth makes as you say them. *Splink* has the following phonemes: /s/p/l/i/n/k/ – for the /s/ we curve our tongue and put it behind the gums of our upper teeth, while our lips come together for /p/, and we put our tongue behind our teeth for /l/ and so on. Each makes a distinctive sound. As advanced readers, we may not be aware of each sound in a word and perhaps think, incorrectly, that clusters such as *spl* are a single sound, but for inexperienced readers this can present problems. If a child cannot hear all of the sounds within a word, he may not be able to read it accurately or spell it in a correct or at least phonically plausible way.

Now let's look at the second question. Did you identify *these*, *time* and *rode* as having split vowel digraphs? A digraph has two letters making one sound, so the /ck/ in *back* makes a single /k/ sound and the /ou/ in *sound* makes a single /ow/ sound. In *these* the e and e make the /ea/ sound, while in *time* it is the i and e that make the /ie/ sound and in *rode* it is o and e which make the /oa/ sound. Think of words that have the same vowels making a digraph without a letter separating them, for example, *tree*, *tie* and *toe*.

Many of us were taught about split vowel digraphs using the term 'magic *e*', that is, the *e* was 'magic' because it transformed a letter's sound into its name: for example, adding *e* to *rod* created *rode*, adding *e* to *win* created *wine* and adding *e* to *hat* created *hate*. The term 'magic *e*' tends not to be used in many modern phonics programmes and children are taught instead to use the term 'split vowel digraph'. The following chapter will look in more detail at grapheme–phoneme correspondence and will examine more of the terminology associated with systematic synthetic phonics. In Chapter 4, you will find out more about decoding and encoding, and there will be further opportunities to practise segmenting words into phonemes.

Those seeking more advice and guidance on this should:

- Become familiar with a range of phonics programmes such as Letters and Sounds, Jolly Phonics, THRASS and Read Write Inc. These widely used schemes offer guidance on terminology and enunciation and provide resources that can be used to teach phonics successfully.

- Visit classrooms where effective phonics sessions are being taught. Seek the advice of colleagues who are experienced in planning and delivering high-quality phonics.

- Research the subject using printed publications and the Internet.

The frustrated child

There are some children for whom the techniques already discussed in this chapter will not be wholly successful and they may continue to struggle with phoneme–grapheme correspondences (see Chapter 11 for further assessment and intervention strategies). They may not be making the same progress as their peers and may be finding phonics a challenge. These children may benefit from:

- Discrete, daily phonics as part of a small group or on an individual basis. The well-planned use of adult support in the classroom may allow children to take part in focused group work with specific targets to meet their individual needs.

- Using a multi-sensory approach. This will encourage children to access and practise phonics in as many different ways as possible with a wide range of interactive teaching techniques and activities. Ideas to support this can be found in Chapter 8.

- Regular and consistent repetition of the key areas of challenge through revisiting and reviewing.

- Frequent assessment that will inform the teacher of progress made and when it is appropriate to move the child on.

Further challenges

In the final part of this chapter we will look at some of the issues which may arise for learners and their parents and carers. We should be constantly aware that just as we have to acquire new knowledge in order to teach effectively, so parents and carers and children may be unfamiliar with terminology and fail to understand the rationale behind the way in which we teach.

Parental knowledge and attitudes

Parents and carers can be a valuable support in the teaching of reading, spelling and phonics and it is in schools' best interests to harness and guide that support. Of course, most parents are not phonics specialists or school educators and may not feel confident about the best ways to support their children in learning phonics and using phonic strategies to read and spell. Parents and carers may themselves have developed approaches which may be inconsistent with the school's approach or have indeed been ineffectively taught phonics during their own childhood. Some parents may use letter names rather than phonemes. It would seem perfectly reasonable to use the letter names when children are surrounded by these and accompany their parents and carers to B&Q, M&S, TGI Friday's and so on, and then watch TV programmes on the BBC and ITV. As we saw in Chapter 1, there can also be sound educational reasons for teaching letter names at an early stage. However, children also need to develop an understanding of the common sounds letters can make and it will be helpful if parents and carers can support teachers by using these too. In addition, it will be useful if they pronounce letter sounds without using the *schwa*. It is important to encourage parents and carers to use good phonic strategies to support their children's learning, and at the same time ensure that they feel that phonics is not beyond them.

Parents and carers may question the techniques used in the teaching of systematic synthetic phonics and it is important for teachers to respond to this. This can be done by providing explanations of programmes and teaching techniques used within school; guidance about how parents and carers may successfully support their children at home; and invitations to come into the classroom to see phonics in action.

Parents and carers can be introduced to successful ways in which they can support their children with phonics through:

- Parents' meetings and workshops, perhaps to be held before their child is due to start nursery or school, or soon after the child starts in the Early Years Foundation Stage (EYFS). Examples of good practice and demonstrations of accurate phonic enunciation can be shared by teachers and parents. Parents can be provided with support in effectively guiding their children in spelling and reading tasks.

- Leaflets, phoneme lists, letter formation guidelines and other written information that can be sent home for parents to refer to when working at home with their children.

- Invitations to visit during phonics lessons to ensure that parents have a clear picture of what is being taught and how.

- Suggestions for high-quality websites that support the teaching of phonics, particularly those that are supported by sound tracks so that children and parents can hear the correct enunciation of each phoneme.

Research Focus: Involving parents and carers

It is important that parents and carers understand that learning grapheme–phoneme correspondences is just part of their children's development as readers and that there are many other things they can do to foster their children's reading development. As Gates and Yale state:

> it is clear that breaking the code is not an end – it is one essential step to proficient reading and to a lifetime pursuit of improving reading comprehension. Ultimately, mastery of reading automaticity lures the reader into the incredible world of print.

> (2011, p.338)

Sui-Chu and Willms maintained that 'parental involvement made a significant unique contribution to explaining the variation in children's academic achievement over and above the effects associated with family background' (1996, p.138). Lynch (2002) found eight- and nine-year-olds' self-belief as readers was influenced by their mothers' beliefs in their ability to help their children.

Lloyd (1992), who developed the Jolly Phonics programme, argued that three conditions needed to be met if a comprehensive reading programme was to be taught in a whole-class format: lessons should be engaging and interactive; there should be sufficient resources to support teaching and learning; and 'parents need to be involved enough to understand the program and know how to support their child at home' (cited in McGuinness, 2004, p.138).

Activity

A parent approaches you and explains that he is unsure how to correctly enunciate phonemes and therefore doesn't feel confident in helping his child at home. How would you advise the parent? Which resources would you recommend he uses?

In Chapter 3, we will focus on strategies for teaching words that children use frequently, many of which include phonic irregularities.

Learning Outcomes Review

In this chapter you have reviewed some of the keys to effective phonics teaching, including understanding the importance of correct enunciation of phonemes and, in particular, avoiding adding a *schwa* whenever possible. Issues related to accent and the strategies used by some trainees and teachers have been explored in depth. The importance of being able to discriminate between phonemes in consonant clusters has been further considered, together with strategies to help parents to support their children's reading effectively.

Self-assessment questions

1. What do we mean by correct enunciation of phonemes?
2. What is a schwa sound and why should we try, wherever possible, to avoid using it when pronouncing phonemes?
3. What is a split vowel digraph?

Further Reading

The following websites provide helpful practical guidance on teaching phonics:

Mr Thorne Does Phonics: www.mrthorne.com/or/ (accessed 9/4/18).

Getting Reading Right: www.getreadingright.co.uk (accessed 9/4/18) – enunciating phonemes.

Sonic Phonics: www.TalkingProducts.com (accessed 19/12/14) – produces a set of graphemes on individual plastic pieces with buttons which when pressed emit the correct enunciation of the corresponding phonemes. These are ideal for practising enunciation and for blending activities with children.

For an entertaining and informative exploration of accents, see:

Crystal, B. and Crystal, D. (2014) *You Say Potato: A Book about Accents*. London: Macmillan.

References

Bryson, B. (1990) *The Mother Tongue*. London: Penguin.

Crystal, B. and Crystal, D. (2014) *You Say Potato: A Book about Accents*. London: Macmillan.

Crystal, D. (2005) *How Language Works*. London: Penguin.

Davies, A. and Ritchie, D. (1998) *THRASS: Teacher's Manual*. Chester: THRASS.

DfE (2011) *Teachers' Standards in England from September 2012*. London: DfE.

DfE (2013) *The National Curriculum in England: Key Stages 1 and 2 Framework Document*. London: DfE.

DfES (2007) *Letters and Sounds: Principles and Practice of High Quality Phonics*. London: DfES.

Gates, L. and Yale, I. (2011) 'A logical letter–sound system in five phonic generalizations', *The Reading Teacher*, 64 (5).

Get Reading Right (2012) *Pronouncing the Phonemes*. York: Get Reading Right. Available at www.getreadingright.co.uk/phoneme/pronounce-the-phonemes (accessed 16/3/12).

Jolly Learning (1992) *Jolly Phonics*. Available at www.jollylearning.co.uk/overview-about-jollyphonics/ (accessed 3/2/15).

Lloyd, S. (1992) *The Phonics Handbook*. Chigwell: Jolly Learning.

Lynch, J. (2002) 'Parents' self-efficacy beliefs, parents' gender, children's reader self-perceptions, reading achievement and gender', *Journal of Research in Reading*, 25 (1): 54–67.

McGuinness, D. (2004) *Early Reading Instruction: What Science Really Tells Us about How to Teach Reading*. Cambridge, MA: MIT Press.

Miskin, R. (2006) *Read Write Inc. Phonics Handbook*. Oxford: Oxford University Press.

Mr Thorne (2012) *Mr Thorne Does Phonics*. Available at www.mrthorne.com/or/ (accessed 1/3/15).

Ofsted (2014) *Getting them Reading Early* (Ref: 110122). Manchester: Ofsted. Available at www.ofsted.gov.uk/resources/getting-them-reading-early (accessed 23/12/14).

Sonic Phonics (2011) Product available at www.talkingproducts.com/sonic-phonics.html (accessed 24/12/14).

Sui-Chu, E.H. and Willms, J.D. (1996) 'Effects of parental involvement on eighth-grade achievement', *Sociology of Education*, 69 (2): 126–41.

Chapter 2 Audit and Test

Work through each section below, responding to each question or task. When you have completed each section, you can read the answers at the end of the chapter.

Section 1: Key terminology for challenges

It is important that you understand the terms below before you move on to the next activity. Provide a definition of each and check your definitions against those at the end of the chapter:

Accent
Dialect
Schwa
Enunciation
Grapheme variation
Phoneme variation

Section 2: Phonics problems

Look at each of the following and consider:

a.   why you think the problem arose;

b.   how you might address it.

1.   A child in your Year 2 class often writes *fink, fank* and *fort* etc. for words beginning with a soft *th* like think, thank and thought.

2.   Some children in your new Year 3 class sound out words to spell them, but often add unnecessary letters. For example, there are spellings such as *duogu* for *dog* and *cuatu* for *cat*.

3.   In your Year 1 class several children add an unnecessary *i* to words like *sky (skiy)* and *why (wiy)*.

4.   You inherit a Year 2 class from a teacher from London and find children adding unnecessary Rs to some words such as *fast (farst), plastic (plarstic)* and *path (parth)*.

5.   A girl in your Year 4 class spells *no* as *now, go* as *gow* and *show* as *showa*.

6.   A Year 3 boy regularly confuses long vowel digraphs in simple words such as *rain (rane, rayn), blow (bloa, bloe)* and *team (teme, teem)*.

Section 3: Grapheme variations

Many phonemes can be represented by more than one grapheme. For example, the *k* sound at the beginning of *king* can be made by *ck* at the end of *kick*, *c* in *cat*, *cc* in *account*, *q* in *Iraq* and *ch* in *school*. Look at the graphemes below and see how many alternative ways each can be represented, providing a word for each example.

1. the **sh** sound in shop

2. the **f** sound in fish

3. the **j** sound in jug

4. the **n** sound in not

5. the **ee** sound in feet

6. the **ai** sound in train

7. the **ou** sound in loud

8. the **oo** sound in food

9. the **o** sound in no

10. the **schwa** sound in the

Section 4: Phoneme variations

Just as different graphemes can represent the same sound, so many graphemes can be used for more than one phoneme. For example, *c* can be sounded differently in *cat* and *city*, *ch* can be sounded differently in *chip*, *chef* and *school*, and *o* is sounded differently in *no*, *not* and *woman*.

Look at the graphemes below and see how many alternative phonemes each can be used to represent, providing a word for each example:

1. f

2. g

3. s

4. ou

5. ea

6. ow

7. y

8. ough

9. th

10. k

ANSWERS

Section 1: Key terminology for challenges

It is important that you understand the terms below before you move on to the next activity. Provide a definition of each and check your definitions against those in the glossary.

Accent

A dialect can be spoken with different accents. Our accent is the way we pronounce words, whereas our dialect has a grammatical structure, even if this is not written down as with Standard English.

Dialect

All versions of a language are dialects and include words, phrases and clauses which may not appear in other dialects. Standard English is the dialect which is often accepted as 'correct' and is the version in which English should be written. Dialect should not be confused with accent.

Schwa

A *schwa* is a short vowel sound such as we hear in words like the, pencil, doctor and taken. The symbol often used to show the *schwa* sound in dictionaries is ə. Say each of those words and notice the short sound made by the letters in bold: like th**e**, pencil, doct**or** and tak**e**n.

Enunciation

This means to pronounce or articulate. It is important that we enunciate phonemes clearly and accurately when teaching children. This means avoiding adding additional sounds such as the *schwa* wherever possible. For many letters this is quite easy, for example, f, l, m, n, r, s. For some, however, it is difficult to avoid (b, d, t), but you should try to keep this as short as possible.

Grapheme variation

Many phonemes can be represented by different graphemes. For example, the *ie* sound in *tie* can be represented by *igh* in *high*, *y* in *by* and *eigh* in *height*.

Phoneme variation

Many graphemes can represent different phonemes. For example, g has different sounds in *gate*, *germ* and *regime*.

Section 2: Phonics problems

Study each of the following and consider:

a. why you think the problem arose;

b. how you might address it.

1. A child in your Year 2 class often writes *fink*, *fank* and *fort* etc. for words beginning with a soft *th* like think, thank and thought.

    a. why you think the problem arose:

    this is probably caused either by the child's inability to pronounce *th* correctly or by hearing an adult (perhaps a parent or even a teacher) mispronounce *th*.

    b. how you might address it:

    focus on mouth shape when making the sound. There are many websites (https://www. gov.uk/government/publications/letters-and-sounds) and a DVD which accompanies *Letters and Sounds*, which show mouth actions as phonemes are enunciated.

2. Some children in your new Year 3 class sound out words to spell them, but often add unnecessary letters. For example, there are spellings such as *duogu* for *dog* and *cuatu* for *cat*.

    a. why you think the problem arose:

    this is probably caused by the children having been taught by someone who didn't enunciate correctly, adding a *schwa* sound to consonants – for example, saying *suh* rather than *ss* for *s*.

    b. how you might address it:

    work on correct enunciation for yourself and the children. Talk with parents about correct enunciation. Look at examples online and in the *Letters and Sounds* DVD.

3. In your Year 1 class several children add an unnecessary *i* to words like *sky* (*skiy*) and *why* (*wiy*).

    a. why you think the problem arose:

    this is probably caused by children's pronunciation and the fact that they 'hear' a *y* sound at the end of *why* and *sky* when some people say the words. This leads to them adding an extra letter. Try saying *sky* and *why* and notice what happens in your mouth: you can say the words keeping your mouth wide open at the end or you can bring your tongue up to your palate. If you do the latter you tend to add a slight additional sound.

    b. how you might address it:

    work on correct enunciation for yourself and the children. Look at lots of examples of words which have *y* at the end making an *ie* sound – for example, by, try, my, reply, fly – and talk about how they are spelled.

4. You inherit a Year 2 class from a teacher from London and find children adding unnecessary Rs to some words such as *fast* (*farst*), *plastic* (*plarstic*) and *path* (*parth*).

    a. why you think the problem arose:

    this is probably caused by the children having assumed that there was an *r* in the words due to their previous teacher's pronunciation.

    b. how you might address it:

talk with the children about different accents – there will be several in the class. Play extracts from TV programmes or websites in which people speak with a range of accents. Emphasise that their teacher and others who use a long *a* in some words are not speaking incorrectly, just differently.

5.   A girl in your Year 4 class spells *no* as *now*, *go* as *gow* and *show* as *showa*.

   a.   why you think the problem arose:

this is probably caused by the girl hearing a *w* sound when these words are spoken. Notice how your lips almost meet at the end of such words. Try saying *go away* and notice how you make a *w* sound between *go* and *away*. If children are used to hearing *w* enunciated with a pronounced *schwa* sound, they may assume that an additional letter is needed when spelling words like *flow* and *show*.

   b.   how you might address it:

look at words which have a long *oe* sound at the end and discuss spellings. Focus, in particular, on those which end with *o* and *ow*.

6.   A Year 3 boy regularly confuses long vowel digraphs in simple words such as *rain* (*rane, rayn*), *blow* (*bloa, bloe*) and *team* (*teme, teem*).

   a.   why you think the problem arose:

on the whole these might be considered 'good' spelling mistakes, since they are phonically plausible. The errors probably arise due to a lack of familiarity with the words in print.

   b.   how you might address it:

look at words with long vowel digraphs and discuss spellings. Through discussions and investigations, build sets of word families for long vowel phonemes. For example: rain, pain, gain; seem, street, greet. Talk about spellings which are likely and less likely. For example, words tend not to have *ay* as an *ay* sound except at the end.

Section 3: Grapheme variations

You were asked to look at the graphemes below and see how many alternative ways each can be represented, providing a word for each example. Some possible answers are shown below. You may have thought of many others too.

1. The *sh* sound in *shop* – *ch* in *chef*, *ci* in *delicious*, *ti* in *nation*
2. The *f* sound in *fish* - *ph* in *photograph*, *gh* in *laugh*, *ff* in *off*
3. The *j* sound in *jug* - *g* in *gem*, *dge* in *edge*
4. The *n* sound in *not* - *gn* in *gnat*, *kn* in *knit*, *pn* in *pneumatic*, *nn* in *dinner*
5. The *ee* sound in *feet* - *ea* in *read*, *ei* in *receive*, *ie* in *grief*, *e-e* in *eve*

| 6. The *ai* sound in *train* – *ay* in *day*, *eigh* in *weigh*, *ey* in *grey* |
| 7. The *ou* sound in *loud* – *ow* in *now*, *ough* in *bough* |
| 8. The *oo* sound in *food* – *ew* in *threw*, *ough* in *through*, *u-e* in *rude* |
| 9. The *o* sound in *no* – *ow* in *know*, *oa* in *coat*, *o-e* in *nose* |
| 10. The *schwa* sound in *the* - *a* in *woman*, *or* in *doctor*, *er* in *teacher* |

Section 4: Phoneme variations

You were asked to look at the graphemes and see how many alternative phonemes each can be used to represent, providing a word for each example. You can see some possibilities below, but you probably found more:

| 1. f fat, of |
| 2. g get, germ, gnat |
| 3. s sit, is, sugar |
| 4. ou noun, tough, cough |
| 5. ea head, meat, steak, idea, earth, |
| 6. ow now, know |
| 7. y you, by, easy |
| 8. ough tough, bough, bought, cough, through, though |
| 9. th this, think |
| 10. k kick, know |

What to do next?

Reinforce your knowledge and understanding of phoneme and grapheme variation by doing as many as possible of the following:

1. Observe teachers working with children and note how they model how to choose the most appropriate phoneme grapheme correspondence (GPC).

2. Re-read Chapter 2 to clarify any queries you may have.

3. Decide on a simple rule for the best way to choose the correct GPC for each of the following:

    ai or ay

    ur or ure

    aw or au

3. Grapheme–phoneme correspondences and 'tricky' or common exception words

Learning Outcomes

By the end of this chapter you will:

- understand challenges presented by the English alphabetical system in which 44 sounds are represented by 26 letters and over 400 combinations of letters;
- be able to map 44 phonemes to 26 letters;
- understand strategies for teaching irregular and less common grapheme–phoneme correspondences.

Teachers' Standards

3. Demonstrate good subject and curriculum knowledge:
    - if teaching early reading, demonstrate a clear understanding of systematic synthetic phonics.
4. Plan and teach well-structured lessons:
    - impart knowledge and develop understanding through effective use of lesson time.
5. Adapt teaching to respond to the strengths and needs of all pupils:
    - know when and how to differentiate appropriately, using approaches which enable pupils to be taught effectively.

Criteria for assuring high-quality phonic work (DfE, 2011)

Enable children to start learning phonic knowledge and skills using a systematic, synthetic programme by the age of five, with the expectation that they will be fluent readers having secured word recognition skills by the end of Key Stage 1 (see note 2).

Note 2: Teachers will make principled, professional judgements about when to start on a systematic synthetic programme of phonic work but it is reasonable to expect that the great majority of children will be capable of, and benefit from doing so by the age of five. It is equally important for the programme to be designed so that children become fluent readers having secured word recognition skills by the end of Key Stage 1.

Introduction

Teaching children to read in English is not the same as teaching them to read a transparent orthography such as Italian, Spanish, Finnish or Swahili. It is more complex.

(Dombey, 2006, p.103)

Dombey deals concisely and clearly with one of the major challenges we face when teaching phonics in English: the irregularities in the language which mean that our 44 phonemes can be represented in more than 400 different ways. As we will see in more detail in Chapter 4, unlike many other languages such as Italian, which has only 25 phonemes represented by 24 letters and eight letter combinations, English presents learners with a more complex challenge (see also Chapter 6). As McGuinness maintains, 'There is no question that the high functional illiteracy rate in English-speaking countries is largely a product of our formidable spelling code and the way it is (or is not) taught' (2004, p.41).

The irregularities in English are the result of the language being made up of several different languages, including Germanic languages, French and Latin. Add to this the fact that spellings have changed over the years and even those which have remained constant are often pronounced differently now, and the case for teaching reading through a phonic approach might begin to appear fragile.

However, despite its many contradictions, the English orthography actually has regular spellings for 80–90 per cent of its words (Adams, 1990; Crystal, 2005). It is, therefore, possible to teach children phoneme–grapheme correspondences which will enable them to decode successfully. Nevertheless, they will still encounter many words, including many of the most common 100 words in the language, which may require other strategies. This chapter will look at the reasons for the English language's varied grapheme–phoneme correspondences, and at strategies for teaching and learning the so-called 'tricky' words that are needed if children are to read anything which might engage their interest. As Dombey states: "it's very hard to make a readable text without words such as "a", "the", "I" and "you"' (2006, p.101).

Research Focus: The origins of English's complex orthography

It is interesting to consider how our complex orthography came about. In fact, before the Norman Conquest in 1066, we actually had quite a regular alphabetic system, even though there were more sounds than letters and some letters had to be combined to make some sounds. After 1066, the Normans imposed French as the language of those

→

who ruled the country, while most documents were written in Latin. Many Anglo-Saxon words were re-spelled by French scribes to reflect French spelling so that, for example, *c* replaced *s* before *e* or *i*, as in *cell* and *city* (see Bryson, 1990). In addition, some letters which had previously been pronounced, such as the *k* in *know* and the *g* in *gnaw*, became silent, and the way in which vowels were sounded changed in what has become known as the 'great vowel shift' of the 15th century. In addition, when printing developed in the 15th century, many early printers were German or Dutch and brought their own spellings to texts.

By the 17th century, with a standard spelling system still not in place, scholars began to modify the way in which they spelled some words to reflect their classical origins, so that *dette* became *debt* because it originated from the Latin *debitum* (think of a *debit* from your bank account), and words such as *receipt* acquired a *p*, *rime* became *rhyme*, and *rein* became *reign* with a *g* from the Latin *regno* (see Crystal, 2005).

A further vowel shift is described by Bryson as 'the most remarkable example of pronunciation change arising purely as a whim of fashion' when the English upper-class in southern England changed the way in which they pronounced words such as *dance*, *bath* and *castle* from a short *a* to 'a broad *a*, as if they were spelled *dahnce*, *bahth* and *cahstle*' (1990, p.91). As Bryson states: 'In the normal course of things, we might have expected the pronunciations to drift back. But for some reason they stuck ... helping to underscore the social, cultural, and orthoepic differences between not only Britons and Americans but even between Britons and Britons' (p.91).

Even after Samuel Johnson produced a dictionary in 1755, which did much to establish a spelling system, words have continued to be added to the language in their thousands as the British travelled the world and conquered large parts of it. Add to that the influx of immigrants from around the world bringing new terms for foods and other items (ciabatta, pizza, hamburger, vindaloo, sushi); the influence of American television, which brings us new words and phrases and alternatives to our own (*sidewalk* for pavement; *garbage* for rubbish etc.) and it is easy to see why English has become such a diverse and rich language. It is also easy to see why it has become such a challenging language for many native speakers to learn to read and write.

Attempting to solve the problem

One solution to the irregularities of English spelling was devised by Sir James Pitman (1961) and comprised a restructuring of the alphabet with additions made to cover the 44 phonemes. Children learned the sound–symbol correspondences and were provided with texts in which words were written in the Initial Teaching Alphabet (ITA), as shown in Figure 3.1.

b	c	d	f	g	h	j	k	l	m	n
bed	cat	dog	fish	goat	hat	jug	key	lion	man	nest

p	r	s	t	v	w	y	z	a	e	i
pet	rock	sun	table	voice	win	yet	zip	apple	engine	insect

o	u	æ	ee	ie	œ	ue	wh	ch	ſh	th
hot	umbrella	angel	eel	ice	oat	uniform	wheel	chair	shoe	thumb

ṭh	au	oi	ou	ŋ	ꭥ	ʒ	ɾ	ɑ	ω	ω
that	auto	oil	owl	ring	dogs	garage	bird	father	book	moon

Figure 3.1 Initial Teaching Alphabet (ITA) (www.omniglot.com/writing/ita.htm, accessed 21/12/11)

Activity

The ITA was used in around 16 per cent of schools during the 1960s, but faded away in the 1970s and 1980s and is no longer used in English schools. Why do you think this might be? What do you consider to be the advantages and drawbacks of ITA?

The ITA system was based on 'received pronunciation', so children with other accents could find it difficult to decipher (although look at Chapter 2, which addresses some issues related to accents). However, the main problems were:

- the limited availability of written materials (some reading schemes, including an ITA version of *Janet and John* – a popular reading series used in the 1950s and 1960s – were available);

- the transition to the traditional English orthography, which many children found difficult and to which some attribute later spelling problems.

More recently, Teaching Handwriting Reading and Spelling Skills (THRASS) (Davies and Ritchie, 1998) was introduced as a basis for teaching grapheme–phoneme correspondences. The authors recognised that English has a challenging orthographic system, and so THRASS aimed to provide 'the big picture' of the alphabetic system through its grapheme, word and picture charts which presented the 44 phonemes together with spelling possibilities. Many schools that adopted other systematic synthetic phonics programmes have continued to use the charts to help children with spelling choices. Like ITA, THRASS was based around spelling possibilities for the 44 phonemes, but unlike ITA it presented these using the normal alphabet and does not require children to make a transition to this at age seven as ITA did.

The essence of a systematic synthetic phonics programme is that it should support children's learning in a systematic, sequential way, with graphemes and phonemes being introduced in stages. An initial response from some people to the term 'synthetic phonics', when this approach was recommended in the Rose Review (2006), was that this was akin to ITA, which included an artificial alphabet. In fact, the term 'synthetic' should not be associated with 'artificiality', since it refers to synthesising or blending letters to make words. The association of the term with artificial fibres in clothing, which are created by blending materials together, led some to misunderstand the nature of synthetic phonics. Nevertheless, any phonically based teaching system for English needs to take into account the diversity of the orthographic system.

Case Study: Working with parents who question the importance of phonics teaching

Chloe, a final year BA QTS student, is working with a Year 1 class, and her class teacher invites her to take part in meetings with parents. One parent questions the need for systematic phonics teaching, citing an article she has read in a national newspaper which criticizes the approach and provides extensive examples of phonically irregular words that children meet in their early reading. The parent also says that she does not like the idea of children learning to read in an artificial, 'synthetic' way. The class teacher tells the parent that training to teach phonics is a key part of Chloe's course and asks if she would like to comment, given that she has been required to do a lot of background reading as part of her studies.

Activity

Put yourself in Chloe's place.

- What would you tell the parent about teaching phonics?
- How would you explain what is meant by systematic synthetic phonics?
- What would you tell her about teaching and learning common irregular words?

The 100 most common words

In Chapter 4, you will see that in order to create decodable texts for children it is necessary to include some of the common words that help bind the language together; these are the words that children see and use the most in their early reading and writing. The list contains many words with irregular and uncommon phoneme–grapheme correspondences. The list is shown in Table 3.1, in order of frequency.

Table 3.1 The 100 most common words in the English language, in order of frequency (Masterson et al., 2003)

the	are	do	about	and
up	me	got	a	had
down	their	to	my	dad
people	said	her	big	your
in	what	when	put	he
there	it's	could	I	out
see	house	of	this	looked
old	it	have	very	too
was	went	look	by	you
be	don't	day	they	like
come	made	on	some	will
time	she	so	into	I'm
is	not	back	if	for
then	from	help	at	were
children	Mrs	his	go	him
called	but	little	Mr	here
that	as	get	off	with
no	just	asked	all	mum
now	saw	we	one	came
make	can	them	oh	an

Some of these words are decodable (they can be sounded out by phoneme) at an early stage in children's phonic development. However, nearly half the words in the list are not easily decodable by the time children need to read and write them and have sufficient knowledge of grapheme–phoneme correspondences to be able to read many words in simple texts. Without the ability to read the most common words, children may become frustrated by their attempts at reading. There are many uncommon spelling patterns and tricky words contained within the list, and a range of phonics strategies should be employed to teach these words. The 2013 National Curriculum refers to 'common exception words', rather than 'tricky words'. For example, the programme of study for Year 1 includes:

read common exception words, noting unusual correspondences between spelling and sound and where these occur in the word.

(DfE, 2013, p.20)

It should be noted, too, that most words have some phonic regularity and that it is only parts of some words which are 'tricky'.

Below you will find strategies that may be used to teach the 100 most common words effectively.

Activity

Before reading on, consider which words in the list of the 100 most common are easily decodable and which are not. Make a list of each – you can then check your lists when reading the next section.

Grouping words

Children will learn words more quickly if they have recognised a common pattern or can experience a common theme. Grouping words will allow children to learn more than one word more effectively and quickly.

Grouping by decodable and tricky words

The list of the most common 100 words can be grouped into decodable or tricky words, as shown in Tables 3.2 and 3.3.

Table 3.2 Decodable words (DfES, 2007)

a	dad	but	look	time
an	had	put	too	house
as	back	will	went	about
at	and	that	It's	your

(Continued)

Table 3.2 (Continued)

if	get	this	from	day
in	big	then	children	made
is	him	them	just	came
it	his	with	help	make
of	not	see	don't	here
off	got	for	old	saw
on	up	now	I'm	very
can	mum	down	by	

These can usually be learned by sounding out phonemes and using other word-building techniques practised during phonics lessons and shared and guided reading.

Many of the words such as *got*, *but*, *can*, *dad* are easily decodable, requiring only basic phonemic knowledge involving single-letter phonemes. However, some of these words such as *your*, *very*, *house*, *time* are only decodable once children have learned more phonemes and phonic strategies through *Letters and Sounds* or other phonics programmes (see Chapter 13).

Table 3.3 Tricky words (DfES, 2007)

the	*me*	*said*	*little*	*Mrs*
to	*be*	*have*	*one*	*looked*
I	*was*	*like*	*when*	*called*
no	*you*	*so*	*out*	*asked*
go	*they*	*do*	*what*	*could*
into	*all*	*some*	*oh*	*he*
are	*come*	*their*	*she*	*my*
were	*people*	*we*	*her*	*there*
Mr				

These words cannot be sounded out phonetically at an early stage and are therefore harder to teach and learn. Many have irregular and uncommon phoneme–grapheme correspondences. They can be taught using other phonic strategies discussed below.

Grouping by phoneme and spelling pattern

Some of the 100 most common words can be grouped with others that are similar so that common patterns can be highlighted and words can be taught together. These groups could be:

he, she, we, me, be – with an *e* that makes the *ee* phoneme

no, go, so – with *o* that says its letter name

do, to – with *o* that makes the *oo* phoneme

of, off, on, oh – initial *o* phoneme

can, dad, had, get, big, him, his, not, got, mum, but, put, was – CVC words

for, now, day, saw, her – words which end with vowel digraphs

Mr, Mrs – titles that require capitalisation and are abbreviations

time, made, came, make, here, like – containing split digraphs

little, people – *le* final phoneme

some, come – rhyming

the, their, there, them, that, they, this, then – initial *th* phoneme

looked, called, asked – *ed* ending

it's, don't, I'm – containing apostrophes

when, what – initial *wh* phoneme

an, as, at, if, in, is, it, of, on, up – a vowel followed by a consonant

to, no, go, he, we, me, be, so, do, (by, my) – consonant followed by a vowel, including the alternative *y*

Mnemonics

This is the practice of improving or helping the memory by using a system, for example, devising an acrostic phrase for a tricky word. It can be a good teaching aid for some of the 100 most common words, particularly some of the tricky words that are not easily decodable. Children enjoy thinking of their own mnemonics and this can be a successful group or individual activity for words that your pupils are finding particularly tricky. Examples include:

said – Sally Ann is dancing

could/should/would – oh you lucky duck

down – ducks only waddle now

come/some – open my ears

were, there, here – every rainbow ends

Activity

Devise some mnemonic reminders for the tricky words *have*, *little* and *their*.

Looks like/sounds like

Some of the tricky words in the list of 100 most common words do not look the way they sound. They may have irregular or uncommon phonemes and spelling patterns which prove challenging for pupils. A simple chant can be used with children which highlights that words may look like one thing but sound like another. Examples may include:

'It looks like *was* but sounds like *woz*.'

'It looks like do but sounds like doo.'

Research Focus: Teaching the whole word

There are some words in the list of the most common 100 that are difficult to group with others and the phonic strategies already discussed simply are not suitable. It is, therefore, sometimes the most successful strategy to teach a tricky word as the 'whole thing' so that children can instantly recognise the word on sight. Children will become familiar and confident using these words with consistent revisiting through games and activities, the use of flash cards and posters in the classroom, and through plenty of opportunities to read and write the whole word in a variety of ways with different materials. A wide variety of ideas to support this can be found in Chapter 8. Nevertheless, we should not rely too heavily on learning whole words as a strategy in early reading.

Williams argues that learning whole words is not enough to become a skilled reader as it relies on visual memory and 'the number of new words encountered soon outstrips the ability to remember them on sight' (2006, p.55). Furthermore, Stuart (2006) found that in order to enter sight vocabulary, words need to be encountered significantly more often than most words appear in everyday reading.

Montgomery (1997) discussed whole-word learning through a 'look and say' approach and maintained that, as early as 1967, Chall's survey of teaching methods 'indicated that to delay the introduction of sound values ... slowed down the acquisition of reading (and spelling) skills' (Montgomery, 1997, p.9). Johnston and Watson advocate that when learning 'tricky' words children's attention should be drawn to the 'pronounceable elements' of the words and point out that 'even the word *yacht*... has a first and last letter which gives a guide to pronunciation' (2007, pp.36–7).

Activity

Look at the next 50 most common words, which are presented in order of frequency in Table 3.4. Notice how many are phonically regular and easily decodable.

Table 3.4 A further 50 most common words in order of frequency (Masterson et al., 2003)

water	away	good	want	over
how	did	man	going	where
would	or	took	school	think
home	who	didn't	ran	know
bear	can't	again	cat	long
things	new	after	wanted	eat
everyone	our	two	has	yes
play	take	thought	dog	well
find	more	I'll	round	tree
magic	shouted	us	other	food

Using some of the strategies described for the 100 most common words, consider:

- Which words might be 'tricky' and why might children find them so?
- How would you help children to learn the words?

Learning Outcomes Review

You should now understand challenges presented by the English alphabetical system in which 44 sounds are represented by 26 letters and over 400 combinations of letters and be able to map 44 phonemes to 26 letters. The chapter has explored strategies for teaching irregular and less common grapheme–phoneme correspondences.

Self-assessment questions

Can you define each of the following terms, which feature in this and previous chapters?

(Continued)

(Continued)

1. Grapheme
2. Phoneme
3. Synthetic phonics
4. Decodable
5. 'Tricky' or common exception word
6. Orthographic system

Further Reading

For a range of interesting chapters about phonics from different perspectives, see:

Lewis, M. and Ellis, S. (eds) (2006) *Phonics, Practice, Research and Policy.* London: Paul Chapman.

For practical suggestions on teaching phonics, see:

Gill, A. and Waugh, D. (2017) *Phonics: Getting it Right in a Week.* Northwich: Critical Publishing.

Glazzard, J. and Stokoe, J. (2013) Teaching Systematic Synthetic Phonics and Early English. London: Critical Teaching, esp. Chapter 4.

Jolliffe, W. (2007) *You Can Teach Phonics.* Leamington Spa: Scholastic.

For guidance on teaching 'tricky' or common exception words, see Chapter 11 in:

Waugh, D., Carter, J. and Desmond, C. (2015) *Lessons in Phonics*. London: SAGE.

References

Adams, M.J. (1990) *Beginning to Read: Learning and Thinking about Print*. London: MIT Press.

Bryson, B. (1990) *The Mother Tongue*. London: Penguin.

Chall, J.S. (1967) *Learning to Read: The Great Debate*. New York: McGraw-Hill.

Crystal, D. (2005) *How Language Works*. London: Penguin.

Davies, A. and Ritchie, D. (1998) *THRASS: Teacher's Manual*. Chester: THRASS.

DfE (2011) *Teachers' Standards in England from September 2012*. London: DfE.

DfE (2013) *The National Curriculum in England, Key Stages 1 and 2 Framework Document*. London: DfE.

DfES (2007) *Letters and Sounds: Principles and Practice of High Quality Phonics*. London: DfES.

Dombey, H. (2006) 'Phonics, practice, research and policy', in M. Lewis and S. Ellis (eds), *Phonics: Practice, Research and Policy*. London: Paul Chapman.

Johnston, R. and Watson, J. (2007) *Teaching Synthetic Phonics*. Exeter: Learning Matters.

Masterson, J., Stuart, M., Dixon, M. and Lovejoy, S. (2003) *Children's Printed Word Database: Economic and Social Research Council Funded Project* (Ref: R00023406). Nottingham: DCSF. Available at www.scribd.com/doc/19010234/14/Appendix-5-The-first--100--high--frequency-words (accessed 17/3/12).

McGuinness, D. (2004) *Early Reading Instruction: What Science Really Tells Us about How to Teach Reading*. Cambridge, MA: MIT Press.

Montgomery, D. (1997) *Spelling: Remedial Strategies*. London: Cassell.

Pitman, J. (1961) 'Learning to read: An experiment', *Journal of the Royal Society of Arts*, 109.

Rose, J. (2006) *Independent Review of the Teaching of Early Reading, Final Report, March 2006* (The Rose Review – Ref: 0201-2006DOC-EN). Nottingham: DfES.

Stuart, M. (2006) 'Learning to read the words on the page: The crucial role of early phonics teaching', in M. Lewis and S. Ellis (eds), *Phonics: Practice, Research and Policy*. London: Paul Chapman.

Williams, M. (2006) '"Playing with words": Level work including vocabulary, phonics and spelling', in R. Fisher and M. Williams (eds), *Unlocking Literacy: A Guide for Teachers*, 2nd edn. London: Fulton.

Audit and test

Work through each section below, responding to each question or task. When you have completed each section, you can read the answers at the end of the chapter. At the end of the chapter, you can also find support for further reading and study related to tricky words.

Section 1: Key terminology for grapheme–phoneme correspondences and 'tricky' words

It is important that you understand the terms below before you move on to the next activity. Provide a definition of each and check your definitions against those at the end of the chapter:

Orthographic system

Decodable

Decoding

Encoding

Phonically irregular

Mnemonic

Over-syllabification

Section 2: Grapheme–phoneme correspondences – 'grotty graphemes'

The phonics programme Read Write Inc. uses the term 'grotty grapheme' for the graphemes which make a word 'tricky'. For example, in *said*, the *ai* in the middle is a short vowel sound rather than the long vowel sound usually made by *ai* (*rain, pain, drain* etc.).

These 'grotty graphemes' become less of a challenge as children develop their knowledge of more complex grapheme–phoneme correspondences. For the purposes of this activity, we have used the grapheme–phoneme correspondences defined in *Letters and Sounds* Phases 2 and 3 as follows:

Phase 2	Phase 3
Set 1: s, a, t, p	Set 6: j, v, w, x
Set 2: i, n, m, d	Set 7: y, z, zz, qu
Set 3: g, o, c, k	
Set 4: ck, e, u, r	
Set 5: h, b, f, ff, l, ll, ss	

Phase 3

Graphemes	Sample words	Graphemes	Sample words
ch	chip	ar	farm
sh	shop	or	for
th	thin/then	ur	hurt
ng	ring	ow	cow
ai	rain	oi	coin
ee	feet	ear	dear
igh	night	air	fair
oa	boat	ure	sure
oo	boot/look	er	corner

Based on knowledge of the grapheme–phoneme correspondences in Phases 2 and 3 above, identify the 'grotty graphemes' in the following common words:

old   was   have   no   he   you

day   saw   were   your   here   they

Section 3: Identifying tricky bits in 50 most common English words

For children with knowledge of the grapheme–phoneme correspondence above, try to identify any tricky bits in the 50 most common words. Consider why they might be tricky. The first few have been done for you and are presented in underlined bold type. Not all of the words contain tricky bits.

the	was	that	th**ere**	then
and	y**ou**	with	out	**were**
a	they	all	this	go
to	on	we	have	little
said	she	are	went	as
in	is	up	be	no
he	for	had	like	mum
I	at	my	some	one
of	his	her	so	do
it	but	what	not	me

(from Masterson et al., 2003)

Section 4: Exploring alternative spellings

You will meet many spelling mistakes from your pupils. To understand why children spell as they do, it is useful to explore possible alternative, but incorrect, spellings for some common words, for example, *fish – phish, once – wons, tough – tuff.*

See how many phonically plausible different ways you could spell each of the following:

germ

school

make

because

could

said

ANSWERS

Section 1: Key terminology for grapheme–phoneme correspondences and 'tricky' words

Orthographic system

> The spelling system of a language, i.e. the ways in which graphemes and phonemes relate to each other. The English orthographic system is more complex than many languages, since most phonemes can be represented by more than one grapheme.

Decodable

> Words which can be easily decoded using phonic strategies, e.g. cat, dog, lamp.

Decoding

> The act of translating graphemes into phonemes, i.e. reading.

Encoding

> The act of transcribing units of sound or phonemes into graphemes, i.e. spelling.

Phonically irregular

> Words that are not easily decoded because they do not conform to common grapheme–phoneme correspondences.

Mnemonic

> A device for remembering something, such as 'ee/ee/ feel the tree'.

Section 2: Grapheme–phoneme correspondences – 'grotty graphemes'

The phonics programme Read Write Inc. uses the term 'grotty grapheme' for the graphemes which make a word 'tricky'. For example, in said, the ai in the middle is a short vowel sound rather than the long vowel sound usually made by *ai* (*rain*, *pain*, *drain* etc).

Look at the words below and identify the 'grotty graphemes':

> old: 'o' grapheme represents the long vowel sound rather than the short vowel sound

> w<u>a</u>s: 'a' grapheme represents an 'o' sound rather than the short vowel sound it usually represents

> ha<u>ve</u>: this is not a split digraph (see Chapter 5). Instead the 've' grapheme makes the 'v' sound

> n<u>o</u>: 'o' grapheme represents the long vowel sound rather than the short vowel sound

> h<u>e</u>: 'e' grapheme represents the long vowel sound rather than the short vowel sound

> y<u>ou</u>: 'ou' grapheme represents an 'oo' sound which is a less common grapheme–phoneme correspondence and has not been taught in Phase 2 or 3

d<u>ay</u>: 'ay' grapheme represents an 'ai' sound. This grapheme–phoneme correspondence has not been taught in Phase 2 or 3

s<u>aw</u>: 'aw' grapheme represents an 'or' sound. This grapheme–phoneme correspondence has not been taught in Phase 2 or 3

w<u>ere</u>: 'ere' grapheme represents an 'ur' sound. This grapheme–phoneme correspondence has not been taught in Phase 2 or 3

y<u>our</u>: 'our' grapheme represents an 'or' sound. This grapheme–phoneme correspondence has not been taught in Phase 2 or 3

h<u>ere</u>: 'ere' grapheme represents an 'ear' sound. This grapheme–phoneme correspondence has not been taught in Phase 2 or 3

th<u>ey</u>: 'ey' grapheme represents an 'ai' sound which is a less common grapheme–phoneme correspondence and has not been taught in Phase 2 or 3.

Section 3: Identifying 'tricky bits' in 100 most common English word

th<u>e</u>	was	that	th<u>ere</u>	then
and	<u>you</u>	with	out	were
a	th<u>ey</u>	<u>a</u>ll	this	g<u>o</u>
t<u>o</u>	on	w<u>e</u>	ha<u>ve</u>	little
s<u>ai</u>d	sh<u>e</u>	are	went	as
in	is	up	b<u>e</u>	no
he	for	had	like	mum
I	at	m<u>y</u>	s<u>ome</u>	one*
of	his	h<u>er</u>	s<u>o</u>	d<u>o</u>
it	but	what	not	m<u>e</u>

*It is not possible to show the phonemes represented by graphemes in the word one.

Section 4: Alternative spellings

Some possible incorrect alternatives include:

germ	jerm, jurm, jirm, gurm, girm
school	skool, skoole, skule, schule, scule, sckule, sckool, sckoole, skewl, skuel, skoul
make	maek, maik, mayk, meak, meyk,
because	becos, bicos, becaus, beecos, beecoz, becoz
could	cud, culd, kud, kuld, kudd, cudd
said	sed, sedd, sayed, sead, psed, psedd (think of pseudonym)

You may have thought of others too, and you may see others when you analyse children's writing. The important thing is to check if children are hearing all the different phonemes in words when they attempt to spell them. They can go on to investigate spelling possibilities and probabilities through word sort activities and through looking at a range of texts.

What to do next?

Reinforce your knowledge and understanding of 'tricky' words by doing the following:

1. Observe teachers teaching children 'tricky' words and note how they help children to remember the tricky bits.

2. Look at a piece of writing produced by a child working in Phase 3 of *Letters and Sounds*, or an equivalent stage in another programme, and analyse the spelling errors to consider why they may have made them and the grapheme–phoneme correspondence that they have drawn on.

4. Decoding and encoding text

Learning Outcomes

By the end of this chapter you should:

- have a clear understanding of the reversible processes of decoding and encoding text;
- understand the importance of providing opportunities for the application of phonic knowledge in reading and writing;
- understand the role of decodable texts in the teaching of reading.

Teachers' Standards

3. Demonstrate good subject and curriculum knowledge:

   - demonstrate a critical understanding of developments in the subject and curriculum areas, and promote the value of scholarship;
   - if teaching early reading, demonstrate a clear understanding of systematic synthetic phonics.

Criteria for assuring high-quality phonic work (DfE, 2011)

Demonstrate that phonemes should be blended, in order, from left to right, 'all through the word' for reading.

Demonstrate how words can be segmented into their constituent phonemes for spelling and that this is the reverse of blending phonemes to read words. Ensure that as pupils move through the early stages of acquiring phonics, they are invited to practise by reading texts which are entirely decodable for them, so that they experience success and learn to rely on phonemic strategies (see note 7).

Note 7: It is important that texts are of the appropriate level for children to apply and practise the phonic knowledge and skills that they have learned. Children should not be expected to use strategies such as whole-word recognition and/or cues from context, grammar or pictures.

Introduction

Decoding and encoding are the mechanisms by which phonics is applied to reading and writing and this chapter will explore not only the importance of these reversible processes, but also how to put them into practice. This chapter will also revisit the difficulties faced by the English alphabetic code and its complex orthography and the need to ensure that teaching the entire alphabetic code is covered, including its more complex aspects. The chapter will particularly review why it is important to provide opportunities for the application of phonic knowledge in both reading and writing. As The Tickell Review of the Early Years Foundation indicated, it is the application of this knowledge that has not always been well addressed:

> *Many children grasp the grapheme–phoneme correspondences in isolation but are not able to, or lack opportunity to, apply their skills in meaningful ways.*

(Tickell, 2011, p.103)

The chapter will conclude with a review of the role of decodable texts and examples of how they are used to support children's reading skills.

Decoding and encoding

It is first important to be clear what the terms mean and then to explore further their interrelationship. 'Decoding' concerns reading the symbols or letters and transferring them into sounds to recover the words. Therefore, when decoding we sound out the letters and blend them together to make a word. 'Encoding' involves spelling and is the process of turning sounds into symbols or letters. These processes of decoding and encoding are reversible and it is crucial, when teaching young children, that we make this explicit by providing opportunities to both read and write graphemes for the corresponding phonemes during every phonics teaching session. In the past, there has often been a focus on phonics for reading to support decoding the text without emphasising that alongside this children should be taught to spell the words. This emphasis on reversibility helps cement the learning for children, for we can always read words we can spell, but we cannot always spell words we can read. Ensuring that opportunities are provided to decode and encode text that work in tandem provides valuable reinforcement of the grapheme–phoneme correspondences. While these two processes are reversible, they nevertheless require different skills. Decoding, or reading, requires recognition memory as the letters act as a prompt. For encoding, the visual prompt is not present and the child must use recall memory, which is more difficult. To spell a word, a child needs to carry out the following tasks:

1. Identify the phonemes in the word (e.g. *read* – /r/ /ee/ /d/ = 3 phonemes).

2. Recall the phonemes in the correct sequence (/r/ /ee/ /d/).

3. Remember how each phoneme is spelled (/r/ 'r', / ee/ 'ea', /d/ 'd' = 'read').

4. Write the correct grapheme to represent each phoneme (*read*).

Activity

Practising decoding and encoding

Work with a colleague or friend to read the words in Table 4.1 to each other and then segment them into phonemes. Count the number of phonemes after segmenting the words and carry out the steps demonstrated above.

Table 4.1 Counting phonemes

Word	Segmented into phonemes	Number of phonemes
splash		
stretch		
spell		
moon		
care		
sauce		
judge		
comb		
sneeze		
caught		

The answers to the activity are given in Table 4.2.

Table 4.2 Answers to exercise 'Counting phonemes'

Word	Segmented into phonemes	Number of phonemes
splash	/s/ /p/ /l/ /a/ /sh/	5
stretch	/s/ /t/ /r/ /e/ /t/ /ch/	5
spell	/s/ /p/ /e/ /ll/	4
moon	/m/ /oo/ /n/	3
care	/c/ /are/	2
sauce	/s/ /au/ /ce/	3
judge	/j/ /u/ /dge/	3
comb	/c/ /o/ /mb/	3
sneeze	/s/ /n/ /ee/ /ze/	4
caught	/c/ /augh/ /t/	3

Segmenting and blending

Closely linked to decoding and encoding texts is the ability to segment and blend words.

Research Focus: Segmenting and blending

McGuinness (2004) cites confusion between segmenting and blending, which leads to the assumption that reading involves blending and spelling involves segmenting. This means that when we read we rapidly translate letters into phonemes and blend them into a word. When we spell, we say the word, segment it into the phonemes and translate each phoneme into a letter or letters. However, as McGuinness states, this is not what happens and she cites the following example:

Children see an unfamiliar word, e.g. sting.

To read it a child sounds out each phoneme: /s/ /t/ /i/ /ng/. They blend it into a word and check the outcome. It is common for beginning readers to segment correctly and blend incorrectly: /s/ /t/ /i/ /ng/: and say 'sing'.

To spell the word sting, the children say the word, hear each segment in sequence and blend the segments into the word as they write.

(2004, p.161)

In reality, segmenting and blending are intimately connected in both reading and spelling. It is not the case that one is purely related to reading and the other to spelling. They are interrelated. For experienced readers the process happens at a phenomenal speed – the same sound-by-sound analysis happens, but the speed makes for automaticity. We only become aware of this interplay when we encounter a word we cannot read or spell.

Activity

Segmenting and blending: The interrelationship

Read the following words slowly and consider the process you undertake. Where possible discuss this with a colleague. You can check the pronunciation in a dictionary.

pyroclastic
oblanceolate
sulphonylurea

Spelling for reading

Research for centuries has shown that spelling has a fundamental success rate in relation to reading. Webster (1793[1968]), in analysing the English alphabetic code, realised this when he wrote a 'speller' and not a 'reader' and put the emphasis on the links between successful spelling and reading. Maria Montessori (1912) also advised teachers to teach spelling first and then for children to use this to read what they have written. In 1985, Frith proposed a six-step model of learning to read and spell, to draw out children's early ability to hear sounds in words. Huxford et al. (1991) showed a progression in which children's ability to spell phonemically regular words preceded their ability to read them. The reading programme *Breakthrough to Literacy* (first published in 1969) advocated a complex system of using language folders with individual words on cards for children to construct sentences. Larger versions of 'sentence holders' and word cards enabled the teacher to model the process. Of course, this system relied on 'look and say' or whole-word recognition rather than phonics; nevertheless, the principle of the interrelationship between writing and reading was present. This illustrates the importance of creating texts for children linked to their phonic knowledge. Such texts can also be linked to a child's experiences and cultural background and therefore become more meaningful.

Case Study: Children creating their own books

In one Reception class, the teacher had taught Phase 2 and some of Phase 3 of *Letters and Sounds* (DfES, 2007) and then provided the children with their own mini-books. On each page, the children were first encouraged to write their names followed by the consonant-vowel-consonant (CVC) word *can*. They then selected a different word from a list that they could decode (e.g. *hop, pop, pat* etc.):

Lucy can hop

Lucy can pop

Lucy can pat

Lucy can tip

Lucy can nip

Lucy can …

The children were encouraged to act out the sentences and to provide an illustration. Books were then taken home to be shared with parents and carers and to be added to with other similar sentences.

English – an opaque alphabetic code

As we have seen in Chapters 2 and 3, one of the essential aspects to understand in relation to the reversible aspects of encoding and decoding is that a writing system is a code with a direct correspondence between the sounds or phonemes and the visual symbols or graphemes. If the code cannot be reversed through encoding/decoding, it is not a code. The problem with the English language is that the code is opaque and there is not a direct correspondence between the 26 letters of the alphabet and the 40+ phonemes. In other languages, this is not the case and the codes are more clearly reversible. Finnish, for example, is nearly completely regular as are Italian, Swedish, Norwegian and German. A review produced by Eurydice on teaching reading in Europe (2011, p.33), reinforces the difficulties for those learning to read in English and states that: *'The development of basic reading skills in orthographically inconsistent languages appears to take more than twice as long as in languages with consistent orthographies.'*

Research Focus: Comparing alphabetic codes

Comparative studies of languages have provided clear evidence of the differences in the transparency of the alphabetic codes.

Venezky (1973) studied 240 Finnish children in grades 1 to 3 and found how easy it was to learn to read and write a transparent alphabet. Children begin reading in Finland at age seven. After one year of tuition, in a reading test of nonsense words denoting the complete Finnish orthography, the children scored 80 per cent and the same test administered to college students showed 90 per cent correct. This showed that it takes only about a year to gain proficiency in Finnish spelling.

Wimmer and Landerl (1997) compared Austrian and English children in a test of German and English words with similar complexity. The English children made twice the number of spelling errors as the Austrian children and, importantly, 90 per cent of the errors made by the Austrian children were phonemically accurate compared to only 32 per cent for the English children.

Geva and Siegel (2000) found a similar pattern in a study of 245 Canadian children who were learning to read and write both English and Hebrew, with English as the first language. Hebrew is a transparent writing system that uses symbols for consonants and diacritic marks for vowels when texts are difficult, as for beginning readers. By the end of the first grade, the children scored 79 per cent correct on the Hebrew reading test but only 44 per cent correct on the English version of the test. Children did not achieve 80 per cent competency until the fifth grade.

Desimoni et al. (2012) in a study of Italian children found that the consistency of the orthography of a language affects reading and spelling acquisition. Likewise Seymour et al. (2003) in a comparison of 14 European languages found striking difference with English-speaking children performing poorly in comparison and, at the end of grade one, they were only demonstrating 34 per cent correct word reading whereas children learning to read in transparent orthographies (Greek, Finnish, German, Italian, and Spanish) were close to maximum expected competence.

Phonics and spelling – the debate

There have been many debates around the connection between phonics and spelling. Some teachers deny an association between phonics and spelling and argue that encouraging children to write words as they sound encourages incorrect spelling. Nevertheless, the English language is an alphabetic system and this does form the basis of spelling words. Gentry (1982) and others have documented examples of children's attempts at phonemic spelling. Gunter Kress (2000) illustrates that very young children often use a mixture of pictures and letters/symbols to convey text.

The encouragement of developmental writing or 'invented spelling' has also been questioned, and when originally proposed as part of the National Writing Project in England (1985–89), developmental writing was intended to include phonically plausible spelling, although this was not widely recognised. The reason for the emphasis that early years educators placed on developmental writing was the motivational effect this had on young children, who previously when asked to write (to produce correct spellings) were often reluctant and would view the task as too difficult.

A range of research studies (Liberman et al., 1974; Lundberg et al., 1980; Bradley and Bryant, 1983; Ehri and Wilce, 1987) have demonstrated that instruction in isolating sounds in words (segmenting) and representing these sounds with letters (spelling) also has a beneficial effect on beginning reading.

Case Study: Children's spelling errors

Analysis of children's spelling errors can be very informative and indicate their level of phonic knowledge and possible gaps. Shahira is working on an English assignment that requires her to identify five spelling errors made by a child, analyse what they tell her about the child's phonic knowledge, and state what specific teaching is required to move the child on further in his/her understanding.

She notes the following errors:

new spelled as *niyoo*

because spelled as *bcoos*

left spelled as *lefd*

too spelled as *tow*

food spelled as *fud*

→

During a tutorial with her mentor, Shahira makes the following notes in preparation for her assignment:

- *new* spelled as *niyoo* – here the child makes a phonemically plausible attempt but has not learned the grapheme-phoneme correspondence for the /oo/ phoneme (spelled as *ew*).
- *because* spelled as *bcoos* – here the child makes a phonemically plausible attempt at the phoneme / / which she represents as *oo*, the '*schwa*': an unstressed vowel sound which is close to /u/ can be spelled in a number of ways. This word is therefore commonly taught as a 'tricky' word and learned as a whole word.
- *left* spelled as *lefd* – the child here makes a common error in spelling the end of the word as *d* instead of *t*. Work on hearing the final sound would help here.
- *too* spelled as *tow* – here the child makes a phonemically plausible attempt but writes the /oo/ phoneme as *ow*. Work on similar words using the graphemes *oo* would help.
- *food* spelled as *fud* – here the child makes a phonemically plausible attempt but writes the /oo/ phoneme as *u*. Again, work on similar words using the grapheme *oo* would help.

Research (Silva and Martins, 2003) suggests that the analysis of spelling errors indicates the level of children's phonological knowledge. There are also patterns of errors, demonstrating:

- phonetically influenced errors on consonants – the /ch/ phoneme sounds as if it starts with a /t/ sound, so is often spelled with the letter t; the phonemes /t/ and /d/ overlap in their pronunciation, and so /t/ is often spelled with the letter *d;*
- omission of unstressed vowels – such as leaving out the letter *i* in *animal;*
- letter name spellings – *lfunt* for elephant; the letter name for *l* is *el*, *f* is *ef.*

The role of decodable texts

The criteria for assuring high-quality phonic work (DfE, 2011) state that phonics teaching should ensure that as pupils move through the early stages of acquiring phonics, they practise by reading texts which are entirely decodable for them so that they experience success and learn to rely on phonemic strategies. Decodable texts contain words that are at an appropriate phonemic level for children to read. Therefore, the first stage books would commonly contain some consonant and short vowel phonemes such as (/s/ /a/ /t/ /p/ /i/ /n/) which are used in a number of simple CVC words. As the activity below demonstrates, such texts are very limited. It is necessary to introduce a small number of high-frequency words such as *the, was, said* in order to create sentences that have some meaning and interest (see Chapter 3). The majority of published phonics schemes include the teaching of a limited number of such words that cannot be decoded easily at the early stages of phonics teaching, and they are often referred to as 'tricky' or 'common exception' words. Such words are introduced to children as difficult, odd, or 'red' words and then are learned as whole words. It is important to limit the number of these words so that children are not using whole-word recognition as a frequent strategy for reading, and that the prime strategy is to decode using phonics.

Decodable texts provide practice for children in reading known phonemes and blending into words. The activity below demonstrates the need for teachers to create sentences and short texts for such purposes. One of the debates that has raged around these texts involves the limited amount of meaning and interest which can be gained from such limited texts. Dombey et al. (2010) and Wyse and Goswami (2008) amongst others have argued that learning to read means learning to make sense of texts. One of the key aims of early reading is to foster a love of reading, and some claim the use of decodable texts does exactly the opposite. However, the proposal is not for children to be solely exposed to decodable texts; this is a small part of the rich diet they should be offered in a language-rich curriculum. Cheatham and Allor (2012) reviewed research into decodable texts and found that decodability is a critical feature with pupils in early phases of reading instruction, which has immediate benefits in increasing the accuracy of what is read. However, they also identify that this is just one feature of developing successful readers. Being read to and enjoying the wonderful world of children's books is another vital part of the curriculum, alongside practising their developing reading skills using decodable texts and examples of sentences and notices in the classroom.

Research Focus: Decodable texts

There is some research to show that for struggling readers a restricted diet of decodable texts may not be helpful. Clark (2014, 2017) argues that simplified text may not only be less stimulating for struggling readers, but also more difficult to comprehend. Price-Mohr and Price (2018, p.5) also found from a small study in one school that:

> children who are not making expected progress in reading, may benefit, in terms of word reading and comprehension, from instructional reading texts that go beyond their presumed decoding ability. They suggest that an assumption that it is easier for children to learn to read using easily phonically decodable words may be unfounded and that the reverse may be true.

Studies also show that there are gender differences in learning to read and, in particular, in using decodable texts. Price-Mohr and Price's research (2017: 613) found:

⟶

statistically significant evidence suggesting that boys learn more easily using a mix of whole-word and synthetic phonics approaches. In addition, the evidence indicates that boys learn to read more easily using the natural-style language of 'real' books including vocabulary which goes beyond their assumed decoding ability.

This emphasises the need to ensure that children are not restricted to purely decodable texts and have access to a wide range of children's books. The Education Endowment Fund's report (2016, p.5), based on a review of research on improving Key Stage 1 Literacy, cites very extensive evidence that children need:

a range of wider language and literacy experiences to develop their understanding of written texts in all their forms.

Activity

Creating decodable books

The use of mini-books that contain simple decodable text at a level that is appropriate for young children is a valuable tool for practising blending phonemes. Examples of these are found in *Phonics: A Complete Synthetic Programme* by Jolliffe (2006) and *Quick Fix for Phonics* (Jolliffe, 2012). You may also like to create your own books by folding several A4 pages in half and stapling along the left-hand edge. On each page write simple sentences using phonemes you have taught; for example, for the phonemes /s/a/t/p/i/n/ you could create the words:

tap, sat, pin, at, pat, nap, nip, ant, tip, in, an

The following simple sentences and phrases could be written into mini-books:

An ant sat	Pat an ant
sat on a pin	tap, tap, tap
in a pin	in a tap
Nip, nip, nip	an ant

You may like to encourage children to create their own illustrations after having read the sentence. Alternatively, you could incorporate a range of pictures obtained from 'clip art' or a similar program. If first books can be personalised to the child, that will help encourage them to read. For example:

Ben sat on an ant.
Nip, nip, nip!

Now look at Table 4.3, which provides possible words for the earlier stages of teaching phonics and, working with colleagues, create some decodable texts.

Table 4.3 Word bank

Phoneme	Possible words
s	as
a	
t	sat, at
i	sit, it, its, is
p	pip, pit, pat, tap, tip, sip
n	nap, nip, nit, an, ant, pan, pin, tan, tin, spin, in, pant, snap, snip

Creating such decodable books provides useful application of developing phonic knowledge, and as the National Reading Panel state:

> *Programs that focus too much on the teaching of letter-sounds relations and not enough on putting them to use are unlikely to be very effective. In implementing systematic phonics instruction, educators must keep the end in mind and ensure that children understand the purpose of learning letter-sounds and are able to apply their skills in their daily reading and writing activities.*

(NICHD, 2000, pp.2–96)

National Curriculum links

The 2013 National Curriculum in England sets out that for pupils in Year 1 they:

> *need to develop the skill of blending the sounds into words for reading and establish the habit of applying this skill whenever they encounter new words. This will be supported by practice in reading books consistent with their developing phonic knowledge and skill and their knowledge of common exception words.*

(DfE, 2013, p.20)

Learning Outcomes Review

The phonemes are constant but the spellings change.

As the research above pinpoints, English is a complex opaque spelling system compared to many other languages. As a result of this the English alphabetic code needs to be carefully taught to ensure that the 40+ phonemes of the language and the common (approximately 176) spellings are fully taught. The code becomes more transparent if it is taught in the way it was written: from sounds to multiple spellings and back to sounds. If this is the case, the consistency of the phonemes becomes clear – the sounds stay the same but the spellings of them do not. This is particularly the case with many vowel phonemes which can be spelled in different ways (e.g. the phoneme /ie/ can be written as *igh* in *light* and *i* in *tiger* or *y* in *fly* or *i-e* in *bike*).

The teaching of reading and spelling needs to be interconnected

This supports the use of different memory skills and aids the learning process. Thus it is important to ensure that decoding (reading) and encoding (spelling) are connected throughout teaching: by looking (visual memory), listening (auditory memory) and writing (kinaesthetic memory). In order to do this, every phonics lesson should provide opportunities for writing the corresponding graphemes for the phonemes, as well as reading words that contain them.

Self-assessment questions

1. Outline the interrelationship between segmenting and blending phonemes.
2. What are some of the difficulties in the English spelling system?
3. What is the role of decodable texts in the teaching of reading?

Further Reading

To explore in more detail the importance of decoding and encoding and how these need to be constantly and reversibly applied, see:

McGuinness, D. (2004) *Early Reading Instruction: What Science Really Tells Us about How to Teach Reading*. Cambridge, MA: MIT Press.

For practical suggestions to support teaching, see:

Jolliffe, W. (2013) *The Primary Teachers' Guide to Phonics*. Witney: Scholastic.

References

Bradley, L. and Bryant, P.E. (1983) 'Categorizing sounds and learning to read – a causal connection', *Nature, 301*: 419–21.

Cheatham, J.P. and Allor, J.H. (2012) 'The influence of decodability in early reading text on reading achievement: A review of the evidence', *Reading and Writing, 25*: 2223–46.

Clark, M.M. (2014) *Synthetic Phonics and Literacy Learning*. Birmingham: Glendale Education.

Clark, M.M. (2017) *Reading the Evidence: Synthetic Phonics and Literacy Learning*. Birmingham: Glendale Education.

Desimoni, M., Scalisi, T.G. and Orsolini, M. (2012) 'Predictive and concurrent relations between literacy skills in Grades 1 and 3: A longitudinal study of Italian children', *Learning and Instruction, 22*: 340–53.

DfE (2011) *Teachers' Standards in England from September 2012*. London: DfE.

DfE (2013) The National Curriculum in England. Available from: https://www.gov.uk/national-curriculum (accessed 2/11/18).

DfES (2007) *Letters and Sounds: Notes of Guidance for Practitioners and Teachers*. Norwich: DfES.

Dombey, H. and colleagues (2010) *Teaching Reading: What the evidence says*. Leicester: UK Literary Association. Available at www.ukla.org/publications/view/teaching_reading_what_the_evidence_says/ (accessed 27/12/11).

Education Endowment Foundation (2016) *Improving Literacy in Key Stage One*. London: Education Endowment Foundation.

Ehri, L.C. and Wilce, L.S. (1987) 'Does learning to spell help beginners learn to read words?', *Reading Research Quarterly, 22*: 47–65.

Eurydice (2011) *Teaching reading in Europe: Contexts Policies and Practices*. Education, Audiovisual and Culture Executive Agency. Available from: https://publications.europa.eu/en/publication-detail/-/publication/816adc3b-ca0f-41e0-9c7c-6892993b3f11/language-en/format-PDF/source-69190744 (accessed 16/4/18).

Frith, U. (1985) 'Beneath the surface of developmental dyslexia', in J. Patterson, J.C. Marshall and M. Coltheart (eds), *Surface Dyslexia*. London: Erlbaum. pp.301–30.

Gentry, R. (1982) 'An analysis of developmental spelling in GNYS AT WRK', *The Reading Teacher, 36*: 192–200.

Geva, E. and Siegel, L.S. (2000) 'Orthographic and cognitive factors in the concurrent development of basic reading skills in two languages', *Reading and Writing: An Interdisciplinary Journal, 12*: 1–30.

Huxford, L., Terrell, C. and Bradley, L. (1991) *The Relationship Between the Phonological Strategies Employed in Reading and Spelling*. London: Blackwell.

Jolliffe, W. (2006) *Phonics: A Complete Synthetic Programme*. Leamington Spa: Scholastic.

Jolliffe, W. (2012) *Quick Fix for Phonics*. Witney: Scholastic.

Kress, G. (2000) *Early Spelling*. London: Routledge.

Liberman, A.M., Fowler, C. and Fischer, F.W. (1974) 'Explicit syllable and phoneme segmentation in the young child', *Journal of Experimental Child Psychology*, 18: 201–12.

Lundberg, I., Olofsson, A. and Wall, S. (1980) 'Reading and spelling skills in the first school years predicted from phonemic awareness skills in kindergarten', *Scandinavian Journal of Psychology*, 21: 159–73.

McGuinness, D. (2004) *Early Reading Instruction: What Science Really Tells Us about How to Teach Reading*. Cambridge, MA: MIT Press.

Montessori, M. (1912) *The Montessori Method* (trans. Anne George). London: Heinemann.

National Institute of Child Health and Human Development (NICHD) (2000) *Report of the National Reading Panel*. 'Teaching children to read: An evidence-based assessment of the scientific research literature on reading and its implications for reading instruction: Reports of the subgroups'. NIH publication no. 00-4754. Washington, DC: Government Printing Office.

Price-Mohr, R. and Price, C.B. (2017) 'Gender differences in early reading strategies: A comparison of synthetic phonics only with a mixed approach to teaching reading to 4–5 year-old children', *Early Childhood Education Journal*, 45: 613–20.

Price-Mohr, R., and Price, C.B. (2018) 'Synthetic phonics and decodable instructional reading texts: How far do these support poor readers?', *Dyslexia*: 1–7.

Seymour, P.H.K., Aro, M. and Erskine, J.M. (2003) 'Foundation literacy acquisition in European orthographies', *British Journal of Psychology*, 94: 143–74.

Silva, C. and Alves Martins, M. (2003) 'Relations between children's invented spelling and the development of phonological awareness', *Educational Psychology*, 23(1): 3–16.

Tickell, Dame C. (2011) *The Early Years: Foundations for Life, Health and Learning* (The Tickell Review). Runcorn: DfE. Available at www.education.gov.uk/tickellreview (accessed 17/3/12).

Venezky, R.L. (1973) 'Letter-sound generalizations of first, second, and third-grade Finnish children', *Journal of Educational Psychology*, 64: 288–92.

Webster, N. (1783[1968]) *A Grammatical Institute of the English Language. Part 1. Facsimile*. Menston: Scholar Press.

Wimmer, H. and Landerl, K. (1997) 'How learning to spell German differs from learning to spell English', in C.A. Perfetti, L. Rieben and M. Fayol (eds), *Learning to Spell: Research, Theory, and Practice across Languages*. Mahwah, NJ: Erlbaum. Pp.81–96.

Wyse, D. and Goswami, U. (2008) 'Synthetic phonics and the teaching of reading', *British Educational Research Journal*, 34(6): 691–710.

Audit and test

Work through each section below, responding to each question or task. When you have completed each section, you can read the answers at the end of the chapter. At the end of the chapter, you can also find support for further reading and study related to decoding and encoding.

Section 1: Key terminology for decoding and encoding text

It is important that you understand the terms below before you move on to the next activity. Provide a definition of each and check your definitions against those at the end of the chapter:

Decoding

Encoding

Segmenting

Blending

Synthetic phonics

Decodable texts

Section 2: Application of phonic knowledge for reading/decoding

By the end of Phase 3 in *Letters and Sounds*, children will have been taught the grapheme–phoneme correspondences which can be found on p.59 in Chapter 3 and the 'tricky' words below.

In Phase 2 of *Letters and Sounds* the tricky words are identified as:	*I the to go no into*
In Phase 3 of *Letters and Sounds* the tricky words are identified as:	*he she we me be was my you her they all are*

Based on these grapheme–phoneme correspondences and tricky words, try to identify words in the following text that children may find difficult to decode because they contain grapheme–phoneme correspondences or are tricky words that children have not yet been taught. Use the example below to help you.

It was a bright **sunny day**. **There** was not a **cloud** in the **sky**. **Both** of the children **wanted** to **play** in the paddling pool in the garden. **They** put on **their** swimming **costumes** and **jumped** into the cool **water** with a **great** splash!

Word	Decoding difficulty at this stage (underlined)	Word	Decoding difficulty at this stage (underlined)
sunny	Children have only been taught the 'ee' grapheme for this phoneme	day	Children have only been taught the 'ai' grapheme for this phoneme
there	Children have only been taught the 'air' grapheme for this phoneme. This is a tricky word taught in Phase 4	cloud	Children have only been taught the 'ow' grapheme for this phoneme
sky	Children have only been taught the 'igh' grapheme for this phoneme	both	Children have only been taught the 'oa' grapheme for this phoneme

(Continued)

(Continued)

Word	Decoding difficulty at this stage (underlined)	Word	Decoding difficulty at this stage (underlined)
wanted	It is not until Phase 6 in *Letters and Sounds* that children are taught that when an /o/ phoneme follows a /w/ phoneme, it is frequently spelled with the grapheme 'a'	play	Children have only been taught the 'ai' grapheme for this phoneme
they	Children have only been taught the 'ai' grapheme for this phoneme	their	Children have only been taught the 'air' grapheme for this phoneme. This is a tricky word taught in Phase 5
costumes	Children have not yet been taught the split vowel digraph for the long vowel phoneme /ue/	jumped	Children are likely to sound out the /e/ and /d/ phoneme rather than modify it to the /t/ phoneme
water	It is not until Phase 6 in *Letters and Sounds* that children are taught that when an /o/ phoneme follows a /w/ phoneme, it is frequently spelled with the grapheme 'a'	great	Children have only been taught the 'ai' grapheme for this phoneme

Try to do the same with the text below.

It was Bob's birthday and he was looking forward to his party. Both he and his sister were blowing up balloons to put on the gate outside, when there was a knock at the door.

Composing decodable sentences for children to read

Now try to write a few decodable sentences for a child to read. Base your word choice on their knowledge of grapheme–phoneme correspondences and tricky words by the end of Phase 3 in *Letters and Sounds*. You may wish to use the example below to help you get started.

At night, the cow on the farm did not sleep. The rain ran down the barn roof until morning.

Section 3: Application of phonic knowledge for spelling/encoding

Use the grapheme–phoneme correspondences which can be found on p.60 in Chapter 3 and the 'tricky' words above to rewrite the two sentences below and adapt spellings accordingly. This will entail misspelling some words, but the activity is designed to focus your attention on the kinds of spelling children may produce at this stage, when they rely upon their knowledge of one grapheme for each of the 44 phonemes.

Example:

The frightened girl, who was dressed in a blue skirt, shouted at the wolf.

may be written as

The (tricky word taught in Phase 2) **frightnd** (not yet been taught 'ed' suffix) **gurl, hoo was** (tricky word taught in Phase 3) **dresst** (not yet been taught 'ed' suffix) **in a bloo skurt, showted** (not yet been taught 'ed' suffix but can hear the separate sounds e/d) **at the wulf.**

Note how the words *frightened*, *dressed* and *shouted* have different misspellings at the end. This is based on the sounds that children can hear for the 'ed' suffix. In Phase 6 of *Letters and Sounds* children develop grammatical awareness, alongside the 'ed' suffix, in order to recognise that the word they are attempting to spell is a past tense word.

Have a go at rewriting the sentences below and consider why the child would misspell some of the words.

1. The baby looked out of the window and waved at the bright yellow moon in the sky.

2. At the weekend, I went to the park in the pouring rain and played on the slide with my friends.

ANSWERS

Section 1: Key terminology for decoding and encoding text

Decoding

The act of translating graphemes into phonemes, i.e. reading.

Encoding

The act of transcribing units of sound or phonemes into graphemes, i.e. spelling.

Segmenting

Splitting up a word into its individual phonemes in order to spell it, i.e. the word *pat* has three phonemes: /p/a/t/.

Blending

Drawing individual sounds together to pronounce a word, e.g. /c/l/a/p/, blended together reads clap.

Synthetic phonics

Synthetic phonics involves separating words into phonemes and then blending the phonemes together to read the word. This compares with analytic phonics in which segments or parts of words are analysed and patterns are compared with other words.

Decodable texts

Texts which can be easily decoded using phonic strategies available to children at a particular stage in a phonics programme, e.g. cat, dog, lamp.

Section 2: Application of phonic knowledge for reading/decoding

Try to identify words in the following text that children may find difficult to decode because they contain grapheme–phoneme correspondences or are tricky words that children have not yet been taught.

It was Bob's **birthday** and he was looking forward to his **party**. He and his **sister were blowing** up balloons to put on the **gate outside**, **when there** was a **knock** at the **door**.

Word	Decoding difficulty at this stage (underlined)	Word	Decoding difficulty at this stage (underlined)
bir**thday**	Children have only been taught the 'er' grapheme and the 'ai' grapheme for the corresponding phonemes in this word	party	Children have only been taught the 'ee' grapheme for this phoneme
sist**er**	Children have only been taught the 'ur' grapheme for this phoneme	**were**	This is a tricky word taught in Phase 4
blo**wi**ng	Children have only been taught the 'oa' grapheme for this phoneme	gat**e**	Children have not yet been taught the split vowel digraph for the long vowel phoneme /ai/

Word	Decoding difficulty at this stage (underlined)	Word	Decoding difficulty at this stage (underlined)
<u>ou</u>ts<u>i</u>de	Children have only been taught the 'ow' grapheme for this phoneme. 'Out' is a tricky word taught in Phase 4. Children have not yet been taught the split vowel digraph for the long vowel phoneme /igh/	when	Children have only been taught the 'w' grapheme for this phoneme
th<u>ere</u>	Children have only been taught the 'air' grapheme for this phoneme. This is a tricky word taught in Phase 4	<u>kn</u>ock	Children have only been taught the 'n' grapheme for this phoneme
d<u>oo</u>r	Children have only been taught the 'or' grapheme for this phoneme		

Section 3: Application of phonic knowledge for spelling/encoding

Have a go at rewriting the sentences below and consider why the child would misspell some of the words.

1.   The baby looked out of the window and waved at the bright yellow moon in the sky.

May be written as

The baibee lukt owt ov the windoa and waivd at the bright yelloa moon in the skigh.

2.   I really enjoyed going to the park in the pouring rain because I played on the slide with my friends.

May be written as

I reely enjoyd goaing to the park in the poring rain beecos I plaid on the slighd with my frends.

Based on knowledge of grapheme–phoneme correspondences in Phases 2 and 3 of *Letters and Sounds*, you will note that there may be more than one phonically plausible way to spell the words above (see Chapter 3).

What to do next?

Reinforce your knowledge and understanding of decoding and encoding by doing the following:

1.   Analyse a decodable text against the corresponding stage within the phonics programme it is designed for, to identify why it is decodable for children at that particular stage.

2.   Compose a piece of decodable text for a child working within Phase 4 in *Letters and Sounds*, or an equivalent stage in another programme, and see if the child is able to decode it.

5. Long vowel digraphs – the advanced alphabetic code

Learning Outcomes

By the end of this chapter you should:

- understand the features of the advanced alphabetic code;
- have developed an understanding of long vowel digraphs, including the most common spelling choices and alternative pronunciations;
- have an overview of how these phonemes can be taught in appropriate ways for young children.

Teachers' Standards

3. Demonstrate good subject and curriculum knowledge:

   - demonstrate a critical understanding of developments in the subject and curriculum areas, and promote the value of scholarship;
   - if teaching early reading, demonstrate a clear understanding of systematic synthetic phonics.

Criteria for assuring high-quality phonic work (DfE, 2011)

Use a multi-sensory approach so that children learn variously from simultaneous visual, auditory and kinaesthetic activities which are designed to secure essential phonic knowledge and skills (see note 5).

Note 5: Multi-sensory activities should be interesting and engaging but firmly focused on intensifying the learning associated with its phonic goal [sic]. They should avoid taking children down a circuitous route only tenuously linked to the goal. This means avoiding over-elaborate activities that are difficult to manage and take too long to complete, thus distracting the children from concentrating on the learning goal.

Introduction

The most complex aspect of teaching phonics, and often the least well taught, has involved the long vowel phonemes and the multiple spelling choices for each. However, it is crucial that children learn the whole of the English alphabetic code, not just a part of it; otherwise, armed with only a part of the code they will never learn to crack it. This chapter will review this complex or advanced part of the alphabetic code and present a range of suitable ways of teaching it effectively. The aim of the chapter is to support a clear understanding of what constitutes the 'advanced alphabetic code', resulting from the complex orthography of written English. It will also examine difficulties that are often experienced in teaching long vowel digraphs, in particular in finding ways to teach these to young children in lively interactive ways. It will support not only an understanding of the most common spelling for these phonemes, but also the multiple ways of spelling the same sound. Alongside this, the chapter will review alternative pronunciations for graphemes – another factor that can cause common confusions. In spite of such complexities of the written English language, the chapter will demonstrate that patterns exist and that these can be utilised effectively in teaching.

Theoretical perspectives/subject knowledge

The alphabetic code

The alphabetic code, or principle, refers to the understanding that letters are used to represent the speech sounds of our language. We use the letters of the alphabet often alone (the basic code), often in twos and in groups of three and four (advanced code) to represent the sounds in our language. If the English language had a consistent and transparent code, every sound would have just one letter assigned to it and it would be very simple to decode. Unfortunately, as we only have 26 letters to represent 44 or more sounds, this means that written English has an advanced code where frequently, sounds are represented by more than one letter and letters represent more than one sound. The alphabetic code is underpinned by the following concepts:

Sounds/phonemes are represented by letters/graphemes.

1. A phoneme can be represented by one or more letters, for example the phoneme /igh/ can be written as *i-e* (in *line*), *igh* (in *sight*), *ie* (in *tie*) or *i* (in *tiger*). A one-letter grapheme is called a 'graph', a two-letter grapheme a 'digraph', a three-letter grapheme a 'trigraph' and occasionally a four-letter grapheme (as in *weigh* = /w/ eigh/): a 'quadgraph'.

2. The same phoneme can be represented (spelled) more than one way, as in /or/ spelled as *or* in *fork*, or *aw* as in *claw* or *oor* as in *door*.

3. The same grapheme (spelling) may represent more than one phoneme, as demonstrated by the letter *s* which may make the sound /s/ in *sip* or /z/ in *laser*.

To summarise the differences between the basic and advanced codes: the basic code consists of learning one spelling choice for each of the 40+ sounds. Most phonics programmes begin with a few consonants and short vowel phonemes (e.g. /s/ /a/ /t/ /p/ /i/ /n/) and then move into blending these into consonant-vowel-consonant (CVC) words (e.g. 'sat', 'tin', 'pin' etc.). Children need to begin by learning one spelling for about 40 of the approximate 44 phonemes in the English language. The advanced code involves mastering the multiple spellings for each phoneme. You may find the chart developed by Debbie Hepplewhite helpful in differentiating the basic and complex alphabetic code. It is available from: http://www.alphabeticcodecharts.com/B1_DH%20Alph%20Code%20overview%20with%20teaching%20points%20colour.pdf

One of the most complex challenges of the alphabetic code is to develop an understanding of the long vowel phonemes. This has commonly presented most difficulties for teachers, particularly in finding suitable ways to teach these to young children. As a result, in the past the long vowel phonemes have often not been taught well, or systematically and therefore the teaching may not have been effective. Cunningham et al. (2004) examined actual and perceived knowledge of phoneme awareness and phonics in teachers of young children and found that not only was their knowledge limited, but also they overestimated what they knew. This can have a serious impact on teaching; therefore having a knowledge of the complex alphabetic code, and how to teach it, is crucial.

Long vowel phonemes

In addition to the five short vowel sounds /a/, /e/, /i/, /o/, /u/ there are 14 long vowel phonemes, as shown in Table 5.1 with their common spellings. Note also the *schwa* phoneme /ə/ (an unstressed vowel sound which is close to the phoneme /u/). There are various spellings of this phoneme including teacher, collar, doctor, about.

Table 5.1 Long vowel phonemes with their common spellings

Phonemes	Grapheme(s)	Common spellings[*]
/ai/	ay, a-e, ai, a	play, take, snail, baby
/ee/	ee, ea, e	feel, heat, me
/igh/	ie, igh, y, i-e, i	tie, fight, my, bike, tiger
/oa/	oa, ow, o-e, o	float, slow, stone, nose
/u/	oo, ou, u	took, could, put
/ue/	ue, ew, u-e	due, grew, tune
/oo/	oo, ue	room, clue
/ow/	ow, ou	cow, loud
/oi/	oi, oy	coin, boy
/ur/	ur, ir, er, ear, or	fur, girl, term, heard, work
/or/	au, or, oor, ar, aw, a	sauce, horn, door, warn, claw, ball
/ar/	ar, a	car, fast (*regional*), ma, pa

Phonemes	Grapheme(s)	Common spellings*
/air/	air, ear, are	hair, bear, share
/ear/	ear, ere, eer	ear, here, deer
/ure/	ure, our	sure, tour

*Other spellings are possible; the ones listed are the most common representations. You may decide to teach the most common representation of each of the long vowel phonemes first and then later gradually teach other ways of spelling the phonemes.

Activity

Check your understanding of long vowel phonemes

Look at the list of words below and see if you can identify those that contain long vowel phonemes:

trail	hope	swan
pay	frog	saw
toy	mouse	fern

The long vowel phonemes commonly contain digraphs (two letters making one sound), e.g. /ae/ written as *ai* or *ay*) or trigraphs (three letters making one sound), e.g. /air/ in *hair* or *bear*.

The following words from the activity above contain long vowel phonemes:

trail /t/ /r/ /**ai**/ /l/	hope /h/ /**o-e**/ / p/
pay /p/ /**ay**/	saw / s/ /**aw**/
toy /t/ /**oy**/	mouse / m/ /**ou**/ /se/
fern /f/ /**er**/ /n/	

Alternative spellings for long vowel phonemes

One of the reasons why long vowel phonemes are complex is that there is a range of alternative spellings for each phoneme. Take, for example, the phoneme /oa/; this can be written in the following ways:

oa – as in *boat*
ow – as in *row*
owoe – as in *toe*
o-e – as in *bone*

Activity

Alternative spellings for long vowel phonemes

How many ways can you find to spell the phoneme /ee/ as in *green?* (There are at least nine).

The phoneme /ee/ (as in *green*) can be spelled in at least nine ways, for example: *ea* (*mean*), *e* (*be*), *ie* (*siege*), *ei* (*deceive*), *e-e* (*serene*), *ey* (*key*), *y* (*folly*), *i* (*radio*), *i-e* (*marine*). Most of these spellings are uncommon and it is important to focus first on the most common spellings when teaching grapheme/phoneme correspondences.

Teaching long vowel phonemes

Considering all the complexities, it seems an insurmountable task to teach this to young children. However, as research has shown (DiLorenzo et al., 2011), this is possible particularly if it is done in lively interactive and multi-sensory ways. This should not detract from the brisk pace of teaching the phonemes and should be introduced alongside introducing each grapheme–phoneme correspondence. There are several ways in which teaching long vowel phonemes can be done effectively with young children:

1. Incorporate actions.
2. Include mnemonics, songs/raps, rhymes and poems.
3. Build a chart as you teach each grapheme–phoneme correspondence to show the phonemes and their alternative spellings.
4. Use visual prompts for each grapheme–phoneme correspondence.

The following section will take each of these methods in turn and provide details of how they can be taught effectively with young children.

1. Using actions

The most well-known scheme that incorporates actions effectively is the Jolly Phonics programme. Each phoneme is introduced with a very brief story and an action. So, for example, when introducing the phoneme /a/ the teacher tells a story about a family having a picnic and suddenly they are invaded by ants. As the ants crawl on the food and onto the family, they say 'a, a, a, a' as if the ants are nipping them. The publisher Jolly Learning provides a range of resources to support the introduction of each of 42 phonemes, and a helpful parents' guide can be downloaded from http://jollylearning.co.uk/parent-teacher-guide/. These actions are particularly useful for helping children to recall the long vowel phonemes, for example:

ou Pretend your finger is a needle and prick thumb saying 'ou, ou, ou'.

oi Cup hands around mouth and shout to another boat saying 'oi! Ship ahoy!'

ue Point to people around you and say 'you, you, you'.

er Roll hands over each other like a mixer and say 'er er er'.

ar Open mouth wide and say 'ah'.

2. Using mnemonics, raps, rhymes and poems

In order to help young children to recall these phonemes, learning a saying or mnemonic can be helpful. This can also be accompanied by an action. As the phonemes are learned, these sayings can be linked together to form a 'rap'. Said in a lively way at the start of each phonics lesson, it acts as revision or 'overlearning' of the phonemes taught and can be a fun way of starting the lesson. Constant practice at saying this rap will support children in remembering the phonemes and their most common spelling choices/graphemes.

When teaching the rap, it is important to follow these steps:

1. Say the phoneme twice, e.g. /ay/ay/.

2. Say the mnemonic, e.g. 'Play with hay'.

3. Say the letter names, e.g. 'A Y'.

4. When accompanied by an action, this would look like those in Table 5.2.

Table 5.2 *Rap plan with actions*

Phoneme	Phoneme (say twice)	Phrase	Letter names	Action
1.	ay/ ay	Play with hay	AY	Pretend to lift a pile of hay
	ai/ai	ai, ai what did you say?	AI	Hand cupped around ear
	a/a	Acorn in an acre	A	Pretend to hold a tiny acorn
2.	ee/ee	Feel the tree	EE	Pretend to hug a tree
	ea/ea	Heat the meat	EA	Pretend to stir with a spoon
	e/e	He and me	E	Point to someone
	y/y	Bony pony	Y	Pretend to ride a pony

(Continued)

Table 5.2 (Continued)

Phoneme	Phoneme (say twice)	Phrase	Letter names	Action
3.	ie/ie	Tie the tie	IE	Pretend to tie a tie
	igh/igh	Light helps sight	IGH	Make a circle with thumb and forefinger and hold around eyes
	y/y	My what a fly	Y	Buzz like a fly
	i/i	Kind tiger	I	Pretend to wave to a tiger

Source: For full details of the above rap, see Jolliffe, 2012, p.106

As in the example of the rap, a rhyme can be helpful in supporting the memory of sounds or in exploring alternative spellings when working on long vowel phonemes.

Activity

Illustrating alternative spellings

Using the poem below, consider what examples of rhymes you might use to illustrate alternative spellings.

> Sounds of the city
> Scamper, scuttle
> Stop and stare
> Cities echoing sounds in the air
> Spring and stretch
> Stride and fuss
> Busy people rushing for a bus
> Circus in the city
> Dresses for a clown
> Stampeding horses make people frown
> Ice-cold drinks
> Sun beats down
> Sweltering people rush out of town

(Jolliffe, 2006)

You may have particularly highlighted 'stare' and 'air', but you may also like to use this rhyme to examine the number of ways of spelling the /s/ phoneme, as follows: 'spring', 'circus', 'city', 'ice', 'fuss'.

3. Build a chart

To support children it is useful to create a chart of phonemes (see Table 5.3) as you teach each one. The process is gradually built up and constantly referred to. Focus on the most common graphemes for each phoneme first, and teach and add those that you feel are most appropriate for the age of the children. You may wish to include pictures to represent each phoneme to make the chart both more useful and more attractive.

Table 5.3 Phonemes chart

/ai/	/ee/	/igh/	/oa/	/u/	/oo/	/ow/	/oi/	/ur/	/or/	/ar/	/air/	/ear/	/ure/	/ə/
ay (day)	ee (see)	ie (tie)	oa (boat)	oo (book)	oo (moon)	ow (cow)	oi (coin)	ur (burn)	au (haul)	ar (car)	air (hair)	ear (fear)	ure (sure)	er (sister)
ai (tail)	ea (beach)	igh (light)	ow (snow)	ou (would)	ue (clue)	ou (shout)	oy (boy)	ir (girl)	or (horn)	a (fast)	ear (bear)	ere (here)	our (tour)	e (wooden)
a (baby)	e (me)	y (my)	o (cold)	u (put)	ew (grew)			er (term)	oor (door)		are (share)	eer (deer)		u (circus)
a-e (make)	y (pony)	i (tiger)	o-e (bone)		u-e (tune)			ear (heard)	ar (warn)					a (about)
		i-e (time)						or (work)	aw (claw)					ar (collar)
									a (call)					or (doctor)

4. Use visual prompts

Visual prompts are another very useful aid in supporting children's recall of long vowel phonemes (and for all phonemes). One well-known programme that uses them is Read Write Inc. You can watch Ruth Miskin teaching long vowel digraphs using such prompts at https://www.youtube.com/watch?v=NRYiOcqyEs8

Prompts are also used in *Phonics: A Complete Synthetic Programme* by Jolliffe (2006) and *Quick Fix for Phonics* by Jolliffe (2012). Some examples are given in Figure 5.1.

Working with parents

To support children in becoming proficient with synthetic phonics, it is extremely important to provide clear information for parents in order to help them understand the process their children will be undertaking. A range of resources is available to help with this, including booklets for parents published by most phonics programmes: as already mentioned,

ay
/ay/ay/ Play with hay, AY

a-e
/a-e/, /a-e/ Take a cake, A-E

Figure 5.1 Examples of visual prompts for learning phonemes

Jolly Phonics provides a very useful booklet available from http://jollylearning.co.uk/parent-teacher-guide/.

Research Focus: Segmenting and blending

The meta-analysis carried out by the National Reading Panel (NRP) made a number of recommendations to support effective phonics teaching, including stating: 'It is clear that the major letter-sound correspondences, including short and long vowels and digraphs, need to be taught' (NICHD, 2000, pp.2–136).

McGuinness identifies a key issue being the delay in teaching all aspects of the alphabetic code and says, 'It is counter-productive to ease children into reading by teaching these elements slowly in disconnected and unrelated bits' (2004, p.324). McGuinness cites the Jolly Phonics programme, where the children involved were the youngest among a range of phonics programmes she studied. They were between 4.8 and 5.0 years old at the start of their phonics programme. This lasted from ten to 16 weeks and children learned the 40+ phonemes and how to write every letter and digraph for them. They could also identify phonemes in all positions in a word and segment and blend phonemes in words. After the training programme, these children were eight months above UK age norms on standardised spelling tests. These gains were not only sustained but increased over time. One of the distinguishing features of Jolly Phonics is the multi-sensory nature of the teaching and, in particular, the actions that are taught for each phoneme. Sumbler (1999) reported in a comparison of different phonics programmes that the time spent learning and using Jolly Phonics actions produced the highest correlation to reading test scores. However, the NRP stated that there was a need for further

→

research to determine the impact of 'active ingredients' (NICHD, 2000, pp.2, 136) such as those used by Jolly Phonics.

An aspect that Henbest and Apel (2017) emphasise is practice in encoding, and giving children the opportunity to consciously work with letters and their sounds to make new words (Weiser and Mathes, 2011). They note the need for further research in this area as:

> The potential effectiveness of encoding practice in a phonics-based program is an important consideration given the relation among reading and spelling and the potential differences in outcomes that may be attributed to whether instruction in spelling is included in phonics-based treatments.
>
> (Henbest and Apel, 2017, p.307)

Given the complexity of the English spelling system, it is not surprising that in the past teachers have either not taught phonics at all, or only taught the more basic elements. The basic code should teach one spelling for each of the 40 phonemes but then move on to teach the advanced code containing the remaining spellings.

One of the notable features of the patterns contained in the English written language is that the parts of words known as 'rimes' contain stable spellings and stable pronunciations. Rimes are parts of words that are spelled the same way, so that in a word such as *cake* the rime is *ake* and the initial consonant or consonants are called the 'onset' of the word. The use of onset and rime, largely derived from the work of Goswami (1995), became very popular as the focus for teaching reading. This approach is what is termed 'analytic phonics', where words are decoded based on patterns with other words. As a method of teaching reading, this has drawbacks in not teaching systematically all 44+ phonemes and their alternative spellings and pronunciations. However, where this has real value is in teaching spelling. Table 5.4 provides a list of 37 rimes that provide nearly 500 words in English.

Table 5.4 The 37 rimes that provide nearly 500 English words (Wylie and Durrell, 1970, pp.787–91)

-ack	-ain	-ake	-ale	-all	-ame	-an	-ank
-ap	-ash	-at	-ate	-aw	-ay	-eat	-ell
-est	-ice	-ick	-ide	-ite	-ill	-in	-ine
ing	-ink	-ip	-ir	-ock	-oke	-op	-or
-ore	-uck	-ug	-ump	-unk			

It is therefore helpful for spelling to learn long vowel phonemes accompanied with the teaching of spelling patterns. Research has shown that the brain is a competent pattern detector, and when a pattern is detected in a word it evokes associations; for example, a word like *complaint* may be associated with spelling patterns in other words such as *paint* and *constraint* (Ehri, 2005).

The Letters and Sounds parents' information booklet provides a range of activities that parents can undertake with children at each phase and is available from www.cornwall.gov.uk/media/3629338/Letters-and-sounds-Info-for-parents.pdf.

Read Write Inc. provides a helpful PowerPoint presentation to download, which takes parents (and anyone new to teaching phonics) through all the sounds and gives the correct enunciation. (See Chapter 12 for details of different systematic synthetic phonics programmes.)

Case Study: Teaching long vowel phonemes

A Year 1 teacher who found teaching long vowel phonemes difficult sets out below how she adapted her teaching to include mnemonics, picture cards and a chart.

I had been teaching phonics for several years and found that the first stages or Phases 1–4 of *Letters and Sounds* (DfES, 2007) seemed quite easy for the children. I had incorporated actions too, which helped. However, once I got to teaching the alternative spellings for the long vowel phonemes, it was really difficult to put this over in a meaningful way for young children. I went on a training course about using multi-sensory techniques and began to use both picture cue cards and mnemonics to help the children recall them. I found some really good ones on the Internet and adapted these. I also created a PowerPoint presentation which was adapted from another idea from a website that had lots of useful resources. The PowerPoint was called 'I say, you say' (www.tes.co.uk/teaching-resource/I-say-you-say-long-vowel-phonemes-6008201/), and I said the phonemes and then with the aid of picture cues the children named words that used that phoneme and grapheme, for example:

I say /oi/, you say.............

The children responded:

We say coin, boil, soil, join (and so on).

What I found particularly effective is the use of picture cards that contain the mnemonic, and I created a chart with these which we add to as I teach another phoneme. We recite it in a lively fun way every day at the start of each phonics lesson. This constant repetition and the visual cues and sayings are really making a difference. I notice that the children's independent writing is reflecting this knowledge too.

Learning Outcomes Review

In English the alphabetic code is complex as we only have 26 letters to represent 44 or more sounds. The basic code consists of learning one spelling choice for each of the 40+ sounds. The advanced code involves mastering the multiple spellings for each phoneme. One of the most complex aspects of this code is to develop an understanding of the long vowel digraphs. Teaching the long vowel phonemes requires multi-sensory methods and a variety of aids to support children in learning them including: mnemonics, raps, rhymes, visual cues, actions and charts. Parents need to be informed of the teaching methods and be provided with a range of ways to reinforce learning at home. The English written language does, however, contain patterns that are particularly useful to exploit in learning spelling. These are the parts of words known as 'rimes', which contain stable spellings and stable pronunciations.

Self-assessment questions

1. Explain the difference between the basic and advanced alphabetic code.
2. Why do the long vowel phonemes cause difficulties for teaching and learning phonics?
3. Name ways in which this difficulty can be supported.

Further Reading

For a chapter exploring issues of the peculiarities of English spelling which supports understanding when teaching long vowel phonemes, see:

Dombey, H. (2006) 'Phonics and English orthography', in M. Lewis and S. Ellis (eds), *Phonics Practice, Research and Policy.* London: Paul Chapman. pp. 95–104.

For further guidance on the simple and complex alphabetic code, see Chapter 4 in:

Glazzard, J. and Stokoe, J. (2013) *Teaching Synthetic Phonics and Early English.* Northwich: Critical Publishing.

References

Cunningham, A., Perry, K., Stanovich, K. and Stanovich, P. (2004) 'Disciplinary knowledge of K-3 teachers and their knowledge calibration in the domain of early literacy', *Annals of Dyslexia*, 54 (1): 139–67.

DfE (2011) *Teachers' Standards in England from September 2012*. London: DfE.

DfES (2007) *Letters and Sounds: Principles and Practice of High Quality Phonics*. London: DfES.

DiLorenzo, K.E., Rody, C.A., Bucholz, J.L. and Brady, M.P. (2011) 'Teaching letter-sound connections with picture mnemonics: Itchy's alphabet and early decoding', *Preventing School Failure*, 55 (1): 28–34.

Ehri, L. (2005) 'Development of sight word reading: Phases and findings', in C. Hume and M. Snowling (eds), *The Science of Reading*. Maldon: Blackwell. pp.135–54.

Goswami, U. (1995) 'Phonological development and reading by analogy: What is analogy and what is not', *Journal of Research in Reading*, 18 (2).

Henbest, V. and Apel, K. (2017) 'Effective word reading instruction: What does the evidence tell us?', *Communication Disorders Quarterly*, 39 (1): 303–11.

Jolliffe, W. (2006) *Phonics: A Complete Synthetic Programme*. Leamington Spa: Scholastic.

Jolliffe, W. (2012) *Quick Fix for Phonics*. Witney: Scholastic.

Jolly Learning (1992) *Jolly Phonics*. Available at www.jollylearning.co.uk/overview-about-jollyphonics/ (accessed 3/2/15).

McGuinness, D. (2004) *Early Reading Instruction: What Science Really Tells Us about How to Teach Reading*. Cambridge, MA: MIT Press.

National Institute of Child Health and Human Development (NICHD) (2000) *Report of the National Reading Panel*. 'Teaching children to read: An evidence-based assessment of the scientific research literature on reading and its implications for reading instruction: Reports of the subgroups', NIH publication no. 00-4754. Washington, DC: Government Printing Office.

Sumbler, K. (1999) 'Phonological awareness combined with explicit alphabetic coding instruction in kindergarten: Classroom observations and evaluation'. Unpublished doctoral dissertation, University of Toronto.

Weiser, B.L. and Mathes, P. (2011) 'Using encoding instruction to improve the reading and spelling performances of elementary students at risk for literacy difficulties: A best-evidence synthesis', *Review of Educational Research*, 81: 170–200.

Wylie, R.E. and Durrell, D.D. (1970) 'Elementary English', *Teaching Vowels Through Phonograms*, 47: 787–91.

Audit and test

Work through each section below, responding to each question or task. When you have completed each section, you can read the answers at the end of the chapter. At the end of the chapter, you can also find support for further reading and study related to vowel digraphs

Section 1: Key terminology for vowel digraphs

It is important that you understand the terms below before you move on to the next activity. Provide a definition of each and check your definitions against those at the end of the chapter:

Vowel digraph

Long vowel phoneme

Short vowel phoneme

Split digraph

Trigraph

Quadgraph

Section 2: Vowel digraphs

A digraph is two letters that are combined to produce one phoneme, e.g. *ee, ch, ow*.

Vowel digraphs can represent a short vowel phoneme, e.g. br**ea**d, l**oo**k.

Can you identify the vowel digraphs representing a short vowel phoneme in the words below?

| said | head | rough | instead | cough |

Vowel digraphs can represent a long vowel phoneme e.g. r**ai**n.

Can you identify the vowel digraphs representing a long vowel phoneme in the words below?

| meet | rain | goat | argue | blow |

Split digraphs represent the long vowel phoneme, but the two letters are split by another letter (a consonant), e.g. m**a**k**e**, l**i**n**e**, h**o**m**e**.

Can you identify the split digraphs in the words below?

| kite | late | note | bike | discrete |

Now sort the words below, taken from Year 1 in the National Curriculum, into three sets of vowel digraphs representing: short vowel phonemes, long vowel phonemes and split digraphs.

sail, clue, slide, slow, road, field, new, goes, sea, lake, hole, join, day, bite, ready, dream, pie, home, true, tame, play, bone, few, time, tree, dead, soap, theme.

Section 3: Identifying vowel digraphs in Year 3–4 spelling list

Look at the example words below taken from the draft National Curriculum at Year 3–4. Identify which words contain a vowel digraph. This could be a long vowel phoneme, a short vowel phoneme, or it could be a split digraph.

accident, advertise, benefit, breath, building, chocolate, congratulate, describe, difficult, experiment, extreme, independent, nephew, often, possess, punctuate, separate, sew, surprise

Section 4: Create a long vowel phoneme chart

There are a many different graphemes that represent a long vowel phoneme. It might be a one- (m<u>i</u>nd), two- (d<u>ay</u>), three- (h<u>igh</u>) or even four- (<u>eigh</u>t) letter grapheme.

Sort the words below into the correct columns based on the long vowel phoneme each contains. This may be represented by a number of different graphemes. There are some examples, already in the table, to help you.

t<u>oy</u>, she, c<u>oa</u>t, tim <u>e</u>, n<u>ow</u>, baby, d<u>ou</u>gh, me, b<u>ow</u>l, l<u>a</u>k<u>e</u>, tiger, st<u>ay</u>, b<u>oi</u>l, h<u>ea</u>t, p<u>ie</u>, b<u>ou</u>gh, b<u>oa</u>t, grey, st<u>ea</u>k, j<u>oy</u>, br<u>ow</u>n, str<u>aigh</u>t, f<u>igh</u>t, st<u>ea</u>l, b<u>o</u>n<u>e</u>, discr<u>e</u>t<u>e</u>, shy, l<u>ou</u>d, sl<u>eigh</u>, c<u>o</u>n<u>e</u>

/ee/	/ie/	/oe/	/ae/	/ow/	/oi/
feel	tie	toe	play	cow	coin
weak	kind	blow	rain	round	boy

Section 1: Key terminology for vowel digraphs

Vowel digraph

Two letters that are combined to produce a long or a short vowel phoneme.

Long vowel phoneme

The long vowel sounds as in *feel* or *cold*.

Short vowel phoneme

The short vowel sounds as in *hat* or *said*.

Split digraph

Two letters, making one sound, but separated by a consonant, e.g. a-e as in cake.

Trigraph

Three letters which combine to make a new sound, e.g. h**air**.

Quadgraph

Four letters which combine to make a new sound, e.g. th**ough**t.

Section 2: Vowel digraphs

You were asked to identify the vowel digraphs representing a short vowel phoneme in the words below?

| S**ai**d | h**ea**d | r**ou**gh | inst**ea**d | c**ou**gh |

You were asked to identify the vowel digraphs representing a long vowel phoneme in the words below? Note that some vowel digraphs include consonants, e.g. ar, ow.

| m**ee**t | r**ai**n | g**oa**t | arg**ue** | bl**ow** |

You were asked to identify the split digraphs in the words below?

| k**i**t**e** | l**a**t**e** | n**o**t**e** | b**i**k**e** | discr**e**t**e** |

You were asked to sort the words below, taken from Year 1 in the National Curriculum, into vowel digraphs representing: short vowel phonemes, long vowel phonemes and split digraphs.

Short vowel digraphs	r**ea**dy, d**ea**d
Long vowel digraphs	s**ai**l, cl**ue**, sl**ow**, r**oa**d, f**ie**ld, n**ew**, g**oe**s, s**ea**, j**oi**n, d**ay**, dr**ea**m, p**ie**, tr**ue**, pl**ay**, f**ew**, tr**ee**, s**oa**p
Split vowel digraphs	sl**i**d**e**, l**a**k**e**, h**o**l**e**, b**i**t**e**, h**o**m**e**, t**a**m**e**, b**o**n**e**, t**i**m**e**, th**e**m**e**

Section 3: Identifying vowel digraphs in Year 3-4 spelling list

You were asked to look at the example words below taken from the draft National Curriculum at Year 3-4, and to identify which words contain a vowel digraph. The vowel digraphs could represent a long vowel phoneme, a short vowel phoneme or could be a split digraph. The words with vowel digraphs appear in bold with the digraphs underlined.

| accident, advert**i**s**e**, benefit, br**ea**th, b**ui**lding, chocol**a**t**e**, congratul**a**t**e**, descr**i**b**e**, difficult, exper**i**m**e**nt, extr**e**m**e**, independent, neph**ew**, often, possess, punctu**a**t**e**, separ**a**t**e**, s**ew**, surpr**i**s**e** |

Section 4: Create a long vowel phoneme chart

You were asked to sort the words below into the correct columns based on the long vowel phoneme each contains. This may be represented by a number of different graphemes.

/ee/	/ie/	/oe/	/ae/	/ow/	/oi/
feel	tie	toe	play	cow	coin
weak	kind	blow	rain	round	boy
she	time	coat	baby	now	toy
me	tiger	dough	lake	bough	boil
heat	pie	bowl	stay	brown	joy
steal	fight	boat	grey	loud	
discrete	shy	bone	steak		
		cone	straight		
			sleigh		

What to do next?

Reinforce your knowledge and understanding of vowel digraphs by doing the following:

1. Observe teachers teaching vowel digraphs. Note whether they represent a long or short vowel phoneme. Collect a bank of ideas and activities for teaching vowel digraphs and the split digraph.

2. Create your own long vowel phoneme chart (as in section 4) and add to it whenever you come across words containing a long vowel phoneme. This will form a useful point of reference for you.

6. Phonics into spelling

Learning Outcomes

By the end of this chapter you should:

- understand that inconsistencies in English spelling result from the fact that the language has developed out of several other languages;
- understand the concept of morphology and how this is relevant to our understanding of spelling and understand the role played by morphemes in modifying words;
- be aware of the value of spelling investigations in supporting knowledge of spelling rules and conventions.

Teachers' Standards

3. Demonstrate good subject and curriculum knowledge:

   - demonstrate a critical understanding of developments in the subject and curriculum areas, and promote the value of scholarship;
   - if teaching early reading, demonstrate a clear understanding of systematic synthetic phonics.

Criteria for assuring high-quality phonic work (DfE, 2011)

Enable children to start learning phonic knowledge and skills using a systematic, synthetic programme by the age of five, with the expectation that they will be fluent readers having secured word recognition skills by the end of Key Stage 1 (see Note 2).

Note 2: Teachers will make principled, professional judgements about when to start on a systematic, synthetic programme of phonic work but it is reasonable to expect that the great majority of children will be capable of, and benefit from doing so by the age of five. It is equally important for the programme to be designed so that children become fluent readers having secured word recognition skills by the end of Key Stage 1.

Introduction

In the previous chapter, we looked at ways in which children's phonic knowledge developed at Phases 5 and 6 of *Letters and Sounds* (DfES, 2007) as they gained more experience of different pronunciations of graphemes. This chapter will clarify how the teaching of systematic synthetic phonics progresses into the teaching of spelling. It will review the importance of morphological understanding and word derivations. A range of examples of investigating spelling rules will be provided, with links to suitable resources.

Research Focus: Successful spellers

Successful spellers are able to make use of the knowledge and skills they acquired through blending and segmenting when they developed their phonic knowledge. As de Graaff et al. maintain,

> [f]or spelling it is necessary that before sounds can be converted into letters, those sounds have to be extracted from the whole-word sound stream, a skill also dependent upon a high-abstraction level. Thus, for skills requiring a higher level of abstraction, a systematic approach appears to be more fruitful than a non-systematic approach.
>
> *(2009, p.331)*

Crystal argues that spelling involves 'a conscious ability to form linear sequences of letters – an ability that is not found in visual pattern recognition (as is required for whole-word reading)' (1987, p.213). He goes on to state that, to be a good speller,

> we need to have both... phonological awareness (to cope with the regular spelling patterns) and a good visual awareness (to cope with the exceptions). Poor spellers, it seems, lack this double skill.
>
> *(1987, p.213)*

Allott (2014) maintains that 'spellings to be learned should be words which pupils are likely to use in their writing but do not already know how to spell' (p.68), and asserts that 'careful focus on the structure of particular words, and discussion of why they are spelled as they are, develops skills which can be transferred to other words' (p.68). As they develop an ability to read and spell longer words, good spellers are able to chunk parts of words and separate words into syllables or units of meaning. In this chapter, we shall explore some of the strategies that can be used to develop both children's ability to spell and their understanding of vocabulary.

Morphemes

Activity

Look at the words below. Now see how many ways you can modify their meanings by adding letters at the beginning or end. For example, *usual* could become *unusual*, *usually* or *unusually*.

like happy port

You may have modified the word *like* into *unlike*, *dislike*, *likeness*, *likely*, *alike* and so on. *Happy* may have become *unhappy* or *happiness,* while among the many possibilities for modifying *port* are *ports*, *export*, *import*, *deport*, *report*, *porter*, *portable* and *deportment.* What you have done is add minimum units of meaning, known as 'morphemes', to words to change or modify their meaning. The words which we began with are usually known as 'root' words, and when we add a morpheme before the root word it is known as a 'prefix', and when we add a morpheme at the end it is known as a 'suffix'. Note that in changing *happy* to *happiness* we had to do more than simply add a suffix: we had to change the *y* in *happy* to an *i*. This is one of the spelling rules that we will explore later in this chapter.

Although the terminology may be unfamiliar, the concept of modifying words in this way is often understood by very young children. Try asking them to name some items which you show them and then ask them to give you words when you show them more than one item. They may not know the word 'plural', but it is likely that most children will be able tell you that you are holding up two pencils or two hands. Because they hear so many plurals which are formed by adding an *s* to a noun, young children tend to apply this rule to all nouns, even those which are irregular such as *man*, *sheep* and *mouse*. People learning English as a foreign language may face similar problems as they try to apply a rule which does not always work.

Morphology and etymology

Pupils should spell words as accurately as possible using their phonic knowledge and other knowledge of spelling, such as morphology and etymology.

(DfE, 2013, p.33, Year 3–4)

If you are to be a successful teacher of spelling, you need to develop your understanding of morphology and be able to explain to children how different morphemes can be added to words to modify their meaning. This will build on children's phonic knowledge as they learn the sounds that single letters and combinations of letters make when used in, for example, prefixes and suffixes. To et al. argue that:

> Because many English words are morphologically related, learning one base word might increase the total vocabulary by a count of several words, if the student learns word formation processes of English.

> For example, if a person learns the word 'love', then morphologically related words (i.e., loveable, lovely) can also be acquired.

> *(2014, p.13)*

Johnston and Watson maintain that 'Children's reading will become more fluent if they recognise these familiar chunks, and thus sound and blend them at the syllable level' (2007, p.44). As well as helping children to identify and pronounce morphemes, it is important that we explain the meanings of the morphemes so that they can read, understand and use them independently.

Activity

Look at the common English prefixes below and decide what each means when used in the adjacent words:

un- in *unhappy*
micro- in *microcosm*
bi- in *bicycle*
pre- in *prenatal*

Un- means *not* and so we can affix it to *happy* to change the meaning to show that someone is *not happy*. *Micro-* (from the Greek *mikros*) means *small*, while *cosm* comes from the Greek *kosmos* which means *a world*, so a *microcosm* is *a small world*. *Bicycles* have two wheels, since *bi-*means *two* and *cycle* refers to *wheels* (from the Greek *kuklos*). *Prenatal* means *before birth*, with *pre-* meaning *before* and *natal* coming from the Latin for birth, *natalis*. While we may not know the origins of some words, we can see that our language is derived from other languages and that this affects the way in which we spell. Often, we have changed spellings over time as well as pronunciations, and this can make discovering word origins (etymology) more of a challenge. However, a basic understanding of how our language has evolved can be a major advantage when it comes to spelling and to understanding unfamiliar words.

As children's phonic knowledge develops and they become more confident about synthesising phonemes, they can begin to cluster or 'chunk' letters more easily, which will help them to read more quickly and spell more accurately. They can then develop their understanding of prefixes and suffixes and their meanings.

Activity

Table 6.1 includes several common prefixes in the left-hand column and a series of root words in the right-hand column. See how many words you can create by matching prefixes with root words. You can use each prefix and each root word as many times as you like.

Table 6.1 Prefixes and root words

Prefix	Root word
un-	play
multi-	market
tri-	store
dis-	scope
re-	plane
micro-	quiet
mega-	invest
super-	fortunate
uni-	form

This kind of activity can help children to appreciate the role of prefixes and can be linked to vocabulary development. For example, they might create a list of new words and then look some of them up in a dictionary to check that they exist and to confirm their meanings. They could go on to use the words in sentences and to research further words with similar prefixes. Similar activities can be done with suffixes, as in the Activity below.

Activity

Look at Table 6.2 and see how many new words you can create by adding suffixes to the root words. Note where you have to make a change to the root word and consider if there is a spelling rule which can be applied when doing the same with similar words.

Table 6.2 Root words and suffixes

Root words	Suffixes
love	-y
hope	-s
match	-ful
make	-ly
box	-es
like	-ing
help	-ed
fun	-ness
fit	-less

As with prefixes, you probably managed to create several words with the same suffix, as well as several with the same roots. This is another activity which children can engage in, and one that will enhance their vocabularies as well as their language comprehension.

When a morpheme cannot stand alone as a word, as with all of the suffixes above, it is known as a 'bound morpheme'; in other words, a morpheme that needs to be connected or bound to a word for it to have meaning.

Case Study: Reinforcing children's understanding of morphemes

To reinforce children's understanding of morphemes, Laura, a third-year trainee, devised a simple game to encourage them to consider a range of possibilities and to expand their vocabularies. The game involved three-syllable words which include a prefix, a root word and a suffix. Laura made a collection of words *(exported, reports, unlikely, delighted)* written on pieces of card which slotted into a card holder with three liftable flaps. She made the card holder by sticking two pieces of card together and leaving a space in which to slot the words on cards. She numbered the flaps 1, 2 and 3.

→

Laura explained to the children that there was a word hidden by the flaps and that they could choose any of the three to be raised to reveal part of the word.

When a flap was lifted she asked children, in a short space of time (around two minutes), to write down as many words as possible which might include the morpheme revealed and have three parts. In the first attempt they revealed the prefix *de*. The children identified *delighted*, *destroyed*, *departed* and so on. When the time was up, Laura asked children to tell her the words they had written and she wrote them on the board. The children had several dictionaries available to them so that they could check that their words existed and verify their meanings. Laura talked with them about the words and their meanings and noted any misconceptions about spellings and about the use of prefixes and suffixes. For example, the children used *dis-* where *un-* was correct, as in *disusually* instead of *unusually*, because they knew that *dis-* and *un-* can have similar meanings.

The words in the case study may be useful for you to use, but you can find many more in *Support for Spelling* (DCSF, 2009). Alternatively, you can do all of this electronically using, for example, a PowerPoint presentation and hyperlinks. This activity not only reinforced the children's understanding of morphemes and their roles, but it also helped develop their vocabularies and their interest in words. This interest can be further developed by exploring 'compound' words.

Compound words

Compound words are words made up of at least two other words. For example, *foot* and *ball* can be put together to make *football* or *hair* and *brush* can combine to make *hairbrush*. Each word is a morpheme in that it is a minimal unit of meaning, but unlike morphemes that are used as prefixes and suffixes (bound morphemes), the words which combine to create compound words can stand alone. They are often known as 'free morphemes'. Children at the end of Key Stage 1 can typically use prefixes and suffixes, as well as splitting compound words into their component parts and using this knowledge to support spelling. Table 6.3 identifies ten high-frequency compound words.

Table 6.3 Ten high-frequency compound words (DCSF, 2009, p.22)

everyone	everybody	everything	nowhere	nobody
somewhere	anyone	anywhere	anybody	someone

These words can be explored with children in a variety of ways. They might begin by trying to separate each of them into two words and go on to look at opposites or antonyms. For example, Table 6.4 shows the words' antonyms (opposites).

Table 6.4 Antonyms for the compound words in Table 6.3

no-one	nobody	nothing	somewhere	somebody
nowhere	someone or no-one	nowhere	nobody	no-one or everyone

In doing this, children begin to see the roles that the different parts of the compound words play and how changing them can create words with different meanings. They may also learn that *no-one* is usually hyphenated or written as two separate words *(no one)* because the double *o* might lead to confusion when pronouncing the word (sometimes read in the same way as *noon*).

Children could go on to investigate other compound words, for example by trying to find them in texts and find out their meanings. They could be given a selection of words to see how many compound words they could create from them, checking that the words they have created actually exist by using a dictionary.

Activity

Look at Table 6.5 in the case study below and see how many compound words you can create.

Case Study: Creating compound words

Table 6.5 Root words

head	hair	brush	teacher
tooth	house	green	farm
school	snow	fall	water
day	class	break	ache

Luke, a second-year undergraduate trainee, asked his Year 4 class to work cooperatively to create compound words from the list in Table 6.5. He encouraged them to share their ideas and to discuss both spellings and meanings. As a group activity, children came up with an agreed combined list and arranged them in alphabetical order before checking them in a dictionary. When they came up with non-existent words, they discussed them and created their own dictionary definitions.

Investigating spelling rules

As a teacher, you will often hear people lamenting 'the fact' that children are no longer taught spelling rules. Of course this is not true, but it is a perception that has been promoted by the popular press. If you ask people to tell you a spelling rule they will usually come up with 'i before e except after c', which is actually full of exceptions and not always very useful. We all know this rule because the rhyme helps us to remember it, but consider the words below and try to think how the rule might be developed:

| being | seeing | heir | reign | reignite |
| their | weird | conscience | science | ancient |

Many teachers add another line to the rule such as 'When you want to say *ee* ...' or 'when it rhymes with *me*'. Others show children that there are exceptions to the rule which arise because our language is derived from so many other languages. Yet others do not bother with the rule, but teach other rules which have far fewer exceptions and wide applicability (see Gentry, 1987). These might include:

- English words don't end with *v*, *q* or *j* (words like *lav* and *satnav* are abbreviations).
- *Q* is followed by *u* in English words (Iraq and Qatar are not English words).

There are many other rules which, while they have some exceptions, can be very useful and might be introduced through investigations.

Activity

Try to devise rules for each of the following.

1. Plurals for words ending with *y*.
2. Changing adjectives ending with *y* into nouns and abstract nouns, e.g. *happy* to *happiness*.
3. Making words ending with *s* into plurals.
4. Adding – *ed* or – *ing* to words.
5. Adding endings to words ending with one *l*, e.g. *careful*.

You will no doubt find that the rules do have some exceptions, but they are far more consistent than 'i before e except after c', and if children attempt to work them out for themselves with guidance, they are likely to remember them and be able to use them when spelling. The rules are:

- **Plurals for words ending with** *y:* for words in which the *y* is preceded by a vowel (*monkey*, *day* etc.), add an *s*. For words in which the *y* is preceded by a consonant, drop the *y* and add *ies*. This rule almost always applies, and the few exceptions include *monies* as a plural of *money* – a word rarely used by most adults, let alone children!

- **Changing adjectives ending with** *y* into nouns and abstract nouns, e.g. *happy* to *happiness:* drop the *y* and replace it with an *i* before adding *–ness*.

- **Making words ending with** *s* into plurals: add *–es*, e.g. *buses*, *misses*.

- **Adding** *–ed* or *–ing* to words: where a word ends with *e* drop the *e* and add *–ed* or *–ing*. Where a word ends with a consonant, simply add *–ed* or *–ing*. There are exceptions to this, e.g. short words such as *be* and *see* do not drop *e* when adding *–ing*.

- **Adding endings to words ending with one** *l*, e.g. *careful*: double the *l* and add *y* or simply add *–ly*.

Test the 'rules' yourself and see how many exceptions you can come up with!

As a trainee teacher or experienced teacher, you will need to decide when to teach spelling rules and when to provide a number of examples which demonstrate a frequent spelling pattern. However, even when looking at common spelling patterns in English, we encounter problems in spelling some words accurately because our language is so rich in homonyms and homophones.

Research Focus: Spelling rules and generalisations

All of the rules in the above activity relate to adding suffixes, which McGuinness maintains are 'well worth teaching, not as rules, but through suitable examples and repetition' (2004, p.280). Goswami and Bryant argued that:

> [o]nce children have the idea that words which have sounds in common often share spelling sequences as well, they have a powerful way to work out how to read and to spell new words.
>
> (1990, p.78)

Mudd (1994) maintains that it is far better to teach children generalisations which have exceptions rather than rules. She cites the example of the 'magic e' (see Chapter 2), which most

→

phonics programmes now refer to as part of a long vowel digraph. The 'magic e', children were told, changes the preceding vowel sound from a short to a long sound, as in *mat* and *mate*. However, Mudd (p.157) provides several exceptions (*stare, compare, one, done, there, where, have, live, prove, none, come, some*), which make 'magic e' a questionable rule, but perhaps a useful generalisation.

The problem of homophones and homonyms

In year 2, pupils move towards more word-specific knowledge of spelling, including homophones.

(DfE, 2013, p.30)

As we have seen in previous chapters, the fact that the generally agreed 44 phonemes in English can be commonly represented by more than 150 different graphemes presents us with problems when reading and spelling. This is somewhat compounded by the fact that we have so many words which sound the same but are spelled differently (*homophones:* meaning 'same sound' from the Greek *homos*, *same* and *phone*, meaning 'sound'). We also have many words which may be spelled the same but have different pronunciations (*homonyms*). Look, for example, at these words:

see, sea

saw, sore

sew, sow

read, reed, red

sight, site, cite

bee, be

rite, write, right

record, record

Once again, the effect of having a language that has evolved from so many others has had an effect upon our spelling system (see Chapter 3). We can also see that we can only know how to pronounce some of the words if we have some context for them. So *read* could rhyme with *red* when it is the past tense of the verb (I *read* the book last week) and with *reed* when it is the present tense of the verb (I love to *read* thrillers). Consider how you would pronounce *record* and how different pronunciations would give different meanings to the word.

English vocabulary is rich with homophones and homonyms, and these are often used in jokes such as: 'Did you hear about the bald man who painted rabbits on his head? He said that from a distance they looked like *hares* (*hairs*).'

However, for people becoming familiar with the language, homophones and homonyms can present problems and cause misunderstandings. *Support for Spelling* stated that in Year 4 children should learn 'to distinguish between the spelling and meaning of homophones' (DCSF, 2009, p.4), and advocated learning homophones alongside other words with similar spellings rather than alongside other homophones. Thus, we might teach *where* alongside *here* and *there* rather than alongside *wear*, and we might learn *wear* together with *hear*, *bear* and *tear* (although *tear* is a homonym, since it can be pronounced in one way when we refer to crying and another when we rip something!). However, as children become more confident about homophones, they might go on to make collections and even create their own jokes involving a play on words or misunderstandings.

A teaching sequence for spelling

Just as *Letters and Sounds* (DfES, 2007) suggests a teaching sequence for phonics, *Support for Spelling* provides a similar structure for teaching spelling:

REVISIT, EXPLAIN, USE

What do we already know?

Oral activities to confirm prior knowledge

Explain purpose of new learning, use vocabulary orally in context

TEACH, MODEL, DEFINE

How the pattern/rule/structure works

Model spelling examples

Define the rules, pattern and conventions

Whole class/individual whiteboard spelling practice

PRACTISE, EXPLORE, INVESTIGATE

Whole class activities

Group work

Extension activities

Independent work

Homework

APPLY, ASSESS, REFLECT

Revise new learning

Apply in writing

Reflect on learning

(DCSF, 2009, p. 10)

This systematic process lends itself to teaching, learning, investigation and assessment and can provide a useful structure when planning spelling lessons. See Chapter 12 for an example of this sequence being used to teach long vowel sounds.

Activity

Consider how you would use the teaching sequence for each of the spelling objectives in Table 6.6.

Table 6.6 Spelling objectives

Y2	To learn how to add common inflections (suffixes) to words
Y3	To spell regular verb endings and to learn irregular tense changes (e.g. go/went)
Y4	To distinguish between the spelling and meaning of homophones

Learning spellings

There are many strategies for learning spellings, and it is important that these are shared with parents and carers as well as children. Pupils are often asked to learn spellings at home, and those who help them may be unaware of some simple ways in which they can do this. The case study below includes some of the most basic strategies, such as identifying the 'tricky' bit of a word and making use of the 'look, say, cover, write, check' strategy. The latter involves studying a word, for example, *separate*, and saying it before covering it and attempting to write it from memory before checking for accuracy. Allied to an ability to identify the 'tricky' parts of words, this can be a very effective approach. Note that we refer to the tricky 'parts' of words rather than to tricky words. As virtually all words include some phonically regular grapheme–phoneme correspondences, it is not the words that are tricky, but parts of the words. The 2013 National Curriculum uses the term 'common exception words' for these words.

The case study below shows how a teacher changed her class's approach and attitude to spelling and some of the strategies she used to do this. Compare the teacher's approach with some of the strategies described in this chapter and consider what else she might do to improve her children's spelling.

Case Study: Part 1 – Developing independent spellers

Laura, a Teach First trainee, found that her Year 3 children were very dependent upon her for help with spellings when writing independently. She felt she should encourage children to think more about spellings and try to work them out for themselves. Most of the children were quite confident in their phonic knowledge and understood and could identify vowel and consonant digraphs, and were able to blend and segment single-syllable words and many two-syllable words. When Laura tried to encourage the children to be more independent, it emerged from both the children and some parents that the children's Year 2 teacher had told them that they must not use words they could not spell, and should always ask for help when they were not sure how to spell a word. The result was that many children produced quite accurate but very boring writing in which adjectives were generally limited to *good, bad* and *nice*.

Laura recalled being told by her English tutor during training that it was important for children to develop as independent spellers and that they needed strategies to help them when they were unable to spell words, which went beyond seeking immediate help from their teacher or teaching assistant. She decided that she wanted to help the children to become more independent as spellers, and talked to colleagues about how she might achieve this. She also read about spelling in a variety of books and articles. Having done this, she concluded that what the children needed was:

- confidence to attempt spellings without worrying that they might be reprimanded if they made mistakes;
- strategies for attempting spellings;
- more opportunities to talk about spelling and to undertake spelling investigations.

Activity

Before reading how Laura planned to develop children's spelling skills, consider how you would approach this with the Year 3 class.

Case Study: Part 2 – Developing independent spellers

Laura decided to introduce the children to some temporary spelling strategies which would enable them to try to spell words when they were writing, without immediate recourse to adult support. She also decided to focus on spelling to a greater extent during shared writing, which would give her an opportunity to model ways of approaching spelling. Further, she would talk to the children about the importance of accurate spelling but explain that learning from mistakes was valuable, and that she would rather they were adventurous with their use of words and made mistakes than played safe and used dull or repetitive vocabulary. If they made mistakes she could help them to learn how to spell words correctly, but if they never strayed from words they knew how to spell their spelling would develop very slowly.

At first, the children continued to ask for spelling help during writing sessions, often forming a queue of pupils clutching spelling dictionaries in which some of the words they requested had already been written by their previous teacher. Laura had to be quite firm in rejecting their requests, but she made a point of touring the classroom during writing sessions rather than engaging in guided work for a couple of weeks, so that she could discuss children's attempts at spelling and guide them on strategies. She encouraged them to try out words on separate pieces of paper to see if they 'looked right', and to segment words and say them aloud before making spelling choices. She also told them that they could write as much of a word as they could, and then leave a space or draw a line to show where they were unable to make an attempt at part of a word.

After a fortnight of shared writing, in which Laura made a point of making occasional spelling errors for children to spot, and also modelled her own attempts at spelling by suggesting possible sound–symbol correspondences and asking for help from the children, she began to notice a change in attitude from her pupils. Rather than following her around the classroom asking for spellings, they often drew her attention to their attempts to spell quite complex words. A key indicator of the success of her approach came when a girl included the word *atrocious* (spelled *atroshus*) in a story when describing the weather. Laura stopped the class and praised her for using such an interesting word and for making a very good and sensible attempt to spell it. When she asked the class for ideas on how the word might be spelled, a child who had used the word *delicious* (misspelled) in a previous lesson and had learned from his mistake, was able to suggest a correct way of spelling *atrocious*. This led Laura to ask the children for other words with similar sounds, and she created a word bank of words ending with *-cious* and *-tious* and displayed the words on the wall.

The children were used to having a weekly list of words on Mondays to copy from the board to learn for a test on Fridays. Laura felt that it would be unwise to change this practice as parents (and some children!) might complain, so she decided to continue with the tests but use the word lists more productively. She introduced a test on Monday before the children saw their list of words, partly so that they could discover if they could already spell some of

$\longrightarrow$

the words. However, the most important aspect of this test was to reveal to the children which parts of the words they needed to focus on when learning them. So, for instance, if they were given the word *pocket* to learn and they spelled it *poket*, they would know that it was the *ck* they needed to focus on when learning independently or with parents and carers.

The Friday tests were made into a more enjoyable and relaxed activity, and she ended the practice of children having to give their mark in front of the whole class. She also took care to differentiate the lists for different spelling abilities and to ensure that children learned words which they were likely to meet during lessons and in their reading.

Laura also reinforced the strategy 'look, cover, write, check' to incorporate *say* after *look*. She modelled this with the children and asked them to learn words with her in guided groups.

By the time there was a parents' evening in November, she found that parents were impressed by their children's improved writing and their more confident approach to spelling. Writing sessions were more productive, and the improved quality of the children's work was commented upon by the literacy coordinator.

The strategies Laura adopted were clearly successful for her class and led to an improvement in both their ability to spell and their attitude to spelling. If children are given a solid foundation in synthetic phonics through a systematic programme, allied to an emphasis on decoding and encoding in which they identify all grapheme–phoneme correspondences in words, they will be well placed to cope with the many challenges that English orthography presents. This will be especially so where their teachers help develop a fascination for words and a range of strategies for learning how to spell them.

Learning Outcomes Review

In this chapter you have seen that inconsistencies in English spelling can present challenges for teaching and learning spelling, but that these can also be turned into opportunities for developing an understanding of the language. An understanding of morphology can help us to break words into segments and units of meaning, and can also develop our ability to spell and to apply our knowledge to new words. Spelling investigations are an important device for supporting knowledge of spelling rules and conventions and for helping internalise these for children.

Self-assessment questions

What do you understand by each of the terms below?

1. Morpheme
2. Etymology
3. Homonym
4. Homophone
5. Prefix
6. Suffix

Further Reading

For an interesting look at strategies for learning spellings and investigating spellings with your class, see Chapter 4 in:

Wray, D. and Medwell, J. (2008) *Primary English: Extending Knowledge in Practice*. Exeter: Learning Matters.

For a fascinating insight into the origins of English words, see Chapter 5 in:

Bryson, B. (1990) *The Mother Tongue*. London: Penguin.

For an interesting history of English spelling, see:

Crystal, D. (2012) *Spell it Out: The Singular Story of English Spelling*. London: Profile Books.

For research and guidance on spelling, see:

Waugh, D., Warner, C. and Waugh, R. (2013) *Teaching Grammar, Spelling and Punctuation in Primary Schools*. London: SAGE.

For simple guidance on teaching 'tricky' or 'common exception' words, see:

Gill, A. and Waugh, D. (2016) 'That doesn't sound right', *Teach Primary*, 10 (5).

Waugh, D. and Gill, A. (2016) 'Tricky customers', *Teach Reading and Writing*.

References

Allott, K. (2014) 'Spelling' and 'Planning for delivery', in D. Waugh, W. Jolliffe and K. Allott (eds), *Primary English for Trainee Teachers*. London: SAGE.

Crystal, D. (1987) *The Cambridge Encyclopedia of Language*. Cambridge: Cambridge University Press.

DCSF (2009) *Support for Spelling*. Norwich: DfES.

De Graaff, S., Bosman, A.M.T, Hasselman, F. and Verhoeven, L. (2009) 'Benefits of systematic phonics instruction', *Scientific Studies of Reading*, 13 (4): 318–33.

DfE (2011) *Teachers' Standards in England from September 2012*. London: DfE.

DfE (2013) *The National Curriculum in England, Key Stages 1 and 2 Framework Document*. London: DfE.

DfES (2007) *Letters and Sounds: Principles and Practice of High Quality Phonics*. London: DfES.

Gentry, R. (1987) *Spel... is a Four-Letter Word*. London: Heinemann.

Goswami, U. and Bryant, P. (1990) *Phonological Skills and Learning to Read*. Hove: Psychology Press.

Johnston, R. and Watson, J. (2007) *Teaching Synthetic Phonics*. Exeter: Learning Matters.

McGuinness, D. (2004) *Early Reading Instruction: What Science Really Tells Us about How to Teach Reading*. Cambridge, MA: MIT Press.

Mudd, N. (1994) *Effective Spelling: A Practical Guide for Teachers*. London: Hodder and Stoughton.

To, N., Tighe, E. and Binder, K. (2014) 'Investigating morphological awareness and the processing of transparent and opaque words in adults with low literacy skills and in skilled readers', *Journal of Research in Reading*, 37 (4): 1–18.

Audit and test

Work through each section below, responding to each question or task. When you have completed each section, you can read the answers at the end of the chapter. At the end of the chapter, you can also find support for further reading and study related to spelling.

Section 1: Key terminology for spelling

It is important that you understand the terms below before you move on to the next activity. Provide a definition of each and check your definitions against those at the end of the chapter:

Singular

Plural

Morpheme

Prefix

Suffix

Homonyms

Homophones

Homographs

Compound word

Medial vowel sound

Section 2: Sorting words according to medial vowel sound

Sort the words below into groups according to their medial vowel sound:

mat bed pig dog sun bag pen sit box cup bull frog fan bed mint

Section 3: Modifying words (see also Chapter 12)

Look at the words from the draft National Curriculum listed below which are to be learned in Year 3-4. How many could *NOT* be added to or modified to create new words? Remember, you can often make the words into plurals (e.g. accidents), change nouns to verbs (e.g. bicycle into bicycling), change verbs to nouns (e.g. approve to approval), change adjectives to nouns (e.g. difficult to difficulty) etc.

---

accident, advertise, approve, benefit, behave, bicycle, breath, breathe, building, calendar, certain, concentrate, chocolate, congratulate, conscience, continue, decorate, describe, dictionary, difficult, discover, disturb, early, earn, earth, educate, excite, experience, experiment, explore, extreme, February, grammar, guide, guard, half, heart, immediate, improve, increase, independent, injure, inquire, interest, island, junior, knowledge, library, material, medicine, mention, multiply, murmur, nephew, occasion, often, opposite, paragraph, particular, peculiar, position, possess, produce, professor, promise, property, prove, punctuate, quality, quantity, quarrel, quarter, recite, recover, register, regular, reign, remember, sentence, separate, sew, situate, strength, sufficient, sure, surprise, surround, thought, though, weary

Now see how many words you can create from the 90 above.

What does this activity tell you about teaching vocabulary and spelling?

Section 4: Compound words

Compound words are made up of at least two other words – for example, *foot* and *ball* make *football*, and *head* and *teacher* make *headteacher*. Look at the compound words below and separate them into their constituent parts. The first one has been done for you:

everyone   every + one

everybody

somewhere

anyone

everything

nowhere

nobody

anywhere

anybody

someone

Now look at the table below and see how many compound words you can create using each word as many times as you like.

head	ball	house	hand
ache	tooth	foot	teacher
green	brush	hair	day
birth	play	week	farm

Section 5: Homonyms, homophones and homographs

Look at the words below and decide which are homonyms, which are homophones and which are homographs:

see   sea   record   fast   hoarse   cricket   weather   lead   flee   flew

Section 6: Spelling rules and generalisations

1. Look at the words below, all of which are spelled correctly, and work out a spelling rule for making words which end with *y* into plurals:

   monkeys   babies   keys   ladies   days   hobbies   buggies

2. Look at the words below, all of which are spelled correctly, and work out a spelling rule for adding –ing to words:

    liking   running   dying   seeing   swimming   hoping   hopping   saving   loving

Now work out rules and generalisations which you could teach to children to complete the following:

3. English words don't end with _____. (Give as many letters as possible.)

4. Q is almost always _____.

5. There are many ways to make the /c/ sound in cat (e.g. k, ck), but the following are never found at the beginnings of words: _____.

6. Think about the spelling 'rule' which most people know: 'i before e except after c'.

    a.   Is this a good rule?

    b.   Are there exceptions?

    c.   How could you modify the rule to make it clearer?

ANSWERS

Section 1: Key terminology for spelling

Singular

A word form used to refer to one of something. When more than one is referred to, a plural form is used. Nouns can be singular or plural.

Plural

The plural forms of words show that they refer to more than one item. This usually involves adding an *s* (cats, books) or *es* (matches, buses), but some plurals are irregular. For example, child becomes children, mouse becomes mice and goose becomes geese.

Some nouns remain the same in their plural form as in their singular form, including sheep and the names of many fish (one haddock, two haddock, one salmon, two salmon).

Morpheme

The smallest unit of language that can convey meaning. A morpheme cannot be broken down into anything smaller that has a meaning. A word may consist of one morpheme ('need'), two morphemes ('need/less', 'need/ing') or three or more morphemes ('un/happi/ness'). Suffixes and prefixes are morphemes.

Prefix

Morphemes which are placed at the beginning of a word to modify or change its meaning. For example, dis/like, micro/scope, tri/cycle.

Suffix

Morphemes added to the ends of words to modify their meanings. For example, use and useful or useless; look and looking, looks or looked.

Homonyms

Words with the same spelling and pronunciation but different meanings – for example, left (opposite of right) and left (departed), bark (of a dog) and bark (of a tree). The term *homonym* is often used as a general term for homophones and homographs. Homonym means *same name*.

Homophones

Words which sound the same but have different spellings and meanings are homophones (homo – same, phone – sound). For example sea and see, sew, so and sow, blue and blew, great and grate. Homophone means *same sound*.

Homographs

Words which are spelled the same as other words which mean something different and are pronounced differently. For example, sow (spreading seeds) and sow (a female pig); lead (to take charge or something used to restrain a dog) and lead (a heavy metal), row (argue) and row (in a boat). Homograph means *same writing*.

Compound word

A word made when two words are joined to form a new word – for example, *toothbrush, football, toenail*.

Hyphens are sometimes used to link the two parts of the word – for example: *twenty-seven, self-audit, penalty-taker*.

Medial vowel sound

The medial vowel sound is the sound of the phoneme in the middle of a word, so that hot and cot have the same medial vowel sound.

Section 2: Sorting words according to medial vowel sound

You were asked to sort the words below into groups according to their medial vowel sound. For the words you were given, the groups should be as follows:

mat	*bet*	*pig*	*dog*	*sun*
bag	*pen*	*sit*	*box*	*cup*
fan	*bed*	*mint*	*frog*	*bull*

As children's phonic skills develop they will encounter words in which the medial vowel sounds are the same, but they are spelled differently. For example:

bed and head

hit and hymn

dog and was

By developing children's awareness of medial sounds, as well as initial and final sounds, we help them to develop their phonological awareness and their phonemic awareness (see Chapter 1).

Section 3: modifying words (see also Chapter 12)

Look at the first ten words in the list:

accident, advertise, approve, benefit, behave, bicycle, breath, breathe, building, calendar

All can be modified by adding prefixes and/or suffixes (morphemes). Some examples are given below:

accidents, accidental, accidentally

advertises, advertising, advertised, advertisement

approves, approved, approval, approving, disapprove

benefits, benefited, benefiting

behaves, behaved, behaviour, behaving

bicycles, bicycles, bicycled, bicycling

breaths, breathing, breathed

breathes, breathing

buildings, rebuild, rebuilding

calendars

All of the words in the list of 90 can be modified in some way; often in several ways. When we tried this out with our trainees, the words they found most difficulty in modifying were *February* and *often*, but more than one February would be *Februaries* (*I remember three Februaries ago … or I have lived through some very cold Februaries*), and *often* can become *oftener*, even though we more often use *more often*!

What all of this tells us is that when we teach spellings we should not only focus on individual words, but should also look at how they can be modified to make new words. This will teach children about spelling conventions such as adding *–ing* and *–ed*, and making plurals, and will also broaden their vocabularies and their understanding of how words work. Even if children learned ten new words every week from Year 1 to Year 6 they would only learn around 2,500, which is far fewer than will actually need. Therefore, we need to help them develop an understanding of words and spelling which will enable them to apply their knowledge and understanding to unfamiliar words.

Section 4: Compound words

The compound words can be divided as follows:

everyone   every + one

everybody   every + body

somewhere   some + where

anyone   any + one

everything   every + thing

nowhere   no + where

nobody   no + body

anywhere   any + where

anybody   any + body

someone   some + one

You were asked to look at the table below and see how many compound words you could create using each word as many times as you liked.

head	ball	House	hand
ache	tooth	Foot	teacher
green	brush	Hair	day
birth	play	Week	farm

Possibilities include:

> *headache, headteacher, handball, greenhouse, football, toothache, toothbrush, hairbrush, birthday, weekday, farmhouse, farmhand*

Children encounter lots of compound words in their reading. By helping them to see how these words are created, we can help them to break them down to read and understand them. New compound words are often created for new inventions or situations and many are then included in dictionaries – for example, *jobseeker, supersaver, masterchef.*

Section 5: Homonyms, homophones and homographs

You were asked to look at the words below and decide which are homonyms, which are homophones and which are homographs:

see sea record fast hoarse cricket weather lead flee flew

- *See* and *sea* are homophones because they sound the same but are spelled differently.
- *Hoarse* is a homophone for *horse.*
- *Weather* is a homophone for *whether.*
- *Flee* is a homophone for *flea.*
- *Flew* is a homophone for *flu.*
- *Record* is a homograph because it can be pronounced in more than one way – for example, *I record my favourite programme. Mo broke the record.*
- *Lead* is a homograph because it can be pronounced in more than one way – for example, *My dog has a lead. The lead was stolen from the roof.*
- *Cricket* is a homonym (it can be a sport or an insect).
- *Fast* is a homonym (it can mean *to go without food* or *quick*).

Section 6: Spelling rules and generalisations

1. If a word ends with a vowel before the *y*, add an *s* (*keys, days*).

   If a word has a consonant before the *y*, replace the *y* with *ies* (*baby – babies, hobby – hobbies*).

2. Spelling rules for adding *–ing* to words:

   - for words which end with *y* just add *–ing* (*worrying, marrying*)
   - if the word ends in *e*, drop the *e* and add *–ing* (*have – having, bite – biting*)
   - if the word is short and ends with a vowel and then a consonant, double the consonant and add *–ing* (*run – running, hop – hopping*).

Others:

- if a word has a double *e*, do not drop the second *e* (*free* + *ing* = *freeing*)
- change *ie* to *y* before adding *–ing* (*die* + *ing* = *dying*, *lie* + *ing* = *lying*).

Rules and generalisations which you could teach to children to complete the following:

3. English words don't end with j, v, q (you were asked to give as many letters as possible).

4. Q is almost always followed by u (exceptions such as Iraq and Qatar are not English words).

5. There are many ways to make the /c/ sound in cat (e.g. *k*, *ck*, *cc*, *q* (in *Iraq*), *que* in *cheque* and *plaque*, *ch* in *chemistry*), but the following are never found at the beginnings of words: *ck*, *cc*.

6. Think about the spelling 'rule' which most people know: 'i before e except after c'.

    Is this a good rule? No, because there are so many common exceptions – *their, seeing, being, rein, reign, weigh, height, heir, reinforce* etc.

    a. Are there exceptions? See above.

    b. How could you modify the rule to make it clearer? If you modify the rule to 'i before e except after c when the word rhymes with me' there are fewer exceptions.

What to do next?

Develop your knowledge and understanding of spelling by:

1. exploring morphemes and their meanings;

2. making collections of homographs, homophones and homonyms – you can find these on websites;

3. finding examples of compound words and creating games and activities;

4. making collections of unusual grapheme–phoneme correspondences – for example, in names;

5. considering the value of different spelling rules and generalisations.

7. Teaching phonics in the early years

Learning Outcomes

By the end of this chapter you will have:

- an understanding of methods of teaching phonics linked to a broad and rich language curriculum;
- an overview of appropriate and engaging methods for teaching phonics in the early years;
- analysed case studies of methods of teaching phonics in the early years for key features of effective practice.

Teachers' Standards

3. Demonstrate good subject and curriculum knowledge:

- demonstrate a critical understanding of developments in the subject and curriculum areas, and promote the value of scholarship;
- if teaching early reading, demonstrate a clear understanding of systematic synthetic phonics.

Criteria for assuring high-quality phonic work (DfE, 2011a)

Teachers will make principled, professional judgements about when to start on a systematic, synthetic programme of phonic work but it is reasonable to expect that the great majority of children will be capable of, and benefit from doing so by the age of five. It is equally important for the programme to be designed so that children become fluent readers, having secured word-recognition skills by the end of Key Stage 1.

(Continued)

(Continued)

Early Years Foundation Stage

The Early Years Foundation Stage Framework (DfE, 2014) sets out the following Early Learning Goal for reading:

> Children read and understand simple sentences. They use phonic knowledge to decode regular words and read them aloud accurately. They also read some common irregular words. They demonstrate understanding when talking with others about what they have read.

Introduction

Teaching phonics in appropriate ways for young children is an area of considerable debate. The importance of a play-based curriculum that is not dominated by teacher-directed activities is an a priori principle for early years practitioners. As Nigel Hall states, 'Play offers a chance to be literate' (1991, p.14).

This chapter will engage with that debate and set the teaching of phonics in the early years within a broad and rich language curriculum. It will provide examples of a range of interactive methods that help young children build their phonic knowledge and make suggestions of how this understanding can be extended across the areas of learning and within the indoor and outdoor classroom. Engaging young children in relevant meaningful ways and also making links to their experiences of literacy at home and at school will also be discussed.

Theoretical perspectives/subject knowledge

When to start?

Teaching phonics in the early years needs to be first and foremost based on informal activities in a play context that begins the process of linking sounds to letters. It starts with playing with sounds with babies and enjoying finger rhymes and songs that tune young children into language, as well as being enjoyable for the child and the carer. Alongside this, babies enjoy the experience of being read to and the rhythm of many early picture books written in rhyme or using alliteration – for example, in *We're Going on a Bear Hunt*:

We're going on a bear hunt.

We're going to catch a big one ...

Swishy swashy!

Squelch, squerch! {etc.}

(Rosen and Oxenbury, 1993)

In all of these activities, children are learning to love books, to enjoy playing with language and they are developing phonological awareness. In nursery settings, the skilful practitioner provides informal activities in a play context to help children link sounds to letters, and this should take place (for most children) before the age of five. What matters is the professional judgement of the practitioner as to when it is appropriate to commence a systematic teaching programme. The key is appropriate early years practice (see the Research Focus (p.132) and the study by Stuart, 2006, for further information). As discussed in detail in Chapter 1, it is not always necessary to engage in a lengthy programme of teaching phonological awareness before beginning to teach grapheme–phoneme correspondences. For some children who demonstrate a delay in learning to read, it may be helpful to provide additional teaching of phonological awareness; however, as discussed in Chapter 11, difficulties may also involve deficits in both letter knowledge and expressive vocabulary and thus careful tracking and accurate assessment is vital.

Learning in a language-rich curriculum

Much has been written about a broad and rich language curriculum in which to base all language teaching, including phonics. One of the key considerations is the classroom environment. An effective classroom environment will ensure that every encounter with print will support children to learn more about the nature of our language. To provide for a rich language curriculum, this environment needs to include:

- a range of books (fiction and non-fiction) attractively displayed;
- a comfortable reading area which includes opportunities to listen to audio books;
- a range of big books, including ones made with the class, for example children's photos and a short statement about each child;
- a print-rich environment which includes such aspects as labels for classroom objects, posters, alphabet charts, writing centres and such things as 'graffiti or message walls' for children to write notes or messages for each other;
- a range of phonics resources including magnetic letters and boards, felt and wooden letters, mini-whiteboards and pens;

- role-play areas which include print such as notices and labels and opportunities to write (e.g. shopping lists);

- use of ICT which includes computers with phonic games and interactive whiteboards at a height for children to use;

- puppets, for example a puppet who can only talk in phonemes, thus encouraging children to practise segmenting words into phonemes.

Practitioners working with young children should therefore:

- support children with symbolic representation of ideas through playing, gesturing, drawing, building, labelling, naming, story-telling and writing;

- support children with significant aspects of the language curriculum through:
  o   playing with language
  o   telling stories and sharing books
  o   writing
  o   using 'words about language' (e.g. word, letter etc.).

One of the key issues to be aware of is the importance of the relationships that are built up with young children. Marian Whitehead highlights the importance of providing 'genuinely mutual conversations between children and adults, and between children and children' (2004, p.106). (See Chapter 8 for further information on multi-sensory and interactive approaches.)

The Tickell Review of the Early Years Foundation Stage (DfE, 2011c) echoed the value of conversation and highlights the relationship between what it described as the three prime areas of learning: communication, language and literacy; personal, social and emotional development; and physical development. It states:

> *The new aspects in both communication and language and personal, social and emotional development take account of recent research which recognises the importance of conversation and narrative in children's learning and development.*

> (DfE, 2011c, p.102)

The review also emphasises the importance of applying phonic skills:

> *Experience has shown that one of the stumbling blocks for children and practitioners is the application of phonic knowledge and skills to reading and writing. Many children grasp the grapheme–phoneme correspondences in isolation but are not able to, or lack opportunity*

to, apply their skills in meaningful ways. Thus the new aspects incorporate the acquisition
of phonic knowledge and skills with its application to reading and writing.

(DfE, 2011c, p.103)

The importance of developing oral language skills is also emphasised in the review by the Expert Panel for the Review of the National Curriculum (DfE, 2011b), which identified the connection between oral development, cognitive development and educational attainment. Such development supports what it describes as 'key domains' and it states:

{W}e are persuaded that oral language is inextricably linked to both word reading skills
and to reading comprehension.

(DfE, 2011b, p.52)

Recent government reviews are therefore agreed that providing for a rich language curriculum is a key aspect of effective provision and clearly linked to phonics and early reading.

Case Study: Meaningful literacy experiences

Read the following extract from Saracho (2004, p.204), which provides an example of a rich literacy experience for young children.

Mrs Grey and the children are sitting in a circle on the floor. She shows the children a big book about a picnic and says, 'Today we are going to be reading another big book.' She begins reading the big book and the children smile as the teacher continues.

Mrs Grey: But before we begin our book today, let's do some thinking. Everyone please close your eyes and place your hands on your lap. I'd like you to imagine that you are going on a picnic and that you are in charge of packing the picnic basket. What will you bring? Use your senses to help you remember the things that you will need. Maybe you are standing in the kitchen. What do you see that must be included? Is anyone reminding you that you must bring certain things?

[The students think quietly for a minute or two before the teacher asks them to open their eyes.]

Mrs Grey: Everyone will have a chance to respond so there is no reason to raise your hands. I will call on each one of you, and when I do, please tell me one thing that must be included in your picnic.

[As the teacher listens to each response, she records it on the chalkboard. By the end of the responses, the list looks something like this]:

→

fruit	banana	coke
pizza	apple	lollipops
orange	ice cream in a bowl	pears

Saracho goes on to describe how the teacher engages the children with props including a shopping basket and various objects and, following this, introduces the book entitled *The Picnic*.

Research Focus: Play and literacy

Providing for literacy opportunities within a play context can be particularly effective in motivating and engaging children in learning literacy skills. Nigel Hall's research in this area provides particularly useful examples. He describes an effective literacy-rich environment where a home corner was subjected to a 'print-flood'; this included:

Cookbooks, recipe pads, a recipe notebook, and writing utensils were placed by the stove. Throughout the home corner, a wide range of appropriate literacy materials was provided, including writing utensils.

The home corner also contained a desk area with paper, envelopes, and writing utensils. Newspapers and letters were pushed through the door before each session. Diaries, planners, telephone directories, books, catalogues and other print material were also placed in strategic locations. The children's play was videotaped unobtrusively, and children were free to come round the back and watch the monitor while recording was in progress. In addition, observers took notes while play was in progress.

With these resources added to the home corner, the children's behaviour demonstrated a keen commitment to literacy.

(Hall, 1991, p.14)

He goes on to state:

If literacy-related resources are offered sensitively to children within sociodramatic play, then the relationship between the emergence of literacy and play is not a general one. Play offers a chance to be literate.

(Hall, 1991, p.14)

This example of engaging young children in meaningful literacy experiences embodies a rich language curriculum: one that should form the bedrock upon which to build the teaching of phonics.

Rhymes and songs

Using a range of rhymes and songs is common practice in the early years. Used alongside a systematic phonics programme they can be valuable reinforcement of specific phonemes. Most important is that they are fun and not only do children readily engage with them, but also the act of singing them particularly aids recall. Classic texts such as *This Little Puffin* compiled by Elizabeth Matterson (1969) are on most practitioners' shelves, and we should not forget their potential in supporting the teaching of phonics. The following demonstrates the role of rhymes and songs:

- They can be useful not only for emphasising initial phonemes, but also for consonant-vowel-consonant (CVC) words, consonant blends and long vowel sounds. In addition, rhymes can highlight that words may sound the same but can be spelled differently.

- Making use of incidental moments in the day to sing songs or say rhymes can be very useful in calming children down, and provide a quiet finish to a session.

- Sharing rhyming stories is another way of encouraging the use of rhyme in connection with work on phonological awareness. Examples include: *Ten in the Bed* (Dale, 1990); *The Dog that Dug* (Long and Korky, 1993); *The Trouble with Mum* (Cole, 1986); *Pass the Jam, Jim* and *You Can Swim, Jim* (Umansky and Chamberlain, 1992); and *Each Peach Pear Plum* (Ahlberg and Ahlberg, 1999). In those texts that include repeated refrains, some words may be able to be decoded using children's phonic knowledge.

- Selecting rhymes to support work on different phonemes can be very useful. For some examples, see BBC Words and Pictures (www.bbc.co.uk/wordsandpictures). Such rhymes can be particularly useful for supporting work on CVC words, for example:

  Higglety, piggelty, pop!

  The dog has eaten the mop:

  The pig's in a hurry,

  The cat's in a flurry,

  Higglety, piggelty, pop!

- This can be extended to work on other CVC words that rhyme with *pop*, for example, *mop, top, shop, cop, hop, lop* and so on.

- The use of captions and messages within the context of role-play can also support children's decoding of print. Some examples are shown in Figures 7.1–7.4.

Figure 7.1 You can play in the sand

Figure 7.2   Hop on the mat

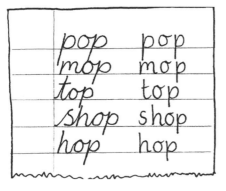

Figure 7.3   Make a list

Figure 7.4   Clap and sing

Puppets

Using puppets with young children is an enjoyable way of encouraging them to engage with learning phonics. Young children will often respond to a puppet where they might be reluctant to say something to a teacher or adult. It is often fascinating to see that in spite of a lack of ventriloquist's skills by an adult, children do believe it is the puppet talking!

Practitioners should model a range of activities using the puppet, such as the puppet who cannot articulate sounds correctly and needs the children's help. Children can then be encouraged to use the puppet, having fun in different ways; for example, having a puppet theatre where two children can play with one puppet each. Practitioners should observe their interactions carefully and intervene at key 'teachable moments' and make links to phonics teaching where appropriate.

Case Study: Using puppets

Harry is a trainee who, as part of his training, is visiting Foundation Stage once a week during the first term of his final year. In this setting, once phonics instruction has begun, the children are divided into groups in order that the teaching can be effectively differentiated. All the teachers have a puppet they use for phonics. Harry has observed some phonics lessons and knows that the puppet is called 'Polly', and Polly can only speak in separate phonemes. Likewise, the children have to speak to the puppet in phonemes. Read the following script of part of the lesson.

Harry: Now let's recall the sounds we learned last week. [He shows the phoneme cards for /s/ and /a/] Can we say together what's on the pictures? Yes – snakes and apples [emphasises the initial sounds]. Now let's repeat these together and watch me for the actions:

/s/ Snakes on slippery sand [moves hand like a snake]

/a/ Ants and apples [fingers crawl up to mouth and then pretend to munch an apple]

Now here's Polly and she is going to say some words using her special way of talking – you will need to listen carefully and see if you can tell your partner the word she says.

/s/ /a/ /d/, /s/ /a/ /t/, /a/ /n/ /t/

Now can you talk in 'Polly talk'? Listen carefully: 'sad'.

Say it to your partner and then altogether, tell Polly. Well done.

Harry sees how this practice in segmenting and blending words using a puppet provides useful reinforcement for the children and engages them in enjoyable ways.

Whiteboards

Providing individual whiteboards for pairs of children, or at times individual children, can be very useful to support children applying their phonic knowledge by writing words containing the phoneme being taught. This will support practice at forming the letters and segmenting words into their constituent phonemes and then writing the corresponding graphemes. This can be incorporated within every lesson using the following procedure:

1. Say a word containing the phoneme being taught and others learned (e.g. for /t/ the word *tap*). Children repeat the word.

2. Now ask children to split (segment) the word into phonemes (e.g. /t/a/p/). They should say each phoneme, counting on their fingers the corresponding number.

3. They then show you how many phonemes (e.g. three for *tap*).

4. Now ask them to write the word on their whiteboards and then to show you.

The use of whiteboards also supports assessment of children's ability to segment words into phonemes and to write the correct letters. Further reinforcement can be provided for children who require additional support.

Magnetic letters

Magnetic letters and magnetic whiteboards can be another very useful resource for teaching phonics. Whole-group modelling by the teacher with magnetic letters works well, so the children can see the letters blending together and they can practise sliding letters together to make words themselves. They then get a turn with their own board to identify the letters and place them together to blend them. For further practice at using letters to make words, the teacher says a word and asks children to work in pairs to make the word using the letters supplied.

Activity

Using resources for interactive learning

Using the examples of resources above, look at Table 7.1 and decide what resources you could use to engage the children.

Table 7.1   Outline lesson plan

Revisit and review	Play a game using phonemes taught: s, a, t, p, i, n
Teach	Introduce new phonemes *b* and *u* and teach mnemonics, CVC segmentation using phoneme frame Letters: *s, b, u, t* Words: *bus, tub*
Practise	Hear, say, read and write: letters using *t, b, u*
Apply	Play 'Guess my word' where children have to listen to phonemes and blend them into words

Learning in context across different areas of learning

Read the extract of a case study below taken from the archived National Strategies website and consider how the application of phonics is encouraged across different areas of learning, indoors and outdoors.

Phonics sessions in the EYFS unit take place every day.

Nursery children enjoy games from Phase 1 of the Letters and Sounds document. Nursery Phase 1 sessions last a maximum of ten minutes and all sessions are fun and active. For those children who are ready, oral blending and segmenting are part of the daily routine, e.g. 'Please put on your c-oa-t'. Nursery children sing songs (Take Ten) and play games linked to Phase 1, paint with decorators' brushes and water, and draw pictures and mark make with chalk on the blackboard outside.

At the end of the year the majority of Reception children were working at Phase 4. The 'Fitzy' markings on the playground are often used for the practice part of their session. Opportunities to apply phonics skills and knowledge are always available beyond the main phonics session, either outside or inside. For example the children enjoy making a magic brew by reading instructions, writing their own recipes or making a price list for a table top sale. They can often be seen walking around with a clipboard and pencil or lying on the carpet with a whiteboard and pen. Magnetic letters are always accessible and a great favourite especially with those with less well developed fine motor skills. The children are very eager to read their reading books and they confidently read the labels, notices and words around the classroom.

84% of Reception children were secure at Phase 3 and above by the end of the Summer Term. All children look forward to their daily phonics session. They know it is going to be a fun time with lots of opportunities to be active.

(http://wsassets.s3.amazonaws.com/ws/tlr/files/downloads/pdf/35759_node.pdf –accessed 2/5/18)

Research Focus: Starting systematic teaching of phonics

Stuart (2006, p.23) examines the question of when to start teaching phonics and cites her research study (1999) carried out in five schools in one inner-London LEA, prior to the introduction of the National Literacy Strategy.

One hundred and twelve children in six Year R classes were given one hour per day literacy teaching for 12 weeks. In three classes, the teaching was based around the use of 'big books', with teachers particularly asked to spend time on word level work, including letter–sound relationships. In the other three classes, phoneme segmentation and blending skills and grapheme–phoneme correspondences were taught, using Jolly Phonics and with strict adherence to that programme.

In relation to the issue of how early can this kind of teaching be profitably introduced, it was shown that immediately after the 12-week intervention 95 per cent of children in the

$\longrightarrow$

Jolly Phonics intervention could correctly indicate the printed letter that represented a given phoneme for more than half (13+) of the letters of the alphabet, and 84 per cent of them could recall the correct phoneme for more than 20 graphemes (Jolly Phonics teaches one grapheme for each phoneme in English, so children are immediately taught one writing pattern for each long vowel: for example, *ee* as in *green* and *mean*, /ae/ as in *maid*, *made* and *may* etc.). The comparative figures for children in the 'big book' intervention were 63 per cent and 58 per cent respectively. Moreover, the mode (the most frequently occurring score) for letter sound recognition in the Jolly Phonics group was 25 (on a test with 26 items) and for letter sound recall it was 21 (on a test with 42 items). Comparative figures here for the 'big book' group were 18 and 0 respectively. Thus that most of these five-year-olds appeared ready and able to learn about letter sounds and grapheme–phoneme correspondences, provided these were taught in a systematic, structured and fun way.

The debate over a focus on teaching phonics with young children continues to rage amongst academics (see Davies, 2012). The core concern voiced by the National Association for the Teaching of English (NATE, 2014) is the danger of focusing on decoding to the detriment of a quest for meaning and enjoyment in reading. Both NATE and the United Kingdom Literacy Association (UKLA) highlight the need for a balance in teaching reading and David Reedy from the UKLA (2012) cites the Ofsted report *Excellence in English: What We Can Learn from 12 Outstanding Schools* (2011), which provides examples of excellent practice. One case study cited by Ofsted (2011) is Clifton Green primary school in York where phonics is an important ingredient in the teaching of reading, but only part of much wider provision for developing literacy. Ofsted also state, in their *Getting Them Reading Early* programme to support inspectors' subject knowledge of phonics, that studies of effective practice show:

Phonics is only part of learning to read. Engagement with stories is evident here, feeding into the children's oral language development, their knowledge of stories and of literary language, providing models for their own spoken and written language. A varied diet of stories listened to forms part of an overall rich curriculum.

(Ofsted, 2014, p.27)

Examples throughout this chapter demonstrate how the teaching of phonics can be embedded in a rich literacy learning environment.

Working with parents and carers

A considerable amount of research has been carried out in the last four decades on the impact of the home–school literacy interface. This has ranged from the seminal work of Weinberger

(1996), which identified the rich and varied literacy experiences of young children at home, and McCarthey (2000), who identified some of the reasons for the gulf between home and school literacy environments. Marsh's research in this area found that

> {e}xisting theories of literacy in the early years place undue emphasis on 'quality' picture books, traditional forms of print literacy, individualised writing practices and literacy-related play activities which are based on middle-class cultural norms. These need to be challenged effectively if the literacy traffic between home and nursery is to flow in both directions for families in all socioeconomic and cultural groups.
>
> *(Marsh, 2003, p.380)*

Marsh's study also found that

> {m}ost of the parents were unable to provide examples of the ways in which home literacy practices impacted on the nursery curriculum, although all were able to provide instances of activities which were brought from nursery to home and felt that these were examples of home-nursery overlap.
>
> *(2003, p.379)*

and there were examples of

> innovative practices which aimed to remedy this situation by incorporating media texts into a family literacy programme.
>
> *(2003, p.379)*

Young et al. emphasise the vital importance of the support from home and that

> {r}eading in the early years is a complex and purposeful socio-cultural, cognitive and linguistic process. Informal reading instruction starts well before children arrive in the classroom and then later on needs the support of families to continue the work of the reading teacher.
>
> *(2012, p.52)*

As discussed in Chapter 5, the importance of working with parents in developing children's literacy and phonics skills is crucial and, alongside this, it helps make meaningful links between home and school.

Adams' findings (1990) fully recognise the importance of the home and community on beginning reading preparedness, recommending the necessity of such mediated learning opportunities as:

- developing young children's literacy understanding through regular reading aloud;

- the importance of the spoken word;

- learning the letters of the alphabet;

- learning how print and words 'work' on the page of a book;

- the importance of teaching children nursery rhymes as prerequisites to developing phonemic awareness and phonics.

Gunn et al. (1995) summarise five areas of emerging evidence that have implications for addressing differences and making a closer match between a child's literacy background and classroom instruction:

Experiences with print (through reading and writing) help preschool children develop an understanding of the conventions, purpose, and functions of print.

Children learn how to attend to language and apply this knowledge to literacy situations by interacting with others who model language functions.

Phonological awareness and letter recognition contribute to initial reading acquisition by helping children develop efficient word-recognition strategies (e.g. detecting pronunciations and storing associations in memory).

Socioeconomic status does not contribute most directly to reading achievement. Rather, other family characteristics related to context are more explanatory such as academic guidance, attitude toward education, parental aspirations for the child, conversations in the home, reading materials in the home, and cultural activities.

Storybook reading, as well as the nature of the adult–child interactions surrounding storybook reading, affects children's knowledge about, strategies for, and attitudes towards reading.

(1995, p.16)

Name writing

The most significant piece of meaningful writing for young children is their first name (Hall and Robinson, 2003). Whitehead (2004) suggests that 'games with names' can be a powerful way into early writing and communication if we follow children's developing interests and observations and provide plenty of examples of names in use. Children's interest is usually accompanied by a desire to write or 'make them' (Makin and Whitehead, 2004). Children can be encouraged to make their marks in wet sand, mud, clay or with paints, pencils and crayons, or in different places such as the playground notice board, the fencing around the garden and so on. Both-de Vries and Bus reinforce the importance of children's names as a springboard for literacy: 'We hypothesize, therefore, that children's understanding of writing as an alphabetic system starts with letters from their own name' (2008, p.39).

Importance of developing vocabulary

Vocabulary is one of the most robust long-term predictors of good literacy development (Snow, 2005). Research has shown that children with large oral vocabularies are unlikely to have problems learning to read (Snow, 2005; Hart and Risley, 1995) – a finding that highlights the huge social class differences in vocabulary size amongst preschool-aged children, which become particularly important towards the end of primary school.

Conversation is the most effective way for children to practise and refine their language skills, including vocabulary. The ongoing verbal give-and-take provides valuable opportunities for speaking and listening, and the child gets immediate feedback. Dudley-Marling and Searle (1991) recommended using 'talk around the edges' (i.e. informal exchanges between children in the classroom) instead of the formal question/answer routines.

Learning Outcomes Review

This chapter has reviewed how to provide a broad and rich language curriculum and how the practitioner can support children within this context. It has discussed when to start systematic phonics teaching and it has provided exemplification of a range of resources to support this. It has also reviewed the importance of making links between literacy experiences at home and at school.

Self-assessment questions

1. Name some ways in which play can support children's early literacy development.
2. How can practitioners make meaningful links between home and school to support literacy development?
3. How can resources support fun engaging ways of teaching phonics to young children?

Further Reading

For detailed guidance on providing a language-rich curriculum, see:

Whitehead, M. (2010) *Language and Literacy in the Early Years*, 4th edn. London: SAGE.

For further information on teaching literacy in the early years and making use of the wider environment, indoors and outdoors, see Chapter 10 in:

Glazzard, J. and Stokoe, J. (2013) *Teaching Synthetic Phonics and Early English*. Northwich: Critical Publishing.

References

Adams, M. (1990) *Beginning to Read: Thinking and Learning about Print.* Cambridge, MA: MIT Press.

Ahlberg, J. and Ahlberg, A. (1999) *Each Peach Pear Plum*. London: Puffin.

Both-de Vries, A.C. and Bus, A.G. (2008) 'Name writing: A first step to phonetic writing? Does the name have a special role in understanding the symbolic function of writing?', *Literacy Learning and Teaching*, *12* (2): 37–55.

Cole, B. (1986) *The Trouble with Mum*. London: Mammoth.

Dale, P. (1990) *Ten in the Bed*. London: Walker Books.

Davies, A. (2012) 'A monstrous regimen of synthetic phonics: Fantasies of research-based teaching "methods" versus real teaching', *Journal of Philosophy of Education*, 46 (4): 560–73.

DfE (2011a) *Teachers' Standards in England from September 2012*. London: DfE.

DfE (2011b) *The Framework for the National Curriculum. A report by the Expert Panel for the National Curriculum review*. London: DfE.

DfE (2011c) *The Early Years: Foundations for Life, Health and Learning – An Independent Report on the Early Years Foundation Stage to Her Majesty's Government*. London: DfE.

DfE (2014) *Statutory Framework for the Early Years Foundation Stage*. London: DfE.

Dudley-Marling, C. and Searle, D. (1991) *When Students Have Time to Talk: Creating Contexts for Learning Language*. London: Heinemann.

Gunn, B., Simmons, D. and Kameenui, E. (1995) *Emergent Literacy: A Synthesis of Research*. Eugene, OR: University of Oregon.

Hall, N. (1991) 'Play and the emergence of literacy', in J. Christie (ed.), *Play and Early Literacy Development*. Albany, NY: State University of New York Press.

Hall, N. and Robinson, A. (2003) *Exploring Writing and Play in the Early Years*. London: Fulton.

Hart, B. and Risley, T.R. (1995) *Meaningful Differences*. Baltimore, MD: Paul H. Brookes.

Jolly Learning (1992) *Jolly Phonics*. Available at www.jollylearning.co.uk/overview-about-jollyphonics/ (accessed 3/2/15).

Long, J. and Korky P. (1993) *The Dog that Dug*. London: Red Fox.

Makin, L. and Whitehead, M.R. (2004) *How to Develop Children's Early Literacy: A Guide for Professional Carers and Educators*. London: Paul Chapman.

Marsh, J. (2003) 'One-way traffic? Connections between literacy practices at home and in the nursery', *British Educational Research Journal*, 29 (3).

Matterson, E. (1969) *This Little Puffin*. London: Puffin.

McCarthey, S.J. (2000) 'Home–school connections: A review of the literature', *Journal of Educational Research*, 93 (3): 145–53.

NATE (2014) *Phonics Instruction and Early Reading: Professional Views from the Classroom*. www.nate.org.uk/cmsfiles/papers/Phonics_and_early_reading.pdf (accessed 21/12/14).

Ofsted (2011) Excellence in English: What Can We Learn From 12 Outstanding Schools. Manchester: Ofsted.

Ofsted (2014) *Getting Them Reading Early: Distance Learning Materials for Inspecting Reading*. London: DfE. Available from: https://www.gov.uk/government/publications/getting-them-reading-early (accessed 2/5/18).

Reedy, D. (2012) 'Misconceptions about teaching reading: Is it only about phonics?', *Education Review*, 24 (2): 50–60.

Rosen, M. and Oxenbury, H. (1993) *We're Going on a Bear Hunt*. London: Walker Books.

Saracho, O. (2004) 'Literacy and language development: Supporting literacy-related play: Roles for teachers of young children', *Early Childhood Education Journal*, 31 (3): 201–6.

Snow, C.E. (2005) 'What counts as literacy development', in K. McCartney and D. Phillips (eds), *Handbook of Early Child Development*. Oxford: Blackwell. pp.274–95.

Stuart, M. (1999) 'Getting ready for reading: Early phoneme awareness and phonics teaching improves reading and spelling in inner-city second-language learners', *British Journal of Educational Psychology*, 69: 587–605.

Stuart, M. (2006) 'Learning to read: Developing processes for recognizing, understanding and pronouncing written words', *London Review of Education*, 4 (1): 19–29.

Umansky, K. and Chamberlain, M. (1992) *Pass the Jam, Jim* and *You Can Swim, Jim*. London: Red Fox.

Weinberger, J. (1996) *Literacy Goes to School: The Parent's Role in Young Children's Literacy Learning*. London: Paul Chapman.

Whitehead, M.R. (2004) *Language and Literacy in the Early Years*. London: SAGE.

Young, J., Walsh, M. and McDonald, L. (2012) 'Revelations on the teaching of reading in the early years of schooling', *Journal of Catholic School Studies*, 84 (1): 44–54.

Audit and test

Work through each section below, responding to each question or task. When you have completed each section, you can read the answers at the end of the chapter.

Section 1: Key terminology for Phonics in the Early Years

It is important that you understand the terms below before you move on to the next activity. Provide a definition of each and check your definitions against those at the end of the chapter:

Language-rich curriculum

Quality first teaching

Phonological awareness

Oral segmenting and blending

General sound discrimination

Alliteration

Voice sounds

Section 2: The Independent Review of the Teaching of Early Reading (The Rose Review)

Access the review through the web link below and read Aspect 2: pp.29–35.

http://webarchive.nationalarchives.gov.uk/20130401151715/https://www.education.gov.uk/publications/eOrderingDownload/0201-2006PDF-EN-01.pdf

Now complete the activity below.

Why does Rose think these are so significant in the teaching of early reading?

1. Speaking and listening

2. Language-rich curriculum

3. Quality first teaching

4. Discrete teaching of phonics

Section 3: Phonological awareness

Phonological awareness is an important prerequisite for successful reading development. In most systematic synthetic phonics programmes, the early phases focus on developing children's phonological awareness. Phase 1 in *Letters and Sounds* includes a range of activities, designed to develop phonological awareness, that are separated into seven aspects.

Aspect 1: General sound discrimination – environmental sounds

Aspect 2: General sound discrimination – instrumental sounds

Aspect 3: General sound discrimination – body percussion

Aspect 4: Rhythm and rhyme

Aspect 5: Alliteration

Aspect 6: Voice sounds

Aspect 7: Oral blending and segmenting

Read the description of the activities below, taken from Phase 1 in *Letters and Sounds,* and decide which of the aspects of phonological awareness above they are designed to teach.

Story sounds

As you read or tell stories, encourage the children to play their instruments in different ways (e.g. *Make this instrument sound like giant's footsteps, ... a fairy fluttering, ... a cat pouncing, ... an elephant stamping).* Invite them to make their own suggestions for different characters (e.g. *How might Jack's feet sound as he tiptoes by the sleeping giant? And what about when he runs fast to escape down the beanstalk?).* As the children become familiar with the pattern of the story, each child could be responsible for a different sound.

I spy

Place on the floor or on a table a selection of objects with names containing two or three phonemes (e.g. zip, hat, comb, cup, chain, boat, tap, ball). Check that all the children know the names of the objects. Then you, or perhaps a puppet, say *I spy with my little eye a z-i-p.* Then invite a child to say the name of the object and hold it up. All the children can then say the individual phonemes and blend them together: 'z-i-p, zip'. When the children have become familiar with this game, use objects with names that start with the same initial phoneme (e.g. cat, cap, cup, cot, comb, kite). This will really encourage the children to listen and then blend right through the word, rather than relying on the initial sound.

Playing with words

Gather together a set of familiar objects with names that have varying syllable patterns (e.g. pencil, umbrella, camera, xylophone). Show the objects to the children, name them, and talk about what they are used for. Wait for the children to share some of their experiences of the objects; for instance, some of them will have used a camera. Then encourage them to think about how the name of the object sounds and feels as they say it. Think about the syllables and clap them out as you say each word. Then clap the syllables for a word without saying it and ask: *What object could that be?*

As children gain confidence, try some long words like *binoculars, telephone, dinosaur.*

Bertha goes to the zoo

Set up a small toy zoo and join the children as they play with it. Use a toy bus and a bag of animal toys with names starting with the same sound (e.g. a lion, a lizard, a leopard, a llama and a lobster) to act out this story. Chant the following rhyme and allow each child in turn to draw an animal out of the bag and add an animal name to the list of animals spotted at the zoo.

Bertha the bus is going to the zoo, Who does she see as she passes through?... a pig, a panda, a parrot and a polar bear.

Section 4: The power of play

Design a different activity for each of the areas below to teach the skill of oral blending:

- Sand/water area
- Role-play area
- Small world area, e.g. vehicles, animals etc.
- Listening area

ANSWERS

Section 1: Key terminology for phonics in the early years

Language-rich curriculum

A curriculum that has speaking and listening at its centre. Links are made between language and practical experiences. It provides an environment rich in print and provides many opportunities to engage with books.

Quality first teaching

Quality first teaching includes a blend of whole-class, group and individual activities designed to match work to children's different but developing abilities.

Phonological awareness

The ability to attend to the phonological or sound structure of language as distinct from its meaning.

Oral segmenting and blending

Blending and segmenting words without using knowledge of grapheme–phoneme correspondence, i.e. without showing written forms.

General sound discrimination

The process of allowing children to become attuned to the sounds around them.

Alliteration

A sequence of words beginning with the same sound – for example, seven silly sailors sat upon a seat.

Voice sounds

In early stages of phonological development children engage in activities to help them distinguish between different vocal sounds. This might include oral blending and segmenting.

Section 2: The Independent Review of the Teaching of Early Reading

You were asked why Rose maintains the following are so significant in the teaching of early reading.

1. Speaking and listening

    Phonics involves both auditory and oral skills. Developing speaking and listening skills develops children's vocabulary and helps them to learn to listen attentively and speak confidently. Children will find decoding words that are already part of their vocabulary easier than those that are not. Their listening skills will be needed to enable them to hear the separate phonemes in words.

2. Language-rich curriculum

    A language-rich curriculum includes: the use of play, story, songs, rhymes and drama. These familiarise children with letters, words and sounds. Both their vocabulary and interest in reading is developed through allowing them time to talk with adults and each other about feelings and experiences.

3. Quality first teaching

    Quality first teaching matches work to children's different but developing abilities. It supports the identification of children who demonstrate potential difficulties with reading. It involves providing appropriate support which minimises the risk of children falling behind. Quality first teaching includes a blend of whole-class, group and individual work.

4. Discrete teaching of phonics

    Teaching phonics discretely allows children to focus on word-recognition skills, for reading and spelling, without being distracted by other aspects such as reading for meaning. This is a time-limited approach which will eventually be taken over by work which develops comprehension.

Section 3: Phonological awareness

You were asked to read the description of the activities, take from Phase 1 in *Letters and Sounds*, and decide which of the aspects of phonological awareness they are designed to teach.

Activity	Aspect of phonological awareness
Story sounds	Aspect 2: General sound discrimination – instrumental sounds
I spy	Aspect 7: Oral blending and segmenting
Playing with words	Aspect 4: Rhythm and rhyme
Bertha goes to the zoo	Aspect 5: Alliteration

Section 4: The power of play

You were asked to design a different activity for each of the areas below to teach the skill of oral blending. Suggested activities are shown below, but you may have thought of others which are just as good.

Area	Activity to teach the skill of oral blending
Sand/water area	Hide some farm animals in the sand tray, e.g. sheep, pig, goat. Ask the children to see if they can find the sh-ee-p. The children need to blend the phonemes to work out which animal they are to look for. They then look for the corresponding animal in the sand tray. Continue by sounding out the names of the other animals.
Role-play area	Set up the role-play area as a café. Pretend to be a customer but when you order say 'I would like a cup of t-ea please', and ask the child to tell you what you have ordered. Continue ordering things but sound them out and allow the child to blend in order to work out what you have ordered.
Small world area	Use the farm animals and a tractor and trailer. Ask the child (in role as the farmer) to collect the p-i-g and put it in the field. The child has to blend the phonemes to work out which animal needs to go into the field, collects it with the tractor and trailer and places it in the field.

(Continued)

(Continued)

Area	Activity to teach the skill of oral blending
Listening area	Record a popular story and laminate some pictures from it. When you record the story, sound some words out, e.g. Tom went to the p-ar-k. Leave time for the child to find the corresponding picture as part of your recording. At the end of the story the child should have the correct pictures for the words that you sounded out in.

What to do next?

Reinforce your knowledge and understanding of teaching phonics in the early years by doing the following:

1. Spend some time in an early years setting. Note any activities in which children's phonological awareness is being developed. You can use the seven aspects in Phase 1 of *Letters and Sounds* to help you.

2. Observe adult/child interaction and consider how it is developing speaking and listening skills and vocabulary development.

8. Multi-sensory and interactive methods

Learning Outcomes

By the end of this chapter you should:

- know a range of interactive and multi-sensory methods that will enhance (but not dominate) the teaching of phonics;
- know a range of resources, including puppets, interactive whiteboards, magnetic and electronic resources to support multi-sensory and interactive approaches to teaching and learning phonics.

Teachers' Standards

3. Demonstrate good subject and curriculum knowledge:

    - if teaching early reading, demonstrate a clear understanding of systematic synthetic phonics.

4. Plan and teach well structured lessons:

    - impart knowledge and develop understanding through effective use of lesson time.

5. Adapt teaching to respond to the strengths and needs of all pupils:

    - know when and how to differentiate appropriately, using approaches which enable pupils to be taught effectively.

Criteria for assuring high-quality phonic work (DfE, 2011)

Enable children to start learning phonic knowledge and skills using a systematic, synthetic programme by the age of five, with the expectation that they will be fluent readers having secured word recognition skills by the end of Key Stage 1 (see note 2).

Note 2: Teachers will make principled, professional judgements about when to start on a systematic, synthetic programme of phonic work but it is reasonable to expect that the great majority of children will be capable of, and benefit from doing so by the age of five. It is equally important for the programme to be designed so that children become fluent readers having secured word recognition skills by the end of Key Stage 1.

Introduction

What do we know about successful teaching and learning, and how can this inform the way in which we teach systematic synthetic phonics?

We know that children tend to be more engaged in learning when they have opportunities to participate and to interact, and that by using the range of their senses they can be helped to remember and recall information. While learning styles for individuals such as visual, aural, read/write and kinaesthetic (VARK) have been questioned and criticised by many (Coffield et al., 2004; Pashler et al., 2008), this does not mean that varying teaching and learning approaches for a group of children should not be seen as a valid and effective way of working. Indeed, The Rose Review maintained that:

> *Multi-sensory activities featured strongly in high-quality phonic work and often encompassed, variously, simultaneous visual, auditory and kinaesthetic activities involving, for example, physical movement to copy letter shapes and sounds, and manipulate magnetic or other solid letters to build words.*

> (2006, para.57, p.21)

The Review found that successful teaching included mnemonics such as pictures of items which began with letters (e.g. a snake for *s*). Handwriting was often learned kinaesthetically and early, for example through writing in sand, in the air and so on (see later in this chapter). As will be seen later in this chapter, there are many ways in which kinaesthetic methods can be applied to help children internalise the shape and formation of letters. Rose found that such multi-sensory approaches appealed to both boys and girls.

This chapter will look at some of the reasons why interactive, multi-sensory teaching and learning is so appropriate for teaching phonics and will explore a range of practical strategies for use in the classroom, some of which might be extended to the home where children can work with parents or carers to reinforce their learning in school. There will also be a focus on creating a classroom environment that promotes multi-sensory learning.

Research Focus: Multi-sensory phonics

Ofsted (2010) produced a report, *Reading by Six*, that drew on the practice of 12 English schools from diverse communities which it deemed outstanding in the teaching of reading. All of the schools adopted 'a rigorous, intensive, and systematic' (p.3) approach to teaching phonics. One of the key criteria identified by Ofsted for effective, systematic, synthetic phonics programmes is that they should *use a multi-sensory approach so that children learn variously*

→

from simultaneous visual, auditory and kinaesthetic activities which are designed to secure essential phonic knowledge and skills.

(2010, p.42)

However, a supplementary cautionary note is added:

Multi-sensory activities should be interesting and engaging but firmly focused on intensifying the learning associated with its phonic goal [sic]. They should avoid taking children down a circuitous route only tenuously linked to the goal. This means avoiding over-elaborate activities that are difficult to manage and take too long to complete, thus distracting the children from concentrating on the learning goal.

(2010, p.43)

Activity

In the light of the comments above, consider the structure and activities in the lesson described below. Do you consider them valid or 'over-elaborate'? Think about how you might teach a similar class about the /t/ sound.

Perkins (2012, pp.63–6) describes phonics teaching in a Reception class in which the whole group is taught in a multi-sensory way. An initial sound and the shape of a grapheme is taught through a story and song, with children drawing the grapheme in the air and on the carpet. Before the group session, objects had been hidden around the classroom for children to find and identify with adult help. They then went on to work out the initial phoneme for the objects, all of which began with /t/. In a story, the teacher told the children about strange sounds she heard while having a picnic. These turned out to be teddies playing tennis, and every time the ball was hit it made the sound /t/. The teacher and her assistant went on to play tennis with a racquet and foam ball with children saying /t/ every time the ball was hit. Thus, through a range of multi-sensory activities children were able to see the /t/ sound in context as well as to learn how it could be represented in writing.

An environment in which to learn

Consider how you learn a second or third language. Do you do this by simply being surrounded by native speakers of the language or by having a teacher speak in the language to you for long periods? Or do you learn most effectively when you are able to take part in activities; use the language in real or created situations; receive feedback on your progress; use your senses, including looking at objects which are named in the language, and taste food? Most people would agree that the more interactive, multi-sensory approach works best for them, so what implications does this have for the way in which we learn about our own language and, in particular, how we learn about its phonology and the relationship between its letters and sounds?

One of the key things to consider is the environment in which children learn. Rose cited the importance of a broad, rich language curriculum and 'opportunities for young children to learn co-operatively in language-rich contexts' (2006, para.102, p.32). This means providing plenty of opportunities not only for seeing and sharing exciting and interesting texts, but also for language play, including games and activities which are multi-sensory. These games and activities may well centre on children's phonic development, but they will include experience of a wide range of literature, so that children can discover the pleasure that can be derived from independent reading. This literature should include texts which will be of interest to the children, but may also be beyond their current reading levels. After all, if children can see what they will be able to do independently and well once they have acquired phonic skills, they will understand why they need to acquire them. Their language comprehension skills may be such that they can learn a lot about the content of the texts, even when they cannot read some or all of the words. As Hall has argued, 'Phonics teaching is far from all that beginning readers need to become successful readers' (2006, p.21). (See Chapter 7 for more information on creating a broad and rich language curriculum.)

The multi-sensory classroom environment

Classroom displays, labels and signs can all contribute to supporting the teaching of phonics and early reading. Clear, large lettering in a suitable and consistent font will make written text around the classroom more accessible to children, while well-placed letter and phoneme posters or signs will give children a continual point of reference to check their own understanding.

Textured letters on felt, carpeting or fine-grained sandpaper can be available so that children can trace and feel the letter shapes. Children can contribute to phonics-based displays by producing

Activity

Draw a plan for a display of letters and sounds in your classroom. Include areas for *high-frequency* and *tricky or common exception words,* phonemes to be taught and revisited, and a space for children to display their own phonics-based writing.

large colourful letters, graphemes and words using a range of writing and drawing media. A dedicated display for *Letters and Sounds* or other phonics-based programmes is a useful area in the classroom to continually enhance phonics teaching and to allow children access to visual clues and key information to support their learning.

Additional learning areas in the multi-sensory classroom

In addition to the main teaching areas in the classroom, many teachers provide spaces for children to practise and experiment with phonics and spelling. Often children are offered the opportunity to choose which areas to work in rather than being directed by the teacher, and use the areas independently. However, they provide excellent opportunities for teachers to engage children in discussion, to play phonic activities and games, and to assess children's phonic ability. Look at the suggestions below and consider, by attempting the activities, how you might make use of such areas in your classroom.

Role-play area

An area for children to engage in phonics through play may:

- be designed to reflect places children visit in everyday situations. Examples could include eating establishments such as a café or take-away restaurant; shops and services, including supermarket, post office and travel agent; leisure venues such as a campsite; other common landmarks such as a building site, hospital or garden centre;

- include opportunities for children to practise phonics by encouraging speaking, listening and writing through tasks related to the chosen role-play area. Examples could include shopping lists, menus, food and goods orders, receipts and bills, prescriptions and so on.

Activity

With a group of peers or colleagues, choose a theme for a role-play area and devise a phonics-based activity that could be carried out by a group of four children.

Writing area

When creating an area for children to engage in phonics through experimenting with writing:

- provide a range of writing media for children to experiment with – crayons, chalk, felt tips, pencils, dry wipe pens;

- offer a range of materials for the children to write on – paper of different texture, size and colour, envelopes, whiteboards;

- present the writing area as an open-ended opportunity where children are engaged in free writing of their own choice, or structure the area and provide a scaffold for a particular outcome (i.e. write a shopping list, design a postcard, address an envelope etc.).

Activity

With a group of peers or colleagues, devise a writing task that will allow a child to revisit chosen words with the /sh/ phoneme independently.

Reading area

When providing an area for children to engage in phonics through reading and discussing a variety of texts:

- offer a range of reading materials for the children to choose from including fiction, poetry, information texts, magazines and children's newspapers, brochures and leaflets, published texts and books that the children have made themselves and e-books available online accessed on a computer;

- allow children the opportunity to read alone and with others and encourage discussion about what they read. Use recording devices to allow children to save discussions about what they have read, record their own texts and make simple book reviews for others to consider.

Construction area

Providing an area for children to engage in phonics through describing what they build and by writing labels, signs and captions can enable them to:

- engage in discussions during which they describe and explain their model;

- write labels, captions and signs to accompany their models. They can draw and label plans and ideas for what they may build.

Painting area

In creating an area for children to engage in phonics through experimenting with mark-making and writing with a variety of media:

Activity

A group of children have built models using LEGO®. How will you provide the opportunity for the children to describe and label their models?

- offer a variety of paints and art media and encourage children to produce letters, graphemes and words;
- let children add sand and PVA glue to produce textured letters for use in a tactile way.

Modelling area

An area with malleable materials that can be used to experiment with moulding phonics-related shapes might include:

- playdough, plasticine and other modelling materials which can be used to shape and form letters, graphemes and words.

Sand/water area

Children can engage in phonics through games and activities in a sand/water area which can be:

- an excellent medium to hide letters, graphemes and words in order to play phonic-based games such as hunt the letter, build a word with the letters chosen and so on.

Activity

Devise a word-building game where children choose combinations of letters hidden in the sand.

Quiet area

A quiet area for children to engage in phonics through games and activities could include:

- phonics-based games and activities, including wordsearches, crosswords, letter jigsaws, matching games, word bingo and so on;
- playing games in pairs and small groups which offers opportunities for discussion and negotiation.

Activity

Design a game to be played by four children which allows them to use CVC word-building skills.

Listening area

A listening area can enable children to engage in phonics through listening to and discussing a variety of recorded media and might:

- offer a range of things for the children to listen to, including recorded stories, a variety of music, a sound quiz and so on, and engage the children in discussions about what they have heard.

Developing phonological awareness: Parents and early schooling

Layton et al. maintain that nursery rhymes, jingles and word games 'act as a trigger for raising phonological awareness' (1997, p.11). They stress the value of language play in and of adults emphasising the rhythm of rhymes and accentuating it with body movements. They go on to stress the important role that parents can have in developing a firm foundation for their children's literacy development and suggest guidance which might be given to them on rhyme and rhyme play. These include:

- listening to and saying nursery, number and action rhymes;

- playing games such as 'I hear with my little ear something that rhymes with ...';

- making up stories of rhyming words including nonsense words.

The early phases of most systematic synthetic phonics programmes focus on developing children's phonological awareness (see Chapter 1) and recommend a range of activities which are both multi-sensory and interactive in order to do this. Phase 1 of *Letters and Sounds*, for example, includes seven aspects:

Aspect 1: General sound discrimination – environmental sounds

Aspect 2: General sound discrimination – instrumental sounds

Aspect 3: General sound discrimination – body percussion

Aspect 4: Rhythm and rhyme

Aspect 5: Alliteration

Aspect 6: Voice sounds

Aspect 7: Oral blending and segmenting

(DfES, 2007, p.1)

It can be seen that these aspects are very strongly oral and aural, and are designed to help children develop their ability to hear and discriminate between sounds as they prepare for subsequent phases in which they will relate phonemes to graphemes. Each aspect is divided into three strands:

- tuning into sounds (auditory discrimination);

- listening and remembering sounds (auditory memory and sequencing);

- talking about sounds (developing vocabulary and language comprehension).

Consider these three strands for a moment. At the earliest phases of a systematic synthetic phonics programme, children might engage in activities in which they listen to different instruments or objects which can be used to make noises and develop their ability to identify them aurally. They might go on to play games which involve listening to and repeating sequences of sounds: perhaps sequences of claps or animal noises that they can repeat. When talking about sounds and developing vocabulary and language comprehension, they might listen to and learn rhymes or songs and talk about the stories they tell. Now consider the same three strands and how they might apply to a later phase in children's development of phonological awareness and phonemic awareness.

Activity

Consider how you could use multi-sensory and interactive approaches to develop children's understanding of split vowel digraphs such as *a-e* in *take*; *i-e* in *time*; *o-e* in *hope*; *u-e* in *tube* and *e-e* in *these* (see Chapter 3).

An interactive approach to accessing phonics

A key element in children's acquisition of phonemic awareness is their ability to segment words into phonemes. A range of multi-sensory and interactive activities can be used to encourage children to access and practise phonics in as many different ways as possible.

- Children can become 'Robbie the Robot' (see Jolliffe, 2006, p.39) to sound out phonemes in words. As the child says each phoneme in a word aloud, arms can be moved in the style of a robot or children can imagine they are pressing buttons on their robot chest. This will emphasise each phoneme in the word.

- 'Brain buttons' can be used in a similar way to the sound buttons found in *Letters and Sounds* (DfES, 2007). As the child says each phoneme in a word aloud, he uses his finger to press an imaginary button on his forehead – the 'brain button'! This will emphasise each phoneme in the word.

- Children can be assigned or choose a 'sound partner' to play phonics games; for instance, they can sound out phonemes for their partner to build into words. Sound partners can also be used for peer support and for checking the correct use of phonic knowledge by their friends.

- An interactive whiteboard (IWB) can be used to support the teaching of phonics. A huge variety of online games and resources are available for use in the classroom. The sound facilities provided with an IWB can be used for children to hear the correct enunciation of phonemes. Children can use the touch-screen, electronic pens and keyboard to write letters, graphemes and words.

Activity

With a partner, practise using 'Robbie the Robot' and 'brain buttons' to sound out the words *fish*, *crunch*, *shirt*, *playing*, *softest* and *splash*.

Research Focus: Multi-sensory approaches to handwriting and spelling

Johnston and Watson (2007, pp.35-6) maintain that letter formation should be taught from the outset using a multi-sensory approach, with children forming letters with their hands in the air and on whiteboards and paper, so that they learn the visual appearance and the sound of a letter at the same time in order to consolidate it in their memory. As children's phonic knowledge increases, matching writing individual letters and digraphs, trigraphs, quadgraphs in flowing handwriting will help them to internalise English spelling patterns (Farmer et al., 2006).

→

Reading by Six maintains that:

> *Multi-sensory approaches to phonics can – and should – support children in recalling the shape of a letter and, if physical movement is involved, the direction in which to form a letter. Writing 'in the air', on the back of another child with a finger, on the hand or in sand are all useful gross motor activities and, if taught properly, they reinforce the way in which the letters should be formed.*

> *(Ofsted, 2010, para.67, p.30)*

It is, then, important to provide children with the opportunities to write letters, graphemes and words in many different ways and with a wide variety of media. Children are often expected to write small letters in a restricted space in more formal workbooks and on work-sheets; however, they often benefit from experimenting with writing letters and graphemes in other situations and with the freedom of producing many sizes of letters.

Media to write on

- There are endless sources for media to write on and stimulate children's interest in writing, such as the ideas given below. Offer a wide variety of paper to write on varying in colour, thickness, size and texture. This gives the children a variety of visual effects as they form chosen letters, graphemes and words. Different sizes of paper, especially non-ruled, allow for unrestricted letter size. Ruled paper with lines of different widths can be provided to scaffold letter size.

- Provide whiteboards with drywipe pens of different nib sizes and colours. Writing on a whiteboard feels very different from paper. It provides a temporary record that can be easily erased or altered, which sometimes allows the child more freedom to have a go. Whiteboards can be photocopied if a permanent record of what the child has recorded is needed.

- Allow children to trace letters, graphemes and words in the air, both following letter shapes that they can see, and independently without a shape to trace. Large letters, graphemes and words can be printed and displayed for the children to trace and there are also a number of 'magic pencil' websites and PowerPoint presentations online that can be used on an IWB. Children are encouraged to use their 'writing finger', which is usually part of their preferred writing hand.

- Use sand trays and the classroom or outdoor sand area to trace letters into the sand. This provides a tactile experience and also leaves a lasting impression that can be seen after the letter has been formed. Other materials such as rice, glitter and so on can be added to or replace the sand to create other effects and an alternative tactile experience.

- Allow children to use computers and other electronic devices with screens and keyboards to practise phonics writing and to play phonic-based games. Children can easily access an IWB, which is a useful tool to see phonics in written and printed form (see Chapter 14).

- Children can trace letters, graphemes and words on to rough carpet and other textured surfaces with their fingers.

- Tools and fingers can be used to scratch letters into modelling materials. If clay is used, this can be used for printing once dry.

- Children can use their bodies, perhaps during PE or in a larger space than the classroom, to make letter shapes. Trickier letters could be made by a group of children working as a team. Large letter shapes, graphemes and words can be marked on the ground, perhaps with chalk on the playground, so that the children can trace the shapes with their feet.

Activity

A small group of pupils in your class struggle to read and spell some of the *Letters and Sounds* Phase 3 high-frequency words (*he, she, we, me, be, was, my, you, her, they, all, are*). Plan a series of activities using a selection of the ideas above to revisit, practise and apply these words successfully.

Media to write with

There are several different writing implements that may be used in the classroom setting, and some suggestions are given below:

- Provide the children with a variety of pencils, both drawing and colouring pencils. Pencils of different thickness would be useful to experiment with. Pencil grips can be used by those children who need extra support with pencil hold, leading to improved letter formation.

- Crayons of varied thickness and colour can be used to write and colour letters, and can also be used to create rubbings.

- Felt tips and other pens can allow the children to produce bright, colourful and permanent letters and words. These could be incorporated into displays in the classroom to be accessed by the other children.

- A keyboard for computers and other electronic devices with screens is a quick and accessible way for children to record phonics. Fonts and the colour and size of text can be altered to suit the age and ability or specific needs of the children.

- Chalk is a useful medium to use outside the classroom as it can be used effectively on large surfaces such as a wall or the playground and can be easily removed. Children can experiment with creating oversized and colourful letters.

- Provide a variety of paints and other art media such as pastels, glitter glue, charcoal and so on for the children to create letters. They can be painted free-hand or traced within a template. Sand and other similar materials can be added to the paint to produce a textured surface which the children can use to trace with their fingers when dry.

- Magnetic and other shaped letters and graphemes are excellent tools for quick and temporary ways of recording phonic knowledge and for playing phonic games.

Activity

You have been asked to order new resources for your classroom ready for the next academic year. What will you include in your order to ensure that your pupils can be engaged in phonics writing in a multi-sensory way?

Case Study: Using multi-sensory activities with a mixed-age class

Sara was in her final year as a trainee teacher and was working with a class which comprised the whole of Key Stage 1 in a small rural school. She was keen to put into practice many of the interactive and multi-sensory activities she had learned as part of her course, but she discovered that some of the Year 2 children found some of the activities too 'young' for them. She was eager to involve all of the children and knew that some of the Year 2 children's phonic knowledge and understanding was not at the level it should be, and that some were behind some of the Year 1 children.

Sara decided to create reading material with the children related to their interests and to other areas of the curriculum currently being studied. The children had recently visited a farm and so she borrowed a model farm, complete with animals, barns, tractors and people, and asked the children to work in groups to set it up on a table in the classroom. They could then name the farm and the people and animals and machinery. With the help of the teacher and a teaching assistant, the children produced name cards and then used these, together with other cards featuring some of the most common words, to make up sentences about the farm. She found that some children enjoyed acting out some of the scenarios they created and some performed these for the rest of the class, while Sara showed large cards with the names of characters to the children. These were then used to practise decoding during group work.

The practical suggestions in this chapter will, we hope, provide you with ideas for developing your own multi-sensory, interactive classroom in which children can develop their reading skills in a lively and positive environment. Ideally, children will arrive at school having listened to stories, songs and rhymes at home and having played language games with their parents, carers and older siblings. Of course, not all children are so fortunate and sometimes these essential aspects of language development can be dependent upon teachers' input. However, there are lots of ways in which parents and carers of all children can be encouraged to help their children, especially when given the right guidance.

In Chapter 10 we shall look at planning for teaching phonics and at a teaching sequence advocated for effective teaching and learning. As we consider this sequence, it is important to keep in mind the need to engage and interest children by using a range of pedagogical strategies to ensure that lessons are both multi-sensory and interactive. As Brien maintains,

> *There is a strength in the unvarying model of the discrete phonics lesson. Many children thrive on the security of a routine, particularly one which gives a new success every day. The consistent approaches to discrete phonics lessons could, without excellent teaching, also be a weakness as it is very easy to allow something so routine to become repetitive and dull.*

(2012, p.70)

Learning Outcomes Review

You should now know a range of interactive and multi-sensory methods that will enhance (but not dominate) the teaching of phonics. Using a range of resources, including puppets, IWBs, magnetic and electronic resources to support multi-sensory and interactive approaches to teaching and learning phonics will enhance your teaching.

Self-assessment questions

What do you understand by the following terms:

1. multi-sensory?
2. kinaesthetic?

See the Glossary at the end of the book for definitions.

Further Reading

For practical guidance on teaching phonics, look at:

Jolliffe, W. (2007) *You Can Teach Phonics.* Leamington Spa: Scholastic.

For practical ideas on creative approaches to teaching SSP, see Chapter 5 in:

Glazzard, J. and Stokoe, J. (2013) *Teaching Systematic Synthetic Phonics and Early English.* Northwich: Critical Publishing.

For a theoretical perspective on teaching systematic synthetic phonics which will be invaluable both in developing your practice and in informing any academic studies, try:

McGuinness, D. (2004) *Early Reading Instruction: What Science Really Tells Us about How to Teach Reading.* Cambridge, MA: MIT Press.

For examples of multi-sensory teaching on film, see:

Ofsted (2014) *Getting Them Reading Early: Distance Learning Materials for Inspecting Reading.* London: DfE.

References

Brien, J. (2012) *Teaching Primary English.* London: SAGE.

Coffield, F., Moseley, D., Hall, E. and Ecclestone, K. (2004) *Learning Styles and Pedagogy in Post-16 Learning: A Systematic and Critical Review.* London: Learning and Skills Research Centre.

DfE (2011) *Teachers' Standards in England from September 2012.* London: DfE.

DfES (2007) *Letters and Sounds: Principles and Practice of High Quality Phonics.* London: DfES.

Farmer, S., Ellis, S. and Smith, V. (2006) 'Teaching phonics: The basics', in M. Lewis and S. Ellis (eds), *Phonics, Practice, Research and Policy.* London: Paul Chapman, pp.34–44.

Hall, K. (2006) 'How children learn to read and how phonics helps', in M. Lewis and S. Ellis (eds), *Phonics, Practice, Research and Policy.* London: Paul Chapman.

Johnston, R. and Watson, J. (2007) *Teaching Synthetic Phonics.* Exeter: Learning Matters.

Jolliffe, W. (2006) *Phonics: A Complete Synthetic Programme.* Leamington Spa: Scholastic.

Layton, L., Deeny, K. and Upton, G. (1997) *Sound Practice: Phonological Awareness in the Classroom.* London: Fulton.

Ofsted (2010) *Reading by Six.* London: Paul Chapman.

Pashler, H., McDaniel, M., Rohrer, D. and Bjork, R. (2008) 'Learning styles: Concepts and evidence', *Psychological Science in the Public Interest*, 9 (3).

Perkins, M. (2012) *Observing Primary Literacy*. London: SAGE.

Rose, J. (2006) *Independent Review of the Teaching of Early Reading, Final Report, March 2006* (The Rose Review – Ref: 0201-2006DOC-EN). Nottingham: DfES.

Audit and test

Work through each section below, responding to each question or task. When you have completed each section, you can read the answers at the end of the chapter.

Section 1: Key terminology for multi-sensory approaches

What is meant by a multi-sensory approach to teaching phonics and reading?

It is important that you understand the terms below before you move on to the next activity. Provide a definition of each and check your definitions against those at the end of the chapter:

Visual

Auditory

Kinaesthetic

Multi-sensory classroom environment

Interactive approaches to phonics

Section 2: Phonics scenarios

Consider each of the following scenarios and decide how you could use multi-sensory approaches to enhance teaching and learning.

1. A lesson to develop blending of phonemes for the following letters: *s a t p i n.*

2. A lesson to develop understanding of consonant digraphs *ch sh th .*

3. A lesson to develop understanding of the split vowel digraph.

Section 3: Case study of teaching

Read the case study of a phonics lesson and identify where the teacher uses visual, auditory and kinaesthetic approaches.

Tina wanted to reinforce her Year 1 class's ability to segment and blend, so she created the Phonics Fairy, who wore a cloak and held a magic wand. For phonics lessons, Tina donned the cloak and explained that the children were going to play pass the parcel; but instead of passing a parcel they were going to pass a box of words. When the music stopped the person holding the box had to take a word out and segment it (i.e. l-o-g rather than reading the word log). The Phonics Fairy then waved the magic blending wand and said the word. After a while some of the more able children took turns to wear the cloak and become the Phonics Fairy.

In subsequent lessons, Tina placed verbs in the box and explained that when the music stopped the person holding the box had to look at a word but not show it to anyone, and then mime an action. She included verbs such as hop, wave, stamp and clap. After the mime children had to raise their hands and ask what the word was by segmenting their suggestions – for example, 'Is it s-t-a-m-p?'. The Phonics Fairy would then blend the phonemes to make the word and ask the child who had mimed if that was correct.

ANSWERS

Section 1: Key terminology for multi-sensory approaches

What is meant by a multi-sensory approach to teaching phonics and reading?

You were asked to define the following key terms:

Visual

Visual approaches to phonics involve activities which encourage children to look at different resources, graphemes etc.

Auditory

Auditory approaches to phonics involve activities which encourage children to listen to different resources, phonemes etc.

Kinaesthetic

Some people learn better using some form of physical (kinaesthetic) activity: hence the use of actions to accompany phonemes and graphemes in Jolly Phonics.

Multi-sensory classroom environment

A classroom in which children can use all of a range of senses (hearing, seeing, feeling, moving).

Interactive approaches to phonics

An interactive approach ensures that children are actively involved in their learning and take a full part in lessons.

Section 2: Phonics scenarios

You were asked to consider each of the following scenarios and decide how you could use multi-sensory approaches to enhance teaching and learning. We hope you will find the suggestions below helpful, but do try to develop and modify them to meet your class's needs.

1. **A lesson to develop blending of phonemes for** *s a t p i n*

    Try making large cards with a letter on each. Ask six children to come to the front of the class and to stand in a line. Ask the rest of the class to suggest ways in which groups of three children holding cards could arrange themselves to make words (for example, sat, pin, nip, tap, tan). Ask another child to write the words on the board and have a class competition to see how many can be made. Each time a word is made, ask the children to segment it and then blend it into a whole word.

2. **A lesson to develop understanding of consonant digraphs** *ch sh th*

    Try collecting pictures and small objects which include the digraphs *th*, *sh* and *ch*. Give each child three cards with one of the digraphs on each card. Put the pictures and objects in a large box and then take them out one at a time and ask questions such as: Which grapheme does this begin with? Which grapheme does this end with? Children should then hold up the correct card.

This can be developed into a more physical activity if you have a large space such as the school hall to work in. Put the graphemes on large pieces of paper on the wall in three different parts of the room. Get the children to sit around you in the middle of the room; take items out one by one and ask children to go to the part of the room where the appropriate digraph can be found. If some go to the wrong place, segment the word carefully and ask them to repeat it. Once everyone is in the right place, ask the class to segment and blend the word.

3. **A lesson to develop understanding of the split vowel digraph**

Make some cards with split digraphs ensuring the space between the vowels is sufficient to place a letter card in it. Give every child two consonant cards and ask them to practise sounding the letters.

Put the split digraph cards on the wall and ask if anyone can use both of their letters to make a word. For example, for the split digraph *a-e* someone with *s* and *m* would be able to make *same*, and for *i-e* someone with *b* and *t* could make *bite*. Each time someone can make a word, ask the children to segment and then blend it. Have a child write the words created on the board and challenge the children to see how many words they can make.

You could modify the activity by placing consonant cards in the middle of each table and asking groups to discuss which letters could be used. This could become an inter-group competition if you feel this is appropriate.

Section 3: Case study of teaching

You were asked to read a case study of a phonics lesson and identify where the teacher uses visual, auditory and kinaesthetic approaches.

Auditory approaches featured throughout, especially when children listened to words being segmented and blended.

Visual elements included reading the words from the box.

Kinaesthetic approaches included miming the words and actions, and passing the parcel.

What to do next?

Reinforce your knowledge and understanding of decoding by doing as many as possible of the following:

1. Observe phonics lessons in school and make a note of the multi-sensory strategies used by teachers.

2. Look at worksheets for phonics lessons and see how you could teach the same things using interactive and multi-sensory methods.

3. Build up a bank of resources to support multi-sensory teaching and learning. These do not need to be very sophisticated and might include: grapheme cards with single letters and digraphs; split digraph cards; a collection of pictures and objects; sand trays for finger writing letters.

9. Teaching a systematic structured progression

Learning Outcomes

By the end of this chapter you should:

- understand the essential components of a systematic structured progression;
- have reviewed examples of a systematic and structured progression.

Teachers' Standards

3. Demonstrate good subject and curriculum knowledge:

    - demonstrate a critical understanding of developments in the subject and curriculum areas, and promote the value of scholarship;
    - if teaching early reading, demonstrate a clear understanding of systematic synthetic phonics.

Criteria for assuring high-quality phonic work (DfE, 2011a)

The programme should be designed for the teaching of discrete, daily sessions progressing from simple to more complex phonic knowledge and skills and covering the major grapheme–phoneme correspondences (see Note 3).

Note 3: The programme should introduce a defined initial group of consonants and vowels, enabling children, early on, to read and spell many simple CVC words.

The programme should provide fidelity to the teaching framework for the duration of the programme, to ensure that these irregular words are fully learned (see Note 6).

Note 6: The programme should not neglect engaging and helpful approaches to the more challenging levels where children have to distinguish between phonically irregular graphemes and phonemes.

Introduction

Since The Rose Review (2006) was published, there has been an ongoing commitment by governments to ensure that synthetic phonics is taught systematically. This chapter explores in detail what this means: in essence, that it should be explicit, organised and sequenced and it should cover all the grapheme–phoneme correspondences in the English language. Detailed discussion of examples will enhance understanding of a systematic and structured approach. Research findings that substantiate this approach will also be reviewed. In particular, the chapter discusses why it is important to ensure that phonics is taught in a systematic progression and whether this should be through adherence to one specific programme. The chapter also reviews a range of activities to support teaching in this way.

Theoretical perspectives/subject knowledge

A focus on ensuring systematic teaching of phonics was highlighted in The Rose Review, emphasising the importance of teaching a systematic structured progression. It stated that

> {p}honic work should teach these skills and knowledge in a well defined and systematic sequence.
>
> (2006, para.45–6)

The principles for high-quality phonic work embodied in this report also state that such teaching should be

> systematic, that is to say, it follows a carefully planned programme with fidelity, reinforcing and building on previous learning to secure children's progress.
>
> (2006, para.45–6)

The issue of 'fidelity' to the programme has created some confusion in the intervening period, and a commonly held interpretation is that teaching should be restricted to one phonics programme, as long as that programme meets the criteria for high-quality phonics work. However, the term refers more broadly to fidelity to a framework or structure. The revised *Criteria for Assuring High-quality Phonic Work* (DfE, 2011b) explicitly states that such fidelity is to 'the teaching framework'. This should ensure that all of the 40+ phonemes and their alternative spellings and pronunciations are taught and applied in reading and writing. Alongside this, high-frequency words with irregular spellings (such as *the*, *was* and *said*) need to be explicitly taught, as is discussed in more detail later in this chapter. The key, therefore, is that such an entire framework should be covered, and it does not mean that this needs to be restricted to one specific programme. In practice, schools often find that adhering to one programme that meets the criteria for high-quality phonics teaching ensures that this happens. The important aspect is that teaching should be carefully structured, cover all grapheme–phoneme correspondences and, as is explored in Chapter 11, it should enable children's progress to be clearly assessed and tracked.

The Ofsted survey (2008) following The Rose Review aimed to ascertain the extent to which a sample of schools understood were acting upon the key concept of 'fidelity to the programme', identified in The Rose Review as an essential aspect of successful phonics teaching. Of the 20 schools Ofsted visited, all but one demonstrated 'fidelity' to the programme mainly by the use of one specific scheme, and in many cases this was *Letters and Sounds*.

Another review by Ofsted, *Reading by Six*, reinforced the importance of systematic phonics teaching and stated that

> {a} sample of 12 of these schools finds that their success is based on a determination that every child will learn to read, together with a very rigorous and sequential approach to developing speaking and listening and teaching reading, writing and spelling through systematic phonics.

> {…}The diligent, concentrated and systematic teaching of phonics is central to the success of all the schools that achieve high reading standards in Key Stage 1. This requires high-quality and expert teaching that follows a carefully planned and tightly structured approach to teaching phonic knowledge and skills. Pupils are given opportunities to apply what they have learned through reading – including time to read aloud to adults to practise their decoding skills – writing and comprehension of what they are reading.

> (2010, p.4)

To summarise, systematic phonics within a structure was a key component alongside the application of these skills in reading and writing.

To explore more fully what is meant by systematic phonics teaching, Ehri et al. state that '[p]honics instruction is systematic when all the major grapheme–phoneme correspondences are taught and they are covered in a clearly defined sequence' (2001, p.394). In addition, Torgerson et al. state that systematic phonics is: 'Teaching of letter–sound relationships in an explicit, organized and sequenced fashion, as opposed to incidentally on a "when needed" basis' (2006, p.8).

The Education Endowment Foundation (EEF), in a review of research into *Improving Literacy in Key Stage One* (2016, p.8), highlight that: 'There is strong evidence to support the use of a systematic phonics programme with pupils in Key Stage 1.' They state that teachers should: 'explicitly teach pupils a comprehensive set of letter–sound relationships through an organised sequence'. It is also emphasised that a phonics programme should be taught using effective pedagogy which should ensure that:

- pupil progress is monitored and that teaching should be responsive to the diagnosis of needs of the pupils (see Chapter 11 for further guidance on this);
- all staff involved in teaching the programme should be sufficiently trained to do so;
- a programme should be implemented as intended by the developer.

The criteria for phonics programmes

The criteria for phonics programmes, as set out by the Department for Education, stipulate that:

> *High-quality systematic, synthetic phonic work will make sure that children learn:*
>
> - *grapheme–phoneme (letter–sound) correspondences (the alphabetic principle) in a clearly defined, incremental sequence;*
> - *to apply the highly important skill of blending (synthesising) phonemes, in order, all through a word to read it;*
> - *to apply the skills of segmenting words into their constituent phonemes to spell; and that*
> - *blending and segmenting are reversible processes.*

(DfE, 2011b)

To be more explicit, the detailed features of a systematic structured progression for teaching synthetic phonics consist of the following:

1. All 40+ grapheme–phoneme correspondences (GPCs) are taught in a clear sequence.

2. The pace of instruction ensures that GPCs are introduced at the rate of about three to five a week, starting with single letters and a sound for each, then going on to the sounds represented by digraphs (e.g. /sh/ and /oo/) and larger grapheme units (e.g. /air/, /igh/).

3. Explicit teaching of blending of phonemes for reading is included, starting after the first few GPCs are taught and continued as more GPCs are taught.

4. Explicit segmenting of phonemes for spelling is provided, again starting after the first few GPCs are taught and working with more GPCs as more are taught.

5. The introduction of the most common spellings for phonemes first and then alternative sounds for spellings and alternative spellings for sounds.

6. The introduction of strategies for reading and spelling common high-frequency words containing unusual GPCs.

Case Study: Systematic and structured phonics teaching

As part of her training, Nathalie was required to analyse a set of phonic programme outlines and decide if she felt they met the above criteria. The set included:

Programme 1: This approach teaches children to read larger sub-units of words as well as phonemes. For example, children learn to recognise *st*, *ap*, *eam* as blends so that there are not so

⟶

many separate parts of words to sound out and remember in blending them. The larger units taught might include onsets (i.e. the consonants that precede the vowel such as *st* in *stop*) and rimes (i.e. the vowel and following consonants such as *op* in *stop*), also called phonograms, and spelling patterns characterising the common parts of word families (e.g. *–ack* as in *pack* and *stack*, *–oat* as in *goat* and *float*). Teaching children to analyse and pronounce parts of words provides the basis for teaching them the strategy of reading new words by analogy to known words (e.g. reading *stump* by analogy to *jump*).

Programme 2: Central to this programme is the use of meaningful stories, pictures and actions to reinforce recognition and recall of letter–sound relationships, and precise articulation of phonemes. There are five key elements to the programme:

1. Learning 40+ letter sounds.

2. Learning letter formation.

3. Blending for reading.

4. Identifying the sounds in words for writing.

5. Tricky words that are high-frequency and irregularly spelled.

The programme includes activities and instruction specifically designed to address those skills most needed in the development of early literacy.

Programme 3: In this programme, all the letters are animate characters that assume the shape of the letters and have names prompting the relevant sound: for example, Sammy Snake, Hairy Hat Man, Fireman Fred, Annie Apple. The task of learning the shapes and sounds of all the alphabet letters is lengthy, particularly for children who come to school knowing none. Techniques to speed up the learning process are valuable in helping nursery children prepare for formal reading instruction.

Programme 4: This programme begins by teaching children phonemic awareness in a unique way. Children are led to discover and label the articulatory gestures associated with each phoneme by analysing their own mouth movements as they produce speech. For example, children learn that the word *beat* consists of a 'lip popper', a 'smile sound' and a 'tongue tapper'. Children learn to track the sounds in words with mouth pictures as well as coloured blocks and letters. Most of the time in this programme is spent building children's phonological awareness and their decoding skills, although some attention is given to the recognition of high-frequency words, text reading and comprehension.

Programme 5: This programme is designed around the structure of an Alphabetic Code Overview Chart. The 44+ sounds (phonemes) are always shown in slash marks (/-/) down the left-hand column of the chart and the spelling alternatives (graphemes) of those sounds are presented across the rows. The basis of the programme is to teach the letter–sound correspondence knowledge (letters, letter groups and sounds) of the English Alphabetic Code and how to put this code knowledge to use applying the three skills of:

→

- all-through-the-word 'sounding out' and blending for reading (synthesis-ing);
- segmenting for spelling (splitting up spoken words into their smallest constituent sounds and knowing which letters or letter groups are code for the identified sounds);
- handwriting the letter shapes correctly.

The ultimate aims of the programme include learners gaining an enriched vocabulary and developing their comprehension in the process of learning to read, spell and write in the English language. Learners also benefit from building-up specific spelling word banks into their long-term memory for writing purposes.

There is a self-assessment question related to this case study at the end of the chapter.

Introducing high-frequency irregular words

Another aspect of systematic synthetic phonics as set out in the DfE criteria for high-quality phonic work concerns ensuring programmes should *'ensure that children are taught high-frequency words that do not conform completely to grapheme/phoneme correspondence rules'*, and it also says that there should be

> *fidelity to the teaching framework for the duration of the programme, to ensure that these irregular words are fully learnt.*

(DfE, 2011b)

The National Curriculum (DfE, 2013) sets out in Appendix 1 a list of what is termed 'common exception words', showing in which year group they should be taught. These words are too complex for young children to decode, but unavoidable in reading most texts (e.g. *was*, *said* and *the*). They need to be introduced at a rate of about two or three per week, but the professional judgement of the pace must lie with the teacher or practitioner. Phonics programmes that meet the DfE criteria contain a clear systematic progression for teaching these. However, even these words usually contain some common letter–sound correspondences, and children should have their attention drawn to these so that they do not regard the words as completely random (see Chapter 3).

Teaching high-frequency common exception words

Once children are able to blend CVC words, they should gradually be introduced to 'common exception words', or, as they are often described, 'tricky' words. These should be limited to two or three per week, depending upon the children you are teaching, for example:

1.	said	are	the
2.	come	was	some
3.	once	two	want
4.	there	your	what
5.	where	who	because

It is also helpful to create a display of these for constant reference. These are sometimes called 'red' words – words that cannot be sounded out, as opposed to 'green' words, words that can be. These words can also be printed on red card for emphasis and displayed in the classroom.

Case Study: A systematic approach

Read the example below taken from the Ofsted *Reading by Six* (2010) report of one school visited that demonstrated systematic phonics teaching and consider the following:

1. How does the school provide for systematic phonics teaching?
2. What opportunities are there for children to practise and apply their phonic knowledge?

Fairlawn has a multi-ethnic school population in which 36 home languages are spoken. It welcomes this cosmopolitan mix. When the headteacher, Robin Bosher, arrived in 2002, he found a good school but judged that pupils could achieve much better.

The provision for children's reading is meticulously organised, from when children start in the Fairlawn nursery annexe to their departure as highly literate 11-year-olds. The nursery staff encourage careful listening to sounds and words in a language-rich environment, with specific phonics work four times a week. Children get to know three core books well each half term, and a wide range of resources stimulate interest in reading and writing. Progress is carefully assessed and recorded and there are daily opportunities for reading, ready access to books, and support for parents, including for those whose circumstances make them hard to reach. Systematic phonics teaching is based on Letters and Sounds. *This is embedded in a 20-minute phonics session for the Reception and Key Stage 1 classes at 11 a.m. every day. The sessions are rigorously structured and taught in a very engaging way, taking the children through a sequence of phases of phonic development. Their reading is consolidated by the books and activities used in the rest of the curriculum. Boxes of banded reading resources are available in every class and children are encouraged to choose books at an appropriate level. The unusually long lunch period includes half an hour that is used for individual and guided reading.*

(Ofsted, 2010, p.11)

Progression and pace

There are strong arguments for a fast-paced programme in order for children to be able to apply their skills in their reading and writing. Phonics teaching in the past used commonly to consist of 'a sound a week' being taught, which meant that it took almost a school year to learn 26 letter sounds. A prolonged pace of teaching means that children begin to use other strategies such as whole-word recognition to read, rather than apply their phonic skills to decode. This can later result in children's progress being limited, particularly as they begin to read a wider range of text, and it also impacts on their spelling ability. Without a thorough and automatic use of phonics for reading and writing, children may struggle with reading and spelling unfamiliar words, which in turn will have a detrimental effect on their comprehension skills.

The Guidance that accompanied The Rose Review from the DfES outlined the progression and pace recommended. This was later embodied in the *Letters and Sounds* (DfES, 2007) phonics framework. This progression is divided into six phases (see Table 9.1).

Table 9.1 Phase 1 from Letters and Sounds phonics framework (DfES, 2007)

Main purpose:
Through speaking and listening activities, children will develop their language structures and increase their vocabulary. In developing their phonological awareness, children will improve their ability to distinguish between sounds and to speak clearly and audibly with confidence and control. They become familiar with rhyme, rhythm and alliteration.
Outcome:
Children explore and experiment with sounds and words. They listen attentively. They show a growing awareness and appreciation of rhyme, rhythm and alliteration. They speak clearly and audibly with confidence and control. They distinguish between different sounds in words and begin to develop awareness of the differences between phonemes.
Typical duration:
This phase reflects the developmental stages for Communication, Language and Literacy in the Early Years Foundation Stage. It paves the way for a programme of systematic phonic work to begin. This starts when the grapheme–phoneme (letter-sound) correspondences are introduced at Phase 2.

This phase was seen as a precursor to a systematic phonics programme, and it stated that teaching should focus on speaking and listening in order to prepare the ground for effective phonics teaching. Children will become increasingly discriminating in identifying and distinguishing between different sounds and phonemes and in articulating them. They will become increasingly aware of the relationship between sounds, letters and words. They will be introduced to a broader range of rhymes and songs with rhythmic patterns. As children are introduced to a phonic programme, they will continue to build their confidence in distinguishing between phonemes.

The *Letters and Sounds* framework that followed this guidance showed that Phase 1 would form the foundation for later teaching, but that the phase was also to be seen as continuous and working alongside later phonic work (see Table 9.2). In practice this has caused some confusion and, as set out in Chapter 1, there was a danger that work on this phase was extended and seen as a 'reading readiness' indicator instead of accompanying the learning of phonemes and the corresponding graphemes.

Table 9.2 Phase 2 from Letters and Sounds phonics framework (DfES, 2007)

Main purpose:
To introduce grapheme–phoneme (letter-sound) correspondences.
Outcome:
Children know that words are constructed from phonemes and that phonemes are represented by graphemes. They have knowledge of a small selection of common consonants and vowels. They blend them together in reading simple CVC words and segment them to support spelling.
Typical duration:
Up to 6 weeks.

In Phase 2 (Table 9.2), teaching focuses on grapheme–phoneme correspondences for a small selection of common consonants and vowels, such as *s*, *a*, *t*, *p*, *i*, *n*, which is a widely used selection. Children will be shown how to blend these together to read simple CVC words and also how to segment them for spelling those words.

Table 9.3 Phase 3 from Letters and Sounds phonics framework (DfES, 2007)

Main purpose:
To teach children one grapheme for each of the 44 phonemes in order to read and spell simple regular words.
Outcome:
Children link sounds to letters, naming and sounding the letters of the alphabet. They recognise letter shapes and say a sound for each. They hear and say sounds in the order in which they occur in the word, and read simple words by sounding out and blending the phonemes all through the word from left to right. They recognise common digraphs and read some high-frequency words.
Typical duration:
Up to 12 weeks.

In Phase 3 (Table 9.3), teaching will focus on all 44 phonemes with their most common graphemes, including digraphs and double letters.

In Phase 4 (Table 9.4), teaching should focus on the skills of blending and segmenting words containing adjacent consonants; they should not be taught in word families, such as *spot*, *spit*, *spin*, as the children will treat *sp* as one unit, and for some children this will be a barrier to learning.

Table 9.4 Phase 4 from Letters and Sounds phonics framework (DfES, 2007)

Main purpose:
To teach children to read and spell words containing adjacent consonants.
Outcome:
Children are able to blend and segment adjacent consonants in words and to apply this skill when reading unfamiliar texts and in spelling.
Typical duration:
4 to 6 weeks.

Table 9.5 Phase 5 from Letters and Sounds phonics framework (DfES, 2007)

Main purpose:
Teaching children to recognise and use alternative ways of pronouncing the graphemes and spelling the phonemes already taught.
Outcome:
Children will use alternative ways of pronouncing the graphemes and spelling the phonemes corresponding to long vowel phonemes. Children will identify the constituent parts of two-syllable and three-syllable words and be able to read and spell phonically decodable two-syllable and three-syllable words. They will recognise an increasing number of high-frequency words automatically. Phonic knowledge and skills will be applied as the prime approach in reading and spelling when the words are unfamiliar and not completely decodable.
Typical duration:
Securing reading and spelling will extend through Year 1.

In Phase 5 (Table 9.5), teaching will focus on long vowel phonemes and the different grapheme correspondences (such as /oe/ *oe, o, oa, ow*). Graphemes that can be pronounced in different ways will be explored (e.g. c in *coat* and *city*). The reverse process of segmenting words into their constituent phonemes applies in the case of spelling.

Table 9.6 Phase 6 from Letters and Sounds phonics framework (DfES, 2007)

Main purpose:
Teaching children to develop their skill and automaticity in reading and spelling, creating ever-increasing capacity to attend to reading for meaning.
Outcome:
Children apply their phonic skills and knowledge to recognise and spell an increasing number of complex words. They read an increasing number of high- and medium-frequency words independently and automatically.
Typical duration:
For the majority of children this phase will begin in and continue through Year 2 so that by the end of that year they should be well on the way to becoming fluent readers. This means that in Year 3 the emphasis will change from teaching word recognition to developing children's language comprehension.

In Phase 6 (Table 9.6), teaching will focus on less common grapheme–phoneme correspondences (e.g. the *s* in *vision* as pronounced /zh/).

Other programmes

Other systematic phonics programmes follow a similar progression (see Chapter 12). Jolly Phonics, for example, has seven steps and then a 'further phonics' stage which introduces less common spellings for long vowel sounds. A downloadable summary of these steps for teaching reading and writing with Jolly Phonics can be accessed from http://jollylearning. co.uk/gallery/steps-for-teaching-jolly-phonics/. One programme that differs and teaches only the most common letter–sound mappings is 'Early Reading Research' (ERR), now known as the Optima reading programme (see: https://optimapsychology.com/programmes/optima-reading/, accessed 2/5/18). A study by Shapiro and Solity (2016) found that while results of this programme compared with *Letters and Sounds* were similar, for those children who showed poor phonological awareness, the simplified programme of ERR was beneficial.

Summary of key aspects of effective progression

It is important to ensure is that any systematic progression in teaching synthetic phonics includes the following:

- It begins with learning grapheme–phoneme correspondences (GPCs), starting with some consonants and short vowels (commonly *s, a, t, p, i, n*) in order to be able to blend these into CVC words from the outset.

- A greater number of GPCs are then taught, including long vowel sounds; different programmes may do this in a different order, but the 40+ phonemes are introduced systematically.

- A small number of high-frequency words that are complex to decode are introduced and taught (commonly three to five per week).

- Alternative pronunciations and spellings for graphemes are then taught.

- The application of GPCs taught in reading and writing is provided throughout.

Research Focus: The background

Ehri et al. (2001) cite Jeanne Chall's (1967) comprehensive review of beginning reading instruction covering studies up to the mid-1960s. Her basic finding was that early and systematic instruction in phonics led to better achievement in reading than later and less systematic phonics instruction. In the 1967 edition of her review, Chall did not recommend any

→

particular type of phonics instruction, but in the 1983 edition she suggested that synthetic phonics instruction held a slight edge over analytic phonics instruction. Chall's finding has been reaffirmed in many research reviews conducted since then (e.g. Adams, 1990; Anderson et al., 1985; Balmuth, 1982; Dykstra, 1968).

Since then, studies to compare systematic phonics instruction with a less structured approach show that 'any kind of well organized and efficient phonics instruction is better than little or no phonic instruction that leaves phonics to chance' (Cunningham and Cunningham, 2002, p.91). Johnston et al.'s (2012) study of the effects of teaching synthetic versus analytic phonics on ten-year-olds who had learned to read using one of these methods as part of their early literacy programme found that group taught by synthetic phonics had better word reading, spelling and reading comprehension.

Systematic or non-systematic?

In 2006, the Department for Education and Skills commissioned the Universities of York and Sheffield to conduct a review of the experimental research on using phonics to teach reading and spelling. In the resulting report, Torgerson et al. found that systematic phonics teaching 'enables children to make better progress in reading accuracy than unsystematic or no phonics, and that this is true for both normally-developing children and those at risk of failure' (2006, p.45). However, Torgerson et al. also stated that the evidence was weak, particularly in contrasting analytic and synthetic phonics where only three randomised control trials had been found.

In Australia, the committee for the National Inquiry into the Teaching of Literacy produced the report *Teaching Reading*. The committee concluded:

> *Thus, the incontrovertible finding from the extensive body of local and international evidence-based reading research is that for children during the early years of schooling, they must first master the alphabetic code via systematic, explicit, and intensive instruction in: phonemic awareness, phonics, reading fluency, vocabulary, and reading comprehension strategies. Because these are foundational and essential skills for the development of competence in reading, writing and spelling, they must be taught early, explicitly, and taught well.*
>
> *(Australian Government, DfEST, 2005, p.25)*

De Graaff et al. (2009) conducted a study in the Dutch language to compare a systematic phonics approach compared with a non-systematic approach. They defined the degree of systematicity using four dimensions. First, in the systematic phonics programme, children encountered a planned set of phonics-through-spelling and synthetic phonics activities. In the non-systematic phonics programme, children were free in choosing exercises during each session. Second, in the non-systematic phonics programme, all ten letters were introduced at the same time. The systematic phonics programme started with five

➡

letters in Stage A. In Stages B and C, the letter set increased with two and three letters, respectively. Third, in the systematic phonics programme, the first five letter sounds were taught explicitly by a first-sound mnemonics procedure. In the non-systematic programme, no such procedure existed. Children were able to learn about the relationship between graphemes and phonemes through the use of a keyboard that produced the phoneme of the key that was pressed. Fourth, in the systematic phonics programme, children learned to spell by gradually increasing the degree of difficulty. For example, children started with spelling the first letter of a word, followed by spelling the last letter of the word and so on. In the non-systematic phonics programme, all spelling exercises were designed such that children were directed to spell the whole word. The findings from the study showed that

> [i]n sum, even in a transparent language such as Dutch, a systematic-phonics approach generally leads to better results than a non-systematic approach.
>
> (De Graaff et al., 2009, p.329)

Developing a prototype

McGuinness' extensive study of existing research and her own empirical studies have led to a prototype for teaching the English Alphabetic Code (2004, p.323), which demonstrates the need to be systematic. It is summarised below:

1. No sight words (except for high-frequency words with rare spellings).

2. No letter names.

3. Sound to print orientation. Phonemes and not letters are the basis for the code.

4. Teach the phonemes only – no other sound units.

5. Begin with the basic code (a one-to-one correspondence between 40 phonemes and their most common spellings).

6. Teach children to identify and sequence sounds in real words by segmenting and blending, using letters.

7. Teach children how to write each letter. Integrate writing into every lesson.

8. Link writing (spelling) and reading to ensure children learn that the alphabet is a code and that codes are reversible: encoding/decoding.

9. Spelling should be accurate, or at a minimum, phonetically accurate.

10. Lessons should move on to include the advanced spelling code (the 136 remaining common spellings).

As discussed in Chapter 1, the use of letter names is a disputed area; however, they can be used as an anchor for children's understanding, as these remain constant while the pronunciations of graphemes may alter. The important point therefore is not to confuse the two when teaching and to focus on teaching a sound-to-print orientation.

Learning Outcomes Review

This chapter has discussed the rationale and the key ingredients for a systematic structured progression in teaching synthetic phonics. It has also provided the key steps in such a progression with examples.

Self-assessment questions

1. Refer to the first case study in this chapter, 'Systematic and structured phonics teaching'. Which of the programmes reflect the criteria for systematic synthetic programmes (DfE, 2011b)?
2. What grapheme–phoneme correspondences are commonly taught first?
3. Why are some high-frequency words taught alongside a systematic teaching of grapheme–phoneme correspondences?
4. What grapheme–phoneme correspondences are commonly taught in the later stages?

Further Reading

For further examples of effective practice of a systematic structured approach, see:

Ofsted (2010) *Reading by Six.* Manchester: Ofsted.

For support with teaching a systematic progression, see Chapter 9 of:

Waugh, D. and Harrison-Palmer, R. (2013) *Teaching Systematic Synthetic Phonics: Audit and Test.* Exeter: Learning Matters.

References

Adams, M.J. (1990) *Beginning to Read: Thinking and Learning about Print.* Cambridge, MA: MIT Press.

Anderson, R.C., Hiebert, E.F., Wilkinson, L.A.G. and Scott, J. (1985) *Becoming a Nation of Readers.* Champaign, IL: Center for the Study of Reading.

Australian Government, Department of Education Science and Training (2005) *Teaching Reading: Report and Recommendations. National Enquiry into the Teaching of Literacy.* Barton: Department of Education, Science and Training.

Balmuth, M. (1982) *The Roots of Phonics: A Historical Introduction*. New York: McGraw-Hill.

Chall, J.S. (1967) *Learning to Read: The Great Debate*. New York: McGraw-Hill.

Cunningham, P.M. and Cunningham, J.W. (2002) 'What we know about how to teach phonics', in A. Farstrup and S.J. Samuels (eds), *What Research Has to Say about Reading*. Delaware, NE: International Reading Association.

De Graaff, S., Bosman, A.M.T., Hasselman, F. and Verhoeven, L. (2009) 'Benefits of systematic phonics instruction', *Scientific Studies of Reading*, 13 (4): 318–33.

DfE (2011a) *Teachers' Standards in England from September 2012*. London: DfE.

DfE (2011b) *Criteria for Assuring High-quality Phonic Work*. Runcorn: DfE. Available at www.education.gov.uk/schools/teachingandlearning/pedagogy/phonics/a0010240/criteria-for-assuring-high-quality-phonic-work (accessed 19/3/12).

DfE (2013) *The National Curriculum in England*. London: DfE.

DfES (2007) *Letters and Sounds: Notes of Guidance for Practitioners and Teachers*. Norwich: DfES.

Dykstra, R. (1968) 'The effectiveness of code- and meaning-emphasis in beginning reading programs', *The Reading Teacher*, 22: 17–23.

Education Endowment Foundation (2016) *Improving Literacy in Key Stage One*. London: Education Endowment Foundation.

Ehri, L.C., Nunes, S.R; Stahl, S.A. and Willows, D.M. (2001) 'Systematic phonics instruction helps students learn to read: Evidence from the National Reading Panel's meta-analysis', *Review of Educational Research*, 71 (3): 393–447.

Johnston, R.S., McGeown, S. and Watson, J.E. (2012) 'Long-term effects of synthetic versus analytic phonics teaching on the reading and spelling ability of 10-year-old boys and girls', *Reading and Writing: An Interdisciplinary Journal*, 25: 1365–84.

Jolly Learning (1992) *Jolly Phonics*. Available at www.jollylearning.co.uk/overview-about-jollyphonics/ (accessed 3/2/15).

McGuinness, D. (2004) *Early Reading Instruction: What Science Really Tells Us about How to Teach Reading*. Cambridge, MA: MIT Press.

Ofsted (2008) *Responding to the Rose Review: Schools' Approaches to the Systematic Teaching of Phonics*. Manchester: Ofsted.

Ofsted (2010) *Reading by Six*. Manchester: Ofsted.

Rose, J. (2006) *Independent Review of the Teaching of Early Reading, Final Report, March 2006* (The Rose Review – Ref: 0201-2006DOC-EN). Nottingham: DfES.

Shapiro, L.R. and Solity, J. (2016) 'Differing effects of two synthetic phonics programmes on early reading development', *British Journal of Educational Psychology*, 86: 182–203.

Torgerson, C.J., Brooks, G. and Hall, J. (2006) *A Systematic Review of the Research Literature on the Use of Phonics in the Teaching of Reading and Spelling*. London: DfES.

Audit and test

Work through each section below, responding to each question or task. When you have completed each section, you can read the answers at the end of the chapter.

Section 1: Key terminology for a systematic and structured programme

It is important that you understand the terms below before you move on to the next activity. Provide a definition of each and check your definitions against those at the end of the chapter:

Fidelity to a programme

Systematic progression

Criteria for assuring high-quality phonic work

Section 2: Criteria for assuring high-quality phonic work

Which of the following are included in the DfE core criteria for assuring high-quality phonic work that identifies the key features of an effective, systematic, synthetic phonics programme? Try to consider a rationale for your choices.

The programme should:

1. include a variety of ready-made resources;

2. teach children to blend phonemes, in order, all through a word to read it;

3. teach children to remember all words by sight;

4. introduce one grapheme–phoneme correspondence a week;

5. teach actions for each grapheme–phoneme correspondence, to help children to remember them;

6. teach all 40+ grapheme–phoneme correspondences in a clear, incremental sequence;

7. teach children a range of different strategies for working out an unknown word, e.g. looking at the picture, using the context of what has been read so far, thinking about what would make sense in the complete sentence;

8. be designed to deliver discrete daily phonics session;

9. allow children to apply their knowledge of grapheme–phoneme correspondences by reading texts which are entirely decodable;

10. be designed to ensure that the vast majority of children have secured word recognition skills by the end of Key Stage 1.

Section 3: Pace and progression

The second column in the grid below does not correctly correspond to the phases from *Letters and Sounds* in the first column. Try to match the statements in the second column with the correct phase, based on the expected length of time spent teaching it and to which year group.

Phase from *Letters and Sounds*	Expected length of time to be spent teaching this phase and to which year group
Phase 1	Up to 6 weeks – Reception
Phase 2	4–6 weeks – Year 1
Phase 3	Throughout Year 2
Phase 4	From Nursery and throughout all phases
Phase 5	Up to 12 weeks – end of Reception
Phase 6	Throughout Year 1

Section 4: A systematic structured approach

The table below provides an overview of the knowledge and skills taught in each of the phases in *Letters and Sounds*. As Phase 1 is addressed in Chapter 7, this activity focuses on phases 2 to 6. It is important to note that Phase 1 teaching should continue throughout all the phases.

Phase from *Letters and Sounds*	Knowledge of grapheme–phoneme correspondences (GPCs)	Skills of blending and segmenting with letters	High-frequency words containing GPCs not yet taught
2	19 letters of the alphabet and one sound for each.	Move children on from oral blending and segmentation to blending and segmenting with letters. By the end of the phase many children should be able to read some VC and CVC words and to spell them, either using magnetic letters or by writing the letters on paper or on whiteboards. During the phase they will be introduced to reading two-syllable words and simple captions.	*the, to, no, go, I*
3	7 more letters of the alphabet. Graphemes to cover most of the phonemes not covered by single letters.	Blend and segment sounds represented by single letters and graphemes of more than one letter, including longer words (e.g. *chip, moon, night, thunder* – choice of word will depend on which GPCs have been taught). Blend to read simple captions, sentences and questions.	*he, she, we, me, be, was, my, you, her, they, all, are.* Emphasise parts of words containing known correspondences.
4	No new GPCs.	Consolidate children's knowledge of graphemes in reading and spelling words containing adjacent consonants and polysyllabic words.	*said, so, have, little, some, come, were, there, little, one, do, when, out, what.* Again, emphasise parts of words containing known correspondences.
5	More graphemes for the 40+ phonemes taught in Phases 2 and 3; more ways of pronouncing graphemes introduced in Phases 2 and 3.	Broaden knowledge of graphemes and phonemes for use in reading and spelling. Learn new graphemes and alternative pronunciations. Become quicker at recognising graphemes of more than one letter in words and at blending the phonemes they represent. When spelling words, learn to choose the appropriate graphemes to represent phonemes and begin to build word-specific knowledge of the spellings of words.	*oh, their, people, Mr, Mrs, looked, called, asked, water, where, who, again, though, through, work, mouse, many, laughed, because, different, any, eyes, friends, once, please.*

Phase from Letters and Sounds	Knowledge of grapheme–phoneme correspondences (GPCs)	Skills of blending and segmenting with letters	High-frequency words containing GPCs not yet taught
6	Word-specific spellings, i.e. when phonemes can be spelled in more than one way, children will learn which words take which spellings (e.g. *see/sea, bed/head/said, cloud/clown*).	Increasingly fluent sounding and blending of words encountered in reading for the first time. Spelling of words with prefixes and suffixes, doubling and dropping letters where necessary (e.g. *hop/hopping, hope/hoping, hope/hopeful, carry/carried, happy/happiness*). Increasingly accurate spelling of words containing unusual GPCs (e.g. *laugh, once, two, answer, could, there*).	As needed.

Reproduced, with minor layout changes, from DfES, 2007.

Use the table above to decide which phase the activities, taken from *Letters and Sounds*, below belong to. Try to consider a rationale, based on the knowledge and skills each is designed to teach.

Activity 1: What's in the box?

Resources

- Set of word cards giving words with adjacent consonants
- Set of objects or pictures corresponding to the word cards, hidden in a box
- Soft toy (optional)

Procedure

1. Display a word card.

2. Go through the letter recognition and blending process.

3. Ask the toy or a child to find the object in the box.

Activity 2: What's missing?

Resources

- Set of any six CVC objects from the role-play area (e.g. **hospital: soap, pen, chart, book, mug**)
- List of nine words for the teacher to read out, which includes the six objects and three additional items (e.g. **bed, sheet, pill**)
- Soft toy (optional)

Procedure

1. Pretext: you (or the soft toy) need to check that you have collected together all the items you need, which are written on your list.

2. Display the six objects.

3. Say one of the words on the list using sound-talk, ask the children to repeat it and then tell their partners what it is.

4. The children look at the items in front of them to see if the object is there.

Activity 3: Phoneme frame

Prerequisite

The children must have an understanding of the grammar of the past tense and experience of segmenting words into phonemes.

Resources

- Set of five-box and six-box phoneme frames drawn on the whiteboard
- Set of five-box and six-box phoneme frames, on laminated card so they can be reused, one per pair of children
- Word cards placed in a bag (e.g. rounded, helped, turned, begged, hissed, wanted, sorted, hummed, waded, washed, hated, greased, lived, robbed, rocked, laughed, called, roasted)

Procedure

1. Pick a word card from the bag and read it out without showing the children.

2. Working with a partner, the children say the word to themselves then segment and count the phonemes. They decide which phoneme frame to use and try writing it with one phoneme in each box.

3. Say *Show me* as the signal for the children to hold up their frames.

4. Demonstrate how to spell the word correctly using a frame on the whiteboard and ask the pairs of children to check their own spellings.

5. Repeat for about six words and look at the words that have been written.

6. What spelling pattern do they all have? Emphasise that even when the final phoneme sounds different (e.g. jumped), the spelling pattern is still the same.

7. Challenge the children to explain why this is (past tense of verbs).

8. Look closely at the phoneme frames.

9. Sometimes the –ed ending is two phonemes (e.g. wanted) and sometimes only one (e.g. grasped).

Activity 4: Quick copy

Resources

- Words using some newly learned graphemes in which all graphemes of two or more letters are underlined (e.g. pound, light, boy, sigh, out, joy).
- Same words without the underlining (e.g. pound, light, boy, sigh, out, joy).

- Magnetic whiteboards with all the appropriate graphemes to make the words, one per child.
- Extra letters to act as foils (e.g. if the grapheme *oy* is needed, provide separate letters *o* and *y* as well).
- If custom-made graphemes are unavailable, attach letters together with sticky tape to make graphemes.

Procedure

1. Display a word in which the grapheme is underlined.

2. Ask the children to make the word as quickly as possible using their magnetic letters and saying the phonemes (e.g. t-oy) and then reading the word.

3. Check that, where appropriate, children are using joined letters, not the separate letters.

4. Repeat with each word with an underlined grapheme.

5. Repeat 1–4 with words without the underlined graphemes, being particularly vigilant that children identify the two-letter or three-letter graphemes in the words.

Activity 5: Buried treasure

Resources

- About eight cards, shaped and coloured like gold coins with words and nonsense words on them made up from graphemes the children have been learning (e.g. jarm, win, jowd, yes, wug, zip), buried in the sand tray.
- Containers representing a treasure chest and a waste bin, or pictures of a treasure chest and a waste bin on large sheets of paper, placed flat on the table.

Procedure

1. Ask the children to sort the coins into the treasure chest and the waste bin, putting the coins with proper words on them (e.g. win) in the treasure chest and those with meaningless words (e.g. jowd) in the waste bin.

ANSWERS

Section 1: Key terminology for a systematic and structured programme

You were asked to provide an explanation for each of the below:

Fidelity to a programme

When teaching systematic synthetic phonics, it is important to adhere to a teaching framework that ensures that all grapheme–phoneme correspondences are taught. This does not necessarily mean that only one programme can be used. However, mixing too many elements from different programmes can result in a lack of essential coherence across a teaching framework.

Systematic progression

An effective systematic, synthetic phonics programme begins with learning grapheme–phoneme correspondences (GPCs) in a specific order. These are used to blend CVC words from the outset. Following on from that, more GPCs are taught until all 40+ phonemes are introduced. Some 'tricky words' that are complex to decode are introduced at a pace of approximately three to five per week. Next, alternative pronunciations and spellings for graphemes are taught. Application of GPCs taught in reading and writing is provided throughout.

Criteria for assuring high-quality phonic work

The DfE provides schools with criteria which defines the key features of an effective, systematic, synthetic phonics programme. Published programmes should meet each of the criteria. This can be accessed at http://www.education.gov.uk/schools/teachingandlearning/pedagogy/a0010240/criteria-for-assuring-high-quality-phonic-work

Section 2: Criteria for assuring high-quality phonic work

You were asked to select which of the following are included in the DfE core criteria for assuring high-quality phonic work that identifies the key features of an effective, systematic, synthetic phonics programme. You were also asked to consider a rationale for your choices.

1.	Include a variety of ready-made resources	No – while this might be desirable, it is not an essential criteria
2.	Teach children to blend phonemes, in order, all through a word to read it	Yes – it is essential for children to learn the skill of blending phonemes, all through a word, from the outset
3.	Teach children to remember all words by sight	No – children should use their knowledge of GPCs and the skill of blending to read words
4.	Introduced one grapheme–phoneme correspondence a week	No – when learning new GPCs, this should be at a pace of between three and five a week, depending on the phase children are working in

5.	Teach actions for each grapheme–phoneme correspondence, to help children to remember them	No – while some programmes use this approach, it is not an essential criterion. There are other ways children can learn the GPCs, e.g. through mnemonics
6.	Teach all 40+ grapheme–phoneme correspondences in a clear, incremental sequence	Yes – this is essential to ensure that GPCs are not missed out and children have an opportunity to revisit, review and apply GPCs that have been taught
7.	Teach children a range of different strategies for working out an unknown word, e.g. looking at the picture, using the context of what has been read so far, thinking about what would make sense in the complete sentence	No – children should use their knowledge of phonics as the prime approach to working out unknown words. Other strategies encourage them to guess a word, rather than work it out. This often leads to guessing an incorrect word
8.	Be designed to deliver discrete daily phonics session	Yes – as this allows suitable attention to be given to securing word recognition skills. Phonics should be viewed as a body of knowledge to be taught rather than a strategy, although opportunities should be sought to allow children to apply aspects of phonic knowledge and skills throughout the curriculum
9.	Allow children to apply their knowledge of grapheme–phoneme correspondences by reading texts which are entirely decodable	Yes – reading decodable texts provides essential practice in reading known phonemes and blending, and increases confidence. This should form part of children's reading diet and should not preclude other reading such as children's favourite books
10.	Be designed to ensure that the vast majority of children have secured word recognition skills by the end of Key Stage 1	Yes – children should have secure phonic knowledge and skills which allows them to be fluent readers and confident writers by the age of seven

Section 3: Pace and progression

You were asked to match the statements in the second column with the correct phase, based on the expected length of time spent teaching it and to which year group.

Phase from *Letters and Sounds*	Expected length of time to be spent teaching this phase and to which year group
Phase 1	From Nursery and throughout all phases
Phase 2	Up to 6 weeks – Reception
Phase 3	Up to 12 weeks – end of Reception
Phase 4	4–6 weeks – Year 1
Phase 5	Throughout Year 1
Phase 6	Throughout Year 2

Section 4: A systematic structured approach

You were asked to use the table, taken from *Letters and Sounds*, to decide which phase each of the activities belongs to. You were also asked to consider a rationale, based on the knowledge and skills each is designed to teach.

Activity	Phase from *Letters and Sounds*	Knowledge and skills the activity is designed to teach
Activity 1: What's in the box?	Phase 4	Reading words containing adjacent consonants by blending phonemes all through the word
Activity 2: What's missing?	Phase 2	Learn to blend phonemes all through the word to read CVC words
Activity 3: Phoneme frame	Phase 6	Reinforce understanding and application of the –ed suffix for the past tense
Activity 4: Quick copy	Phase 5	Recognise two-letter and three-letter graphemes in words and not read them as individual letters
Activity 5: Buried treasure	Phase 3	Practice blending GPCs that have been taught to read words

What to do next?

Reinforce your knowledge and understanding of teaching a systematic and structured programme by doing the following:

1. Ask a teacher which phonics programme is used in their school and use the criteria for assuring high-quality phonic work to find out about its key features and how it is used.

2. Observe a phonics lesson and consider what phonics skills and knowledge are being taught and how it fits in with a systematic approach.

10. Planning for phonics

Learning Outcomes

By the end of this chapter you will:

- have a clear understanding of key aspects in planning an effective phonics lesson;
- have reviewed effective pedagogy for teaching phonics;
- understand the importance of providing opportunities for applying phonic knowledge;
- have reviewed methods of differentiation for teaching phonics.

Teachers' Standards

3. Demonstrate good subject and curriculum knowledge:

    - if teaching early reading, demonstrate a clear understanding of systematic synthetic phonics.

4. Plan and teach well-structured lessons:

    - impart knowledge and develop understanding through effective use of lesson time.

5. Adapt teaching to respond to the strengths and needs of all pupils:

    - know when and how to differentiate appropriately, using approaches which enable pupils to be taught effectively.

Criteria for assuring high-quality phonic work (DfE, 2011)

The programme should be designed for the teaching of discrete, daily sessions progressing from simple to more complex phonic knowledge and skills and covering the major grapheme–phoneme correspondences (see Note 3).

Note 3: The programme should introduce a defined initial group of consonants and vowels, enabling children, early on, to read and spell many simple CVC words.

The programme should provide fidelity to the teaching framework for the duration of the programme, to ensure that these irregular words are fully learned (see Note 6).

Note 6: The programme should not neglect engaging and helpful approaches to the more challenging levels where children have to distinguish between phonically irregular graphemes and phonemes.

Introduction

This chapter provides a clear rationale for the structure of effective phonics lessons and key aspects to bear in mind when planning. Specifically, in this chapter you will look at the key aspects to incorporate when planning for phonics. These include ensuring that the structure of each lesson includes opportunities to revisit aspects taught, to teach something new and to apply and practise that learning. In essence, in every phonics lesson you should ensure that children have opportunities to discriminate the sound aurally, to enunciate the sound and to apply their learning in reading and writing. This chapter will help your understanding of effective practice through case studies and examples of lessons to provide the tools to apply this in different phases and for different contexts. A number of examples from *Letters and Sounds* (DfES, 2007) are used in this chapter, particularly because this is a commonly used programme and many elements are common. Chapter 12 will explore different programmes in more depth.

Theoretical perspectives/subject knowledge

In order to provide for effective phonics teaching whatever the phonics programme used or whatever the particular context, it is necessary to understand some key principles that underpin this. These are incorporated within the DfE (2011) criteria for high-quality phonics programmes. These include:

1. Every lesson should enable opportunities for children to *hear*, *say*, *read* and *write* phonemes and the corresponding graphemes as they are taught.

2. Teaching should make use of the visual, auditory and kinaesthetic memory.

3. Application of phonic knowledge in reading through the use of decodable texts should demonstrate that the purpose of reading is to gain meaning.

4. Coaching is provided for pupils who are learning at a slower pace in order to support the learning through:

    - opportunities for multiple readings of words that are decodable;

    - revisiting and directly teaching grapheme–phoneme correspondences;

    - opportunities provided for writing with teacher-scaffolded interactions;

    - authentic multiple reading and writing activities that mirror the child's world.

5. Teaching is contingent to ongoing formative assessment so that children's responses are built on and developed such that learning is appropriate to the learner.

6. Partner work is encouraged to maximise interaction between pupils and provide more opportunities to practise.

7. A new phoneme is introduced every day (with regular review lessons): the emphasis should be on teaching the 44+ phonemes and their corresponding graphemes quickly so that children are able to apply these skills to their developing literacy skills.

8. Each lesson should include revision of phonemes already taught. This can be done quickly by pointing to letters on a chart and children saying the sounds or using picture cards.

9. The use of alliterative phrases or mnemonics when teaching phonemes is helpful to reinforce the sounds; for example, for the consonant *l*: *lick the lemon lolly.* This should also be accompanied by an action to aid the memory (e.g. licking a lolly).

In summary: lessons should be pacey, interactive and relevant for children.

Planning for systematic teaching

It is important that phonics is taught systematically, discretely and on a daily basis. Thorough planning for this helps promote a clear focus on the teaching of phonics and gives teachers continual opportunities to deliver high-quality phonics teaching. In the publication *Getting Them Reading Early*, Ofsted states that: 'Systematic phonics refers to phonics teaching which is done regularly, discretely, explicitly and in an agreed and rational sequence' (2011, p.14).

As The Rose Review states: 'It cannot be left to chance, or for children to ferret out, on their own, how the alphabetic code works' (2006, para.48) – particularly a code that is as complex as that of English. As discussed in Chapter 9, the systematic and structured teaching of phonics is a crucial aspect.

To put this into practice, thorough ongoing planning, supported by continual focused assessment, is necessary to deliver high-quality systematic phonics. Phonics planning should include and address:

*   the four elements of a well-structured phonics session – revisit and review, teach, practise and apply;

*   activities to teach and support blending for reading and segmenting for spelling;

*   opportunities to learn and practise high-frequency words, tricky words, phonemes and graphemes;

*   continual assessment of children's knowledge and ability.

The four structural elements

Each effective phonics lesson should be structured around four elements as acknowledged in the *Letters and Sounds* framework: revisit and review, teach, practise, and apply. The *Letters and*

Sounds programme promotes these four elements. An example, taken from *Letters and Sounds* (DfES, 2007), shows the suggested sequence for teaching the Phase 2 curriculum:

Revisit and review:

- *Practise previously-learned letters.*
- *Practise oral blending and segmentation.*

Teach:

- *Teach a new letter.*
- *Teach blending and/or segmentation with letters (weeks 2 and 3).*
- *Teach one or two tricky words (week 3 onwards).*

Practise:

- *Practise reading and/or spelling words with the new letter.*

Apply:

- *Read or write a caption (with the teacher) using one or more high-frequency words and words containing the new letter (week 3 onwards).*

Including these four elements in every phonics lesson encourages a fast-paced, well-organised session during which children are given the opportunity to practise skills and knowledge already gained, and to learn new information. It is recommended in different programmes that each element of the lesson should last approximately five to seven minutes, and it is important that lessons are short (about 15–20 minutes maximum), lively and interactive. The most effective ways to utilise this time may include the following ideas:

- **Revisit and review:** teachers and children are able to revise previous teaching and learning. This may be returning to an element of a previous lesson that was not successful, looking again at an aspect from earlier in the current phase, or indeed, recapping material from a previous phase. This element of the lesson allows the opportunity for individuals to accomplish something previously unattained.

- **Teach:** provides plenty of opportunity to introduce new high-frequency words, tricky words and phonemes, unfamiliar concepts and skills. This element of the session can also be used to introduce new games and activities which can then be played in future sessions.

- **Practise:** allows children to consolidate their learning by playing a wide range of games. These games may be designed to use blending for reading or segmenting for spelling skills and techniques. In *Letters and Sounds* the section 'Principles and practice of high-quality phonics' (DfES, 2007) provides guidance and instructions for many different activities and gives suggestions for when these games can be most effectively used.

- **Apply:** gives children the opportunity to use what they have learned successfully in other contexts. This may involve playing games or reading and writing sentences containing key phonemes and words from the teaching element of the session. It also gives teachers the chance to assess whether targets have been achieved and the appropriate knowledge gained, or whether there are opportunities to revisit and review next time.

Blending for reading and segmenting for spelling

Planning for phonics should include direct teaching and activities to teach children how to blend phonemes to allow them to read words, and to segment words into separate phonemes to allow them to spell. Ofsted points out that

> {b}lending and segmenting are, in the words of the Rose Review, 'reversible processes': that is, if you can blend the sounds together to read a word, you should also be able to identify and break down (segment) the individual sounds in a word you hear to spell it. To spell the word, you need to represent each sound you hear by a letter – or more than one letter.
>
> (2011, p.18)

Every phonics lesson should include activities to teach both blending and segmenting.

Blending for reading

Why is blending so important and why should it be included in every phonics lesson? Children need to be able to blend phonemes together in order to be able to read whole words. Ofsted makes it clear that

> {t}he skill of blending sounds together needs to be taught directly. Children may be able to say the sound a letter 'makes' when shown the letter (for instance, on a flashcard), but this does not necessarily mean that they can blend individual sounds together to make a whole word. (Letters do not actually 'make' sounds: they are just a way of representing that sound in writing.)
>
> (2011, p.20)

There are many ideas for activities to teach blending for reading in *Letters and Sounds* (DfES, 2007). Below is an example of one of these activities, taken from Phase 3.

What's in the box?

Resources

- *Set of word cards (e.g. with words containing Sets 6 and 7 letters and Phase 3 graphemes).*
- *Set of objects or pictures corresponding to the word cards, hidden in a box.*
- *Soft toy (optional).*

Procedure

- *Display a word card.*
- *Go through the grapheme recognition and blending process, placing a sound button below each grapheme. Draw attention to the long sound buttons under the two-letter and three-letter graphemes.*
- *Ask the toy or a child to find the corresponding object or picture in the box.*

Variation 1 (to further develop vocabulary)

- *Attach some pictures to the whiteboard using reusable sticky pads or magnets, or display some objects.*
- *Display a word card.*
- *Go through the grapheme recognition and blending process as above.*
- *Ask a child to place the word card next to the corresponding picture or object.*

Variation 2 (when children are confident blenders)

- *Children sit in two lines opposite one another.*
- *Give the children in one line an object or picture and the children in the other line a word card.*
- *Ask the children with word cards to read their words and ask the children with objects or pictures to 'sound-talk' the name of their object or picture to the child sitting next to them.*
- *Ask the children to hold up their words and objects or pictures so that the children sitting in the line opposite can see them.*
- *Ask the children with word cards to stand up and go across to the child in the line opposite who has the corresponding object or picture.*
- *All the children check that they have the right match.*

Planning should include a variety of games and activities for blending to maintain children's interest and to teach a range of blending skills.

Segmenting for spelling

Both blending and segmenting are vital in the teaching of phonics. Children should be able to break words into separate phonemes in order to spell. Segmenting is the reverse of blending. In segmenting, to spell a word the teacher or the child listens to a whole word, identifies the individual sounds (not letters) that make up the word and chooses a letter, or more than one letter, to represent each individual sound.

There are also many ideas for activities to teach segmenting for spelling in *Letters and Sounds* (DfES, 2007). Below is an example of one of these activities taken from Phase 3.

Phoneme frame

Resources

- *Large three-phoneme frame drawn on a magnetic whiteboard.*

- *Selection of magnetic letters or graphemes displayed on the whiteboard (the graphemes should be either custom-made as units or individual letters stuck together using sticky tape, e.g. /oa/).*

- *List of words.*

- *Small phoneme frames, each with a selection of magnetic letters or six-letter or six-grapheme fans, one per child or pair of children.*

Procedure

Words made up of Sets 6 and 7 letters:

- *Say a CVC word (e.g.* jam*) and then say it in sound-talk.*

- *Say another CVC word (e.g.* wet*) and ask the children to tell their partners what it would be in sound-talk.*

- *Demonstrate finding the letter* w *from the selection of magnetic letters and put it into the first square on the phoneme frame; put the letter* e *in the second square, and* t *in the last square. Sound-talk* w-e-t *and then say* wet*.*

- *Say another CVC word (e.g.* zip*) and ask the children to tell their partners what it would be in sound-talk.*

- *Ask the children to tell you what to put in the first square in the phoneme frame, then in the next and so on.*

- *Ask the children to make the word on their own phoneme frames or fans.*

- *If all the children have phoneme frames or fans, ask them to check that they have the same answers as their partners. If the children are sharing, they ask their partners whether they agree.*

- *Ask the children to hold up their phoneme frames or fans for you to see.*

- *Repeat items 4–8 with another CVC word.*

- *Continue with other CVC words.*

Planning should, therefore, also include a variety of games and activities to teach a range of segmenting skills.

Phonemes and graphemes

It is important that phonics lessons include opportunities to learn, practise and revisit the 44+ phonemes and the graphemes they are represented by. *Letters and Sounds* distributes the teaching of these phonemes across several phases, allowing for progression and the systematic development of knowledge and skills. Below is an example of an activity to support the teaching of phonemes and graphemes in Phase 3 of *Letters and Sounds* (DfES, 2007).

Fans

Purpose

- *To find the correct grapheme in response to a sound being spoken.*

Resources

- *Fans with a designated set of graphemes, one per child or pair of children.*

Procedure

- *Say the sound of a grapheme and ask the children to find the letter on the fan and leave it at the top, sliding the other letters out of sight.*

- *If all the children have fans, ask them to check that they have the same answer as their partners. If the children are sharing, they ask their partners whether they agree.*

- *Ask the children to hold up their fans for you to see.*

Variations

- *The children have two different fans each.*

- *The children work in pairs with three different fans.*

High-frequency and tricky words

As discussed in Chapters 3 and 9, high-frequency words are those that appear most often in everyday reading and spelling. Some of these are termed 'common exception words' in the 2013 National Curriculum and are often called 'tricky words' as they cannot be sounded out phonetically and can therefore prove most challenging to read and spell. The 2013 National Curriculum clearly specifies the need to ensure that these words are taught.

Ofsted emphasises that

> {c}hildren should be taught to read words that are not completely phonically regular, often called 'tricky' words in phonic schemes. Children need to be taught to read these tricky words on sight, so that they do not have to spend time puzzling them out. In terms of spelling, children need to remember the tricky parts of a word, that is, the letters that do not match the usual grapheme–phoneme correspondences they have learnt.

> (2011, p.22)

Teachers should plan to include time for teaching or revisiting a small group of tricky words in each phonics lesson. Below is an example of how to teach tricky words, as in *Letters and Sounds* (DfES, 2007) Phase 2.

Teaching the tricky bit in high-frequency words

Resource

- *Caption containing the tricky word to be learned.*

Procedure

- *Explain that there are some words that have one, or sometimes two, tricky letters.*
- *Read the caption, pointing to each word, then point to the word to be learned and read it again.*
- *Write the word on the whiteboard.*
- *Sound-talk the word and repeat, putting sound lines and buttons under each phoneme and blending them to read the word.*
- *Discuss the tricky bit of the word where the letters do not correspond to the sounds the children know (e.g. in* go, *the last letter does not represent the same sound as the children know in* dog).
- *Read the word a couple more times and refer to it regularly throughout the day, so that by the end of the day the children can read the word straight away without sounding out.*

Activity

Reviewing planning

Read the example weekly plan (Figure 10.1 on pages 202–3) and consider:

1. How the four parts of the lesson are specifically planned.
2. How games and various activities provide practice.
3. How assessment opportunities are clearly planned.

Now look at the plan (Figure 10.2 on pages 203–4) and consider how multi-sensory learning is explicitly provided.

Differentiation

The most effective way of differentiating phonics teaching is through group work. Once systematic phonics teaching has begun, it is important to assess children's progress and then group children according to ability. The important point to bear in mind is that children should be grouped and re-grouped for teaching purposes rather than be in fixed ability groups. As the research study below shows (Shapiro and Solity, 2008), this can be mixed with whole-class teaching.

Letters and Sounds, Phase 5, Week 1:
Objectives and criteria for success:
Teach new graphemes for reading p.134 *ay, ou, ie, ea.*
Practise recognition and recall of Phase 2, 3 and 4 graphemes as they are learned.
Practise reading and spelling words with adjacent consonants and words with newly learned graphemes.
Teach reading the words *oh, old, their* p.141.
Teach spelling the words *said, so* p.148.
Practise reading and spelling high-frequency words p.141/p.148.
Practise reading and spelling polysyllabic words p.142 and p.149.
Practise reading sentences p.142.
Practise writing sentences p.149.

Day	Revisit and review	Teach	Practise	Apply	Assessment
Mon.	Recall all GPCs from Phase 2, 3 and 4. Note any children who struggle with this and focus on those for the rest of the week.	Teach reading high-frequency word *old* p.141 and tricky words *oh, their* p.140. Teach *ay* and talk about the difference between this and *ai* and that *ay* usually comes at the end of a word. Blending for activity: *day, play, may, spray, stray, delay.* Use activities from Phase 4 pp.113–15 for blending for reading activities in Phase 5.	Segmenting for spelling activity *stay, tray, clay, pray, play.* Use activities from Phase 4 pp.116–17, for segmentation for spelling activities in Phase 5.	Reading sentences activity Yes/No questions p.142: Can I stay and play? Can I spray the paint? May I stay at home today?	Give the sound when shown any grapheme that has been taught. Begin to write some of the common graphemes when given a sound.

Day	Revisit and review	Teach	Practise	Apply	Assessment
Tue.	Practise recognition and recall of Phase 2, 3 and 4 GPCs. Practise reading high-frequency words p. 141.	Teach *ou* and compare to *ow*. Explain that *ou* rarely comes at the end of a word. Blending for reading activity: *out, cloud, proud, about, scout.*	Segmentation for spelling activity: *sound, found, mountain, sprout, loud, loudest.*	Writing sentences p.149: The sound is loud. I go down now.	Begin to apply phonic knowledge and skill when reading and spelling unfamiliar words that are not completely decodable. Be able to blend and segment in order to read CVC words. Begin to read automatically the words in the list of 100 high-frequency words taught in previous phases. Begin to accurately spell most of the words in the list of 100 high-frequency words. Form each letter correctly.
Wed.	Practise recognition and recall of Phase 2, 3 and 4 GPCs. Practise reading high-frequency words p.141 and spelling tricky words p.148.	Teach spelling tricky words *said, so* p.148. Teach *ie* and compare to I. I is a word on its own, *ie* makes the sound in other words – usually at the end. Blending for reading activity: *tie, pie, lie, die, cried, fried.*	Segmentation for spelling *tried, pie, spied, denied, tie, lie.*	Reading sentences p. 142: I cook a pie.	
Thu.	Practise recognition and recall of Phase 2, 3 and 4 GPCs. Practise reading high-frequency words p.141 and spelling tricky words p.148.	Teach *ea* and compare to *ee*. Blending for reading sentence substitution p.158. *Paul eats peas with his meat/beans/.*	Segmentation for spelling *treat, meat, steam, sea, read, repeat, heap, least.*	Writing sentences p.149: He reads under the tree.	
Fri.	Practise recognition and recall of Phase 2, 3 and 4 GPCs. Practise reading high-frequency words p. 141 and spelling tricky words p.148.	Teach the children how to play 'phoneme spotter' p.145. Start today with reading and listening and see if they can identify any of this week's sounds.	Continue from 'phoneme spotter' by listing the words containing this week's phonemes and their alternatives ay/ ai/ ou/ ow/ ea/ ee.	Use the words generated from before to teach children how to play 'best bet' p.147, with the same sounds.	

Figure 10.1 Example of Letters and Sounds, *weekly lesson plan (Chester)*

Lesson: Phoneme /ai/
1. Review (approximately 5 minutes) Review previous sound by saying first line of vowel rap in a lively fun way with the children: 'ay, ay, play with hay? AY'
Hear it • Help children to practise hearing the sounds by reading a range of words, some containing the phoneme /ay/ (e.g. *day, sold, bone, way, cake, play*). Ask them to put their hands up every time they hear the /ay/ phoneme.
Say it • Using several words containing the phoneme taught, say these slowly in 'robot talk', e.g. /p/l/ay/, /w/ay/, s/ay/. Ask the children to repeat the word (blending the phonemes). • Now ask the children to talk in 'robot talk'. Say a word, e.g. *may* and ask them to segment it using 'robot talk'.
Read it • Show children the following words, which you have written on the whiteboard or easel: *play, say, hay.* • Ask them to read the words to a partner by blending the phonemes then saying the word.

(Continued)

(Continued)

Lesson: Phoneme /ai/

Write it
• Say a word (e.g. *ray*) to the children and ask them to segment the word into phonemes and tell you how many phonemes there are (2) and then write the word on an individual whiteboard and show you.

2. New phoneme: /ai/ (10 minutes)

Hear it
• Introduce the new phoneme by saying several words that contain it *(sail, mail, tail)*. Explain that this is the same sound as /ay/ but they are learning a different way to spell it.

Say it
• Show the children the corresponding phoneme picture card and mnemonic phrase, 'ai/ay/ what did you say?' Ask the children to repeat it several times with you. Say the letter name(s) of the new grapheme: 'AI'.
• Say the rap and ensure that the children do the action (hand cupped around ear): '/ai/ai/ what did you say? AI'.
• Using several words containing the new phoneme, say these slowly in 'robot talk' e.g. /s/n/ai/l/, /m/ai/l/, /t/r/ai/l/ and ask children to tell their partner the word (blending).
• Now ask the children to talk in 'robot talk' by saying a word, e.g. *wail*, and ask them to segment it using 'robot talk' to their partner.

Read it
• Read a range of words that contain the grapheme that you have written on the whiteboard or easel, e.g. *rail, pail, sail*. Ensure that children can identify the grapheme *ai*.
• Ask them to read the words to their partner by blending the phonemes and saying the words.
• Place the phoneme picture card on the wall underneath the previous cards /ay/ to build up the phoneme chart for the long vowel phonemes. Ask the children to tell you the graphemes for the phoneme and repeat the mnemonic phrase for /ai/.

Write it
• Say a word containing the new phoneme to the children, ask them to repeat it and then segment it into phonemes, e.g. *pail*. Ask them to tell you how many phonemes (3) and then to write the word on their whiteboards and underline the grapheme that represents the new phoneme being taught.

Figure 10.2 Lesson plan incorporating multi-sensory learning (Jolliffe, 2007)

Assessment to inform planning

Assessment and target-setting is reviewed at length in Chapter 11; however, it is important to consider how it informs planning. Teachers should be assessing pupils' progress in phonics to both inform future planning and target-setting, and to consider when children are ready to move on to the next phase of teaching. Continuous daily assessment of individual or group understanding and attainment is necessary to allow the teacher to plan the next lesson. Perhaps a tricky word or phoneme has not been mastered by all pupils and therefore could be revisited in a future lesson. This daily assessment is often informal and immediate; for example, the teacher checks children's responses on whiteboards or listens to pupils as they enunciate phonemes. A quick note can be made of those children who have not successfully achieved what was asked of them and revisiting these issues can be planned for a lesson in the near future.

Assessments at the end of a phase of phonics teaching should be carried out to consider whether children are ready to move on to the next phase of teaching. These assessments are often more formal, assessing children on an individual basis and keeping records of attainment for tracking purposes. *Letters and Sounds* offers guidance materials and record-keeping documents to assist with assessment, for example:

By the end of Phase 3 children should:

- *give the sound when shown all or most Phase 2 and Phase 3 graphemes;*

- *find all or most Phase 2 and Phase 3 graphemes from a display, when given the sound;*

- *be able to blend and read CVC words (i.e. single syllable words consisting of Phase 2 and Phase 3 graphemes);*

- *be able to segment and make a phonemically plausible attempt at spelling CVC words (i.e. single syllable words consisting of Phase 2 and Phase 3 graphemes);*

- *be able to read the 'tricky' words* he, she, we, me, be, was, my, you, her, they, all, are;

- *be able to spell the 'tricky' words* the, to, I, no, go;

- *write each letter correctly when following a model.*

The assessment of phonics should also take place as part of wider reading and writing assessments for each child. Children's phonic ability should be taken into consideration when they are both reading (including blending skills) and writing (spelling using segmenting skills). Many assessment materials are provided in different programmes as well as phonics criteria as part of the overall reading and writing assessment process.

Research Focus: Whole-class teaching

Shapiro and Solity (2008) cite recent studies which have shown that supplementary phonological and phonics training can be highly effective, even when delivered to large groups or whole classes of children (Hatcher et al., 2004; Leafstedt et al., 2004). These studies focus mainly on children at risk of developing difficulties, and additional phonological training is thought to be unnecessary for normally developing readers. In fact, Hatcher et al. showed that additional phonological training had no impact on the top two-thirds of readers. Although the UK National Reading Panel report (Torgerson et al., 2006) concluded that systematic phonics training can benefit children at different achievement levels, only four of the 14 studies included in

$\longrightarrow$

the meta-analysis were with normally developing readers. All of these studies involved either additional training outside the classroom or relatively small teaching groups (between ten and 20 children), and all were of short duration (up to ten weeks).

The intervention in Shapiro and Solity's (2008) study covered the teaching of phonological awareness (synthesis and segmentation), phonics, sight vocabulary and reading to and with children. The intervention incorporated phonological and phonics training into whole-class sessions that covered all aspects of reading. They investigated the success of the intervention by comparing the reading development of children receiving the intervention with those attending comparison schools.

They found that children from the intervention schools improved in their reading performance faster than children in comparison schools, and that children at different levels of phonological awareness appeared to benefit equally from the intervention. They also found that the proportion of children classified as having reading difficulties by the end of Year 2 was significantly less. They concluded that 'delivering short, frequent whole-class sessions that include focused phonological and phonics training can have a significant impact on the reading development of children with poor phonological skills' (Shapiro and Solity, 2008, p.617). This study therefore emphasises that effective instruction delivered to all children in the class can be of benefit to all and can reduce the need for additional support.

Devonshire et al. (2013) found that an intervention programme that aimed to teach reading and spelling literacy to five- to seven-year-old children including both word reading and spelling significantly improved the literacy skills of the children. They concluded that early teaching of English literacy should include instruction in morphology, etymology and rules about form, in addition to phonics.

Aligning additional support with core class teaching

Wonder-McDowell, from a two-group, pre-post experimental study, suggested that at-risk second-grade students benefit from supplemental instruction that is aligned with the classroom core-reading programme. They concluded:

> These findings suggest that at-risk students benefit from increased 'FIT' of instruction: (a) with content mirroring the scope and sequence of the core class-room instruction that is highly 'focused' on individual need, (b) in small groups of four or less to increase 'intensity' and (c) that provides a double dose of instruction, increasing instructional 'time'.
>
> (2010, p.57)

This study therefore emphasises that additional instruction which is not coherent or linked with other whole-class teaching is less effective.

High-quality, focused assessment can be used for target-setting. Group and individual targets can be created for areas of underachievement, and these can then be addressed through revisiting and reviewing in future phonics lessons.

Case Studies

1. Staff training

The following case study from Blue Coat School, cited by Ofsted, demonstrates the support for teachers to ensure effective phonics teaching:

> There is a comprehensive internal programme of staff training, as well as training for other schools. The headteacher and reading manager lead this and provide opportunities for about ten to 12 schools each term to visit to see what they are doing. It is a national model school for Read Write Inc. and the headteacher makes presentations to other headteachers about systematic phonics. The school works on five alliterative principles that form part of the programme:
>
> - Participation
> - Praise
> - Pace
> - Purpose
> - Passion
>
> together with two of their own:
>
> - Progress
> - Presence

(2010, p.34)

This case study demonstrates the importance of a whole-school approach to the teaching of phonics.

2. Consistency at Woodberry Down

A further case study cited by Ofsted reinforces the impact of consistency:

> The children are grouped by their attainment in phonics. The staff, however, use a full range of identical strategies across whatever group they are teaching to keep pupils highly involved in their learning. The range of phonemes are run through as a group. Words which are not phonically regular are pointed out and learnt as 'tricky words'.

⟶

The terms 'magnet eyes', 'marshmallow [silent] claps', and 'my turn, your turn' routines (from adults and pupils) are used consistently and with great success. Working with partners is completely consistent, one child acting first as 'tutor', then as pupil. The 'tutor' holds a lollipop stick and points at the words her or his partner has to read so both remain engaged and active. Then they swap roles, repeating the same page in the book. For the pupils, this is fail-safe, interactive learning. The text on which the group works mirrors exactly the phonemes that have been rehearsed or taught and contains the non-phonically regular words that the group has studied. Pupils' reading and writing are therefore systematically and successfully supported and the pupils taste success.

(2010, p.35)

This case study demonstrates consistent strategies used throughout, and this is particularly important where pupils are grouped according to their progress in learning phonics. Therefore, when moving from one group to another as they develop understanding, pupils encounter the same procedures and terminology.

3. Integrated learning in the nursery setting

Busy Bears Children's Day Nursery plan for indoor and outdoor play-based activities, through which phonics is taught as an integrated element of the curriculum. Phonics is taught through the *Literacy* and *Language and Communications* Areas of Learning Development in the EYFS Framework (DfE, 2017). The focus for those children in the nursery, who are 40 to 60 months old, is on Phase 1 of *Letters and Sounds*, and a variety of activities are planned for through free play and adult-led group time.

Children work with things that are familiar to them and they explore their names, common sounds and initial letters of common items through a range of games that use physical, verbal and written means. This might include guessing which hidden everyday object is making a noise, identifying the initial letter of common animals, hunting for letter shapes, finding their own named water bottle and using illuminated whiteboards to write their name. In addition to the planned adult-led activities, the practitioners at the nursery build upon a wide range of child-led activities, where a child's particular interest may spark and lead the learning.

Children are observed and assessed using the EYFS Framework, and records are kept electronically so that links can be made between multiple observations of the child. The next round of planning is completed as a result of the outcomes of the assessments, and so the practitioners are able to meet the needs of the children as they develop.

The nursery offers a wide range of resources and activities that children may engage with independently to develop their early phonics skills, such as a mark-making trolley with a variety of writing media, and food bags and large trays with paint, shaving foam, gloop and sand to draw letter shapes. Games such as *Playdough Disco* and *Squiggle While You Wiggle* help to develop children's fine motor skills, pencil grip and mark-making.

→

Developing early phonics skills is taken into account when the practitioners plan the displays around nursery. Carefully chosen fonts, with the appropriate use of both upper case and lower case letters, are used for signs and labels. Names on pegs and personal belongings, accompanied by a photograph of the child until it is no longer needed, are provided to allow the child to be independent in early letter and name recognition. Children self-register using their names when they arrive and leave each day.

Learning Outcomes Review

This chapter has detailed the essential ingredients for planning effective systematic phonics teaching. It has provided examples of teaching different aspects and reviewed planning. While research has shown that such effective teaching reduces the need for additional support for pupils, the chapter has discussed methods of differentiation based on accurate and ongoing assessment of pupils' progress.

Self-assessment questions

1. Name the four elements that should be contained in a structured phonics lesson, as highlighted in *Letters and Sounds* (DfES, 2007).
2. How can the application of phonic skills in reading and writing be incorporated into lessons?
3. What kind of activities will support multi-sensory teaching?
4. How can differentiation be successfully achieved?

Further Reading

For further information on planning effective phonics lessons, see:

Gill, A. and Waugh, D. (2017) *Phonics: Getting it Right in a Week.* Northwich: Critical Publishing (see especially Day 5).

Hall, K. (2006) 'How children learn to read and how phonics helps', in M. Lewis and S. Ellis (eds), *Phonics, Practice, Research and Policy.* London: Paul Chapman.

For detailed examples of lesson plans, see:

Jolliffe, W. (2012) *Quick Fix for Phonics.* Witney: Scholastic.

For further support with planning, see Chapter 10 of:

Waugh, D. and Harrison-Palmer, R. (2013) *Teaching Systematic Synthetic Phonics: Audit and Test*. Exeter: Learning Matters.

References

Devonshire, V., Morris, P. and Fluck, M. (2013) 'Spelling and reading development: The effect of teaching children multiple levels of representation in their orthography', *Learning and Instruction*, 25: 85–94.

DfE (2017) *Statutory Framework for the Early Years Foundation Stage*. London: DfE.

DfE (2011) *Teachers' Standards in England from September 2012*. London: DfE.

DfES (2007) *Letters and Sounds: Principles and Practice of High-quality Phonics*. Norwich: DfES.

Hatcher, P.J., Hulme, C. and Snowling, M.J. (2004) 'Explicit phoneme training combined with phonic reading instruction helps young children at risk of reading failure', *Journal of Child Psychology and Psychiatry*, 45 (2): 338–58.

Jolliffe, W. (2007) *You Can Teach Phonics*. Leamington Spa: Scholastic.

Leafstedt, J.M., Richards, C.R. and Gerber, M.M. (2004) 'Effectiveness of explicit phonological-awareness instruction for at-risk English learners', *Learning Disabilities Research and Practice*, 19 (4): 252–61.

Ofsted (2010) *Reading by Six*. Manchester: Ofsted.

Ofsted (2011) *Getting Them Reading Early*. Manchester: Ofsted. Available from www.gov.uk/government/publications/getting-them-reading-early (accessed 29/12/14).

Rose, J. (2006) *Independent Review of the Teaching of Early Reading, Final Report, March 2006* (The Rose Review – Ref: 0201-2006DOC-EN). Nottingham: DfES.

Shapiro, L.R. and Solity, J. (2008) 'Delivering phonological and phonics training within whole-class teaching', *British Journal of Educational Psychology*, 78: 597–620.

Torgerson, C.J., Brooks, G. and Hall, J. (2006) *A Systematic Review of the Research Literature on the Use of Phonics in the Teaching of Reading and Spelling*. London: DfES.

Wonder-McDowell, C. (2010) 'The hidden peril of differentiation: Fragmented instruction', *College Reading Association Yearbook*, 31: 45–59.

11. Tracking and assessing pupils' learning and effective intervention

Learning Outcomes

By the end of this chapter you should have:

- an understanding of the importance of tracking and assessing pupils' learning in phonics and how this supports planning for appropriate next steps;
- a knowledge of a range of strategies for assessing and tracking pupils' progress;
- examined methods of additional support for pupils and intervention programmes.

Teachers' Standards

2. Promote good progress and outcomes by pupils:

    - be accountable for pupils' attainment, progress and outcomes
    - plan teaching to build on pupils' capabilities and prior knowledge
    - guide pupils to reflect on the progress they have made and their emerging needs.

3. Demonstrate good subject and curriculum knowledge:

    - if teaching early reading, demonstrate a clear understanding of systematic synthetic phonics.

6. Make accurate and productive use of assessment:

    - know and understand how to assess the relevant subject and curriculum areas, including statutory assessment requirements;
    - make use of formative and summative assessment to secure pupils' progress;
    - use relevant data to monitor progress, set targets, and plan subsequent lessons;
    - give pupils regular feedback, both orally and through accurate marking, and encourage pupils to respond to the feedback.

Criteria for assuring high-quality phonic work (DfE, 2011)

Note 4: If the programme is high quality, systematic and synthetic it will, by design, map incremental progression in phonic knowledge and skills. It should therefore enable teachers to: track children's progress; assess for further learning; and identify incipient difficulties, so that appropriate support can be provided.

Introduction

The focus of this chapter is to support a thorough understanding of methods of assessing and tracking children's phonic knowledge and examples of intervention where appropriate. The chapter reviews the underpinning principles of effective assessment in phonics in detail and demonstrates how formative assessment, or assessment for learning, should regularly inform next steps in teaching. The chapter also examines methods for monitoring and tracking pupils' progress and provides support for diagnostic assessment, including a review of the phonics screening check undertaken at the end of Year 1 (usually aged six). The chapter concludes with examples of appropriate support for pupils to ensure progression.

Theoretical perspectives/subject knowledge

The Rose Review highlighted the importance of developing effective assessment that is 'simple, rigorous and purposeful' (2006: para.61). Such assessment should be continuous and planned to ensure that children have sufficiently grasped aspects taught. In the previous chapter, an example of planning demonstrated how opportunities for assessment were built in on a weekly basis. Working in this way, it is easy to diagnose any problems. It is then possible to re-teach or consolidate learning by providing specific and alternative activities to address the difficulties. It is important that each stage has been achieved to ensure that the children are confident and fluent and ready to progress to the next stage. It is also necessary to ensure that frequent opportunities to review phonemes are taught – it is this process of 'over-learning' that is so important for successful phonics acquisition.

Ofsted's survey *Removing Barriers to Literacy* specifically found that one of the key factors that made a difference was the need to 'teach phonics systematically as part of the teaching of reading and ensure that pupils' progress in developing their phonic knowledge and skills is regularly assessed' (2011, p.8).

Schools in the survey that were successful in teaching phonics demonstrated that 'the assessment of pupils' understanding of letters, sounds and words was frequent and record-keeping was meticulous' (2011, para.49).

Overall the survey found that

> *{t}he most successful schools, colleges and other providers of adult education and training visited made outstanding use of national test and assessment data to raise the expectations of staff and to set sufficiently challenging targets.*

> (2011, p.6)

This highlights the importance of making use of regular assessment and tracking data to plan for appropriate and challenging lessons.

Ongoing formative assessment

Inevitably, some children will make slower progress, which highlights the vital role of assessment for learning in which a teacher carefully provides opportunities in all lessons to check children's progress. The *Letters and Sounds* guidance on assessment and tracking identifies the range of opportunities for assessment:

> *This can be during the discrete daily phonics session, but will also be apparent during shared guided and independent reading and writing sessions.*
>
> *Writing samples provide useful evidence of children's phonic knowledge and ability to apply phonic skills, but evidence obtained through observation of children's approaches to reading unfamiliar words is of equal importance.*

(DCSF, 2009a: 3)

It is also helpful to bear in mind that, as *Letters and Sounds: Notes of Guidance for Practitioners and Teachers* points out,

> *the boundaries between the phases are deliberately porous so that no children are held back, or unduly pressured to move on before they are equipped to do so. It follows that practitioners and teachers will need to make principled decisions based on reliable assessments of children's learning to inform planning for progression within and across the phases.*

(DfES, 2007, p.3)

Case Study: Ongoing assessment

This case study cites two examples of assessment opportunities that can be planned into most phonics lessons.

In one school the Year 1 teacher was working on Phase 5 of *Letters and Sounds* and used two particular activities that enabled her to check children's progress, at a glance, aided by a teaching assistant.

$\longrightarrow$

Phoneme fingers

This activity is used to check children's ability to segment words into phonemes. Here the teacher says a word, e.g. *school,* and then asks the children to work out how many phonemes. Then the teacher says '3-2-1 and show me!' and the children hold up the corresponding number of fingers for phonemes (in this case four). To check understanding, she asks them to pretend to write the graphemes on each finger (see Figure 11.1).

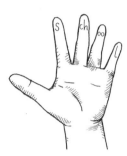

Figure 11.1   Hand showing corresponding graphemes for the word 'school'

Mini whiteboards

This activity provides opportunities for children to apply their knowledge of grapheme-phoneme correspondences by writing words containing a specific phoneme. For example, the teacher has been teaching the phoneme /ay/ and asks the children to write the word *play,* followed by other examples: *day, hay, tray.* She regularly asks the children to work in pairs to do this, so that they support each other. Once they have written the word, she asks them to hold up their whiteboards to show her. Again, at a glance, she can see which children are able to do this successfully.

Tracking

Progress in learning phonics is largely hierarchical, and as children are taught a systematic progression it is important that each child's progress is carefully tracked. The *Letters and Sounds* framework provides such a phonics progress tracking sheet to map children's progress. For a completed example showing children's initials at different stages, see Figure 11.2.

It is important to distinguish on such tracking sheets the difference between the children who are working at a particular phase and those children who are secure at a phase. Children are judged to be secure at a particular phase once they consistently know most of the phonemes associated with that phase, and can apply the skills of blending and segmenting using an appropriate range of grapheme–phoneme correspondences. Teachers need to develop systems such as highlighting names/initials of children to denote when they are secure at a particular phase.

Letters and Sounds provides clear guidance of expectations of what to look for at each phase, as shown below:

> *Children are secure at Phase 3 when they can:*
>
> - *find from a display all or most Phase 2 and 3 graphemes when given the sound;*
> - *blend and read CVC words consisting of Phase 2 and 3 graphemes;*
> - *segment and make a phonemically plausible attempt at spelling CVC words using Phase 2 and 3 graphemes.*

(DCSF, 2009a, p.15)

> *Children are secure at Phase 4 when they can:*
>
> - *give the sound when shown any Phase 2 and Phase 3 graphemes;*
> - *find from a display any Phase 2 and 3 grapheme when given the sound;*
> - *blend and read words containing adjacent consonants;*
> - *segment and spell words containing adjacent consonants.*

(DCSF, 2009a, p.15)

> *Children are secure at Phase 5 when they can:*
>
> - *give the sound when shown any grapheme that has been taught;*
> - *write the common graphemes for any given sound;*
> - *use phonic skill and knowledge as the prime approach to reading and spelling unfamiliar words, including those that are not completely decodable;*
> - *read and spell phonically decodable two-syllable and three-syllable words.*

(DCSF, 2009a, p.16)

As the guidance points out,

> - *{t}he majority of the evidence for the {statements} above can be gathered cumulatively during the daily discrete phonics sessions, particularly during the 'revisit and review' and 'apply' sections. Teachers and practitioners should also, of course, collect additional evidence from their observations of children reading independently, for example in guided reading sessions or in the book corner, or from their writing, either in guided writing sessions or in independent activities.*

(DCSF, 2009a, p.6)

Ofsted (2014, p.20), in a survey of 12 schools showing good practice in assessment, cite a case study of one school which includes phonics:

> *Each class had an identical folder and the contents were in line with what was expected by school leaders – set out in the school's 'non-negotiables'.*
>
> *The folders included guided reading records from Nursery to Year 6, including what was planned, plus the pupils' responses. These were assessed against particular assessment foci and were very thorough and detailed. The Year 6 plans in particular showed that there was a high degree of challenge and expectation of a very mature response from the pupils.*
>
> *Also included were the benchmarking tests for reading and comprehension, reading levels assessed against national curriculum levels, high frequency words checklists and spelling check lists.*
>
> *Folders for younger classes also included a phonics phase tracker and phase assessment grids, plus spelling tests.*
>
> *The cohort action plan was also included as well as reviews of progress for pupils entitled to free school meals.*

Figure 11.2 provides an example of a phonics tracking sheet.

One of the most critical factors is for children to have meaningful opportunities to practise, consolidate and extend their phonic skills and knowledge in a broad range of contexts, and particularly for the Foundation Stage, both indoors and outdoors and throughout the day. Observation of children's achievements in self-initiated activities will help affirm the observations made during adult-led phonics, reading and writing sessions.

Individual assessment

Where teachers have not been able to gather sufficient information from observations to provide a clear picture of children's achievements, or have concerns about a particular child, a more focused adult-led assessment may be undertaken. This can be done in the following ways:

Graphemes and phonemes

- Provide a list of graphemes taught (not in alphabetical order) and ask children to tell you the sounds they make.
- Dictate some letters and appropriate words from taught phonemes for children to write.

Class: Year 2 - Mrs C
Teacher/Practitioner: 2013-14

Progression		Autumn		Spring		Summer	
Phase 1 continuous through Phase 2-6 *Show awareness of rhyme and alliteration. Distinguish between different sounds in the environment and phonemes. Explore and experiment with sounds and words.*	Phase 6 (Year 2) *Working on: recognising phonic irregularities and becoming more secure with less common grapheme-phoneme correspondences. Working on: applying phonic skills and knowledge to recognise and spell an increasing number of complex words.*						Y2
	Phase 5 (Year 1) *Working on: reading phonically decodable two-syllable and three-syllable words.* *Working on: using alternative ways of pronouncing and spelling the graphemes corresponding to the long vowel phonemes.* *Working on: spelling complex words using phonically plausible attempts.*	KL KN CT LT RL IM KR HN AR SS JU	KL KN JT CT LT LB RL IM JS KR HN GR AR HL KWR SS OR OL JU JW CM MB SS AR				Y1
	Phase 4 (Year R/Year 1) *Working on: segmenting adjacent consonants in words and applying this in spelling.* *Working on: blending adjacent consonants in words and applying this skill when reading unfamiliar texts.*	HL KWR OR OL JW CM JT MB LB SS GR AR	JS			YR/Y1	
	Phase 3 (Year R) *Working on: Knowing one grapheme for each of the 43 phonemes* *Working on: reading and spelling a wide range of CVC words using all letters and less frequent consonant digraphs and some long vowel phonemes.* Graphemes: ear, air, ure, er, ar, or, ur, ow, oi, ai, ee, igh, oa, oo *Working on: reading and spelling CVC words using a wider range of letters, short vowels, some consonant digraphs and double letters.* Consonant digraphs ch, sh, th, ng *Working on: reading and spelling CVC words using letters and short vowels.* Letter progression Set 7: y, z, zz, qu Set 6: j, v, w, x	DA BS BR JS	DA BS BR				
	Phase 2 *Working on: Using common consonants and vowels blending for reading and segmenting for spelling simple CVC words.* *Working on: Knowing that words are constructed from phonemes and that phonemes are represented by graphemes.* Letter progression: Set 5: h, b, f, ff, l, ll, ss Set 4: ck, e, u, r Set 3: g, o, c, k Set 2: l, n, m, d Set 1: s, a, t, p						
	Phase 1 (7 Aspects) *Working on: Showing awareness of rhyme and alliteration, distinguishing between different sounds in the environment and phonemes, exploring and experimenting with sounds and words and discriminating speech sounds in words. Beginning to orally blend and segment phonemes.*						

Figure 11.2 *Example of a phonics progress tracking sheet*

Assessing blending skills

- For this, reading non-words is useful in testing their knowledge of phonemes taught. The teacher demonstrates by reading some and stating clearly that they are nonsense words. This is a useful activity in mastering the process of sounding and blending phonemes and demonstrating this, but is only useful for this purpose and, of course, will not assess their comprehension skills. Non-words, or pseudo-words, are used in the DfE phonics screening check for six-year-olds.

Phonics screening check

To assess children's progress, a statutory requirement was introduced in 2012 for children towards the end of Year 1 (age six) to have their phonic knowledge and understanding screened (DfE, 2012). The purpose of the screening check is to assess whether children have achieved the age-expected level of understanding of phonics and to identify children who may be struggling in developing phonics skills. For those children not achieving the expected level, the aim is to provide additional support, as intervention at an early stage is more effective in helping children to achieve good literacy skills.

The screening check contains 40 words, divided into two sections of 20 words each. Both of the sections contain a mixture of real and pseudo (made-up) words. The pseudo-words are designed to test children's ability to know the corresponding phonemes (or sounds) for the graphemes (letters), and also to be able to blend these into whole units or words. The ability to blend sounds is a crucial skill in reading and therefore both aspects need to be assessed. A child may read some words by sight because they are familiar to him or her, while reading pseudo-words aims to test the skill of blending sounds to decode words more accurately.

All the pseudo-words are introduced to children as 'alien' words and there is a picture shown next to each of these words in the check to show an imaginary creature to clearly demarcate these. It is important for children to practise this and ensure that they know these are not real words.

Section 1 of the screening check contains words with a simpler structure, using words with single letters and common consonant and vowel combinations. Section 2 has a variety of more complex structures (such as words which contain blends of three consonants) and/or a split digraph (a sound that is represented by two letters and split by a consonant, e.g. 'tape'), or words with trigraphs (three letters representing one sound, e.g. 'hair', 'air', 'pear').

The expectation for competence in phonics by the end of Year 1 is that children should be able to decode all words (and non-words) containing:

- simple structures with single letters and consonant digraphs (e.g. *clap*)
- two consonants together and a vowel (e.g. CVCC *band* or CCVC *plan*)

Children should also be able to decode most words (and non-words) containing:

- frequent vowel digraphs (e.g. *tray*);
- a single consonant string (e.g. *clip*);
- two consonant strings and a vowel (e.g. CCVCC *clump*).

In addition, children should be able to decode some words (and non-words) containing:

- less frequent vowel digraphs and split digraphs (e.g. *screw* and *tune*);
- a single three-consonant string (e.g. *strap*);
- two syllables (e.g. *cabin*).

The check is administered by an adult (usually a teacher), individually with each child. The child's response to each word is recorded on the mark sheet, denoting if correct or incorrect and any comments noted against incorrect answers, for example, if a child reads some sounds correctly but not all, or if a child tries to give a real word instead of a pseudo-word. The adult can point to whole words, but should not point in a way to support decoding the word.

For more guidance on administering the check and how it is scored, there is a training video available on the Department for Education website at: www.gov.uk/government/publications/ phonics-screening-check-sample-materials-and-training-video (accessed 03/05/18).

Research Focus: The phonics screening check

The introduction of this 'check' (DfE, 2012) for young children aged six has caused considerable controversy. Psychologists at the University of Oxford and the University of York, in a study to evaluate the validity of the check, found that it while it does identify children who may be falling behind, it does not provide teachers with additional information beyond other assessments that are already commonly used (University of Oxford, 2013). It also has disadvantages in terms of the costs incurred and the tendency for schools to teach 'to the test'. Setting the level high for children to meet the required standard, can also cause unnecessary concern for parents and put pressure on young children.

There have also been a number of objections to the statutory nature of the check, with concerns about the resource implications of mandatory testing and the negative consequences when such tests become 'high-stakes' (e.g. Association of Teachers and Lecturers, 2011; Brooks, 2010). A survey of nearly 3,000 teachers, conducted after the administration of the check but before its results, reported that 87 per cent of respondents did not agree with the

$\longrightarrow$

statutory implementation of the check and thought that it should be discontinued (ATL/NAHT/ NUT, 2012). Duff et al. argue that

> *combining our observations about the integrity of the national phonics screening check data with our findings that teachers perform reliable and sensitive assessments of phonics progression, we argue in favour of using resources to continue to train and support teachers in the knowledge, assessment and teaching of early literacy skills.*

> *(2012, p.11)*

Darnell et al. (2017) have questioned the methodology of the screening check and whether the testing of 85 grapheme–phoneme correspondences it is based on is effective. They found that:

> *The GPCs assessed, therefore, do not reflect the full range of GPCs that it is expected will be taught within a systematic synthetic phonics approach. Furthermore, children's ability to decode real words is dependent on their vocabulary knowledge, not just their phonic skills. These results question the purpose and validity of the phonics screening check and the role of synthetic phonics for teaching early reading.*

> *(2017, p.505)*

The inclusion of pseudo-words, or nonsense words, continues to cause considerable debate. Tal and Siegel (1996, p.224) maintain that 'the ability to decode pseudo-words indicates to what extent a child has mastered alphabetic mapping'. However, Gibson and England (2016) argue that the inclusion of pseudo-words within the phonics screening check is based on an assumption that an early ability to read these is associated with later success in reading. This is backed up by research on word identification and pseudo-words fluency tests with Year 1 pupils by Fuchs et al. (2004, p.7), who concluded that the research 'demonstrated the superiority of word identification fluency over nonsense word fluency'. Gibson and England (2016) draw on evidence from comparative European orthographic studies employing pseudo-words and found that in languages such as German, where the correspondence between graphemes and phonemes is more straightforward, there was an advantage is reading nonsense words. However, for English there are some issues. First, there are words that are rare, but are actually real words, such as 'splok', which is used in urban slang to mean the impairment of the ability to smell. Second, they cite the issue of pronunciation so that a pseudo-word such as 'jound' could be pronounced to rhyme with 'found' or 'wound' and such alternatives are not accounted for in the marking guidance. The third issue cited is the difficulty that may be caused by pupils' accents, and while the guidance says that a child's accent should be taken into account, a teacher may have a preference for Received Pronunciation and mark accordingly. The debate over the use of pseudo-words is complex; however, the screening check is mandatory and schools need to prepare children, ensuring a balance between having fun with children with nonsense words and preparing them for the check and yet not putting undue emphasis on them to ensure that success in reading is concerned with deriving meaning from text.

$\longrightarrow$

In order to respond to criticism, the Department for Education published a research report on the check conducted by the National Foundation for Educational Research (NFER) (Walker et al., 2013) which provides evidence of teachers being positive about teaching phonics, although views on the check were mixed and those interviewed claimed that the check would have minimal impact on the standard of reading as it told them nothing they did not know already. A further study published by the DfE/NFER in 2015 reiterated this and concluded that although this revealed that the screening check has had an impact on pupils' attainment in phonics, it had not as yet demonstrated improved attainment in literacy. Results published by the DfE (2017) showed that 81 per cent of pupils met the expected standard of phonic decoding in 2017, which was an increase from 69 per cent in 2013 and from 58 per cent in 2012. The DfE has also provided guidance on how teachers should respond to the results, together with an outline of methods of support for children who did not achieve the required result (DfE, 2013).

Activity

Reading non-words

Now check your phonic knowledge using the grid of non-words in Table 11.1 and rearrange these in the correct columns according to their sounds.

Table 11.1   Phonics for non-word exercises

/ae/ (day)	/oe/ (cold)	/ie/ (tie)	/ee/ (tree)	/ur/ (burn)
laiv	slone	hieb	leat	spay
weaf	poat	reeb	leem	diep
tirl	dight	libe	hie	terv

The correct arrangement is: /ae/ (day): laiv, spay; /oe/ (cold): slone, poat; /ie/ (tie): hieb, dight, libe, hie; /ee/ (tree): leat, leem, weaf, diep, reeb; /ur/ (burn): tirl, terv.

Assessing segmenting skills

Assessing segmenting skills can be done in the following ways:

- by pronouncing a word and asking the child to repeat it and then to tell you the sounds from first to last (or using phoneme fingers as described above);

- by pronouncing a word, asking the child to repeat it and then select appropriate magnetic letters to make the word;

- by asking the child to write the word you say after repeating it.

Group testing of phonic skills

There are also some commercial tests that allow teachers to conduct them with larger groups (for examples, see Johnson and Watson, 2007). These principally consist of sentences with a word missing and the child selects the appropriate word by putting a circle around it. For example:

> The cat sat in the ... (*road, rode*)

Intervention

Assessing and tracking children's progress is necessary in order to support those children who may not have fully grasped some phonemes and the corresponding graphemes.

It is important to consider carefully before withdrawing children from whole-class phonics teaching if they seem to be progressing at a slower pace. They will benefit from the whole-class experience of blending and segmenting and hearing a range of phonemes, in addition to vocabulary development. Further support may be provided individually or in small groups as necessary to supplement this.

When undertaking any intervention programme, it is first important to base this on accurate assessment of the children's needs. It is also important that the children recognise that the goal of all phonics lessons is to achieve fluent word recognition and effortless reading and writing. There is a need, therefore, to continually apply the learning to reading and writing, both during the phonics session and in guided reading and writing sessions, and across the curriculum.

Intervention programmes

One intervention programme based on *Letters and Sounds* (DfES, 2007) is aimed at Key Stage 2 pupils who demonstrate difficulties in reading and writing. The materials are designed to guide teachers, and suitably trained teaching assistants (TAs), in supporting children who may have poorly developed phonic knowledge, skills and understanding. As the programme states:

> {f}or some children, the missing piece of the jigsaw may be specific items of knowledge that require only a few weeks of short, focused sessions. However, other children may not have crucial concepts such as blending and segmenting in place. Some may have a combination of the two and will require a term or more of consolidation. It is crucial, therefore, that

the children's current knowledge is accurately assessed and the gaps identified so that support can be precisely targeted.

(DCSF, 2009b, p.i)

The programme consists of the following steps:

Step 1: Assess current knowledge from a bank of assessment materials.

Step 2: Identify the need and select the appropriate unit (see overview of Units 2, 3, 4 and 5 below).

Step 3: Teach during regular, short, focused sessions.

Step 4: Assess and then prioritise the next section to teach.

The units

- *Unit 2 linked to Phase 2, Letters and Sounds*: Grapheme–phoneme correspondences (GPCs), blending and segmenting; knowledge of the alphabet and letter names.

- *Unit 3 linked to Phase 3, Letters and Sounds*: Consolidation of Phase 2; phonemes consisting of two or more letters (digraphs).

- *Unit 4 linked to Phase 4, Letters and Sounds*: Consolidation of Phase 2 and Phase 3; reading and spelling words containing adjacent consonants and polysyllabic words (*creep*, *bring*, *starlight*).

- *Unit 5 linked to Phase 5, Letters and Sounds*: Consolidation of Phase 2, Phase 3 and Phase 4; alternative spellings for phonemes (/ai/ as in *day*, *came*, *rain*) and alternative pronunciations for graphemes (*ea* as in *eat*, *bread*, *great*).

As Phase 5 is likely to be the area of greatest need at Key Stage 2, this phase has been broken down into four sections, each including groups of graphemes which are most commonly confused by children at Key Stage 2. There is no expectation that all four sections are covered if children are insecure in only one or two. It is important that the specific phonemes/graphemes, which have been identified through assessment as being unknown or confused, are taught directly and applied in reading and writing (DCSF, 2009b, p.3).

Another intervention programme, *Quick Fix for Phonics* (Jolliffe, 2012), provides a three-step catch up procedure to support children needing to improve their phonic knowledge and skills. The steps are:

1. Diagnostic assessment activities to enable accurate evaluation of a child's current level of phonic knowledge.

2. Revisiting consonants and short vowel phonemes with a series of multi-sensory lesson plans.

3. Revisiting long vowel phonemes to support children's understanding of the more complex phonemes and their alternative spellings with a range of activities and lesson plans.

Planning for intervention

It is vital that for those pupils requiring intervention, thorough planning based on the findings of recent assessment is undertaken. This planning should aim to provide daily, systematic phonics teaching. However, it should also take into account wider reading and writing targets for those children who require additional assistance. For those pupils needing intervention, phonics should not only be tackled in isolation but should also be addressed within the wider teaching of reading and writing. The Rose Review summarised the features of effective intervention as follows:

> {N}o matter which provision is applied, the most successful intervention arrangements were planned as part of the total programme for teaching reading and monitored carefully.

> (2006, para.162, p.49)

Therefore, in addition to discrete phonics intervention provision, children should be supported in their learning of phonics while involved in all reading and writing activities.

Grouping and intervention

Effective intervention can often be carried out by teaching those children identified as needing additional support in small groups. It is important that the children in these groups are of a similar ability in order to provide the most suitable support for each individual. Planning for these individuals or groups should be carried out by the class teacher as part of the wider class planning for phonics in order to promote consistency and a systematic approach. It is also important that the adults who lead the intervention groups should maintain records and provide feedback to the class teacher to inform future planning and target-setting. Grouping arrangements may include:

- Additional lessons in small groups, before the lesson to prepare children or after the main lesson to help them catch up. This may be done by the class teacher or teaching assistant.

- One-to-one work with a trained teaching assistant.

- A group of children who are at the same level in reading or phase in *Letters and Sounds* being taught together so that the teaching can focus closely on their needs. This could be arranged across several classes in Key Stage 1. If trained teaching assistants were also involved in this teaching time, then those pupils below target or requiring intervention could be taught in smaller groups.

- Especially in Reception, a mixed-ability class being divided towards the latter part of the academic year for phonic work to enable the younger or less able children to make good progress before Year 1.

- Support for a child or a small group of children within a lesson.

Another important strategy is to ensure that children's literacy learning is developed throughout the curriculum so that attention might be drawn to letter–sound correspondences which occur in vocabulary related to, say, history and science where these have also been taught in literacy lessons. This serves to reinforce the importance and relevance of phonic knowledge as well as developing a more extensive vocabulary.

Activity

Deciding on appropriate intervention

Read the following case study of one pupil who is falling behind his peers:

James is five and has been receiving systematic phonics instruction for nearly 12 months. He has mastered Phases 2 and 3 quite easily and has managed quite well at Phase 4, but now he is working at Phase 5 and gets very confused at the different graphemes for long vowel phonemes. He is reluctant to practise and doesn't seem to enjoy either reading or writing. He is keen at drawing and can represent stories though drawings. His teacher has talked to his parents and discovered he is fascinated with dinosaurs. She decides to use these interests to engage James more in learning phonics, but she is unsure how to do this.

Suggest some ways in which James could be supported both to engage meaningfully with decodable texts and to recall the long vowel digraphs and their alternative spellings.

James needs support through the use of techniques such as mnemonics and multi-sensory teaching to recall the long vowel phonemes. Where this can be linked to a context and a specific interest – in this case dinosaurs – this will provide engagement. Working with James to create his own reading book about dinosaurs, which includes decodable text at his phonic ability level, is one way of doing this.

Research Focus: The Clackmannanshire Study

Implementation

Johnston and Watson found only very low levels of underachievement when a synthetic phonics programme is well implemented. The study carried out in Clackmannanshire, Scotland (Johnston and Watson, 2005) looked at 300 children in the first year of the Scottish primary school system. They compared three different teaching methods: synthetic phonics, analytic phonics, and an analytic phonics method that included systematic phonemic awareness teaching. At the end of the programme, those children who had been taught by synthetic phonics were found to be seven months ahead of the other two groups in reading. While this research has been criticised for not providing sufficient evidence for synthetic phonics (Wyse and Goswami, 2008), there has been further research on the long-term impact of this study on these children at ten years old (Johnston et al., 2012). This found that the group taught by synthetic phonics had better word reading, spelling and reading comprehension skills and therefore the impact was sustained.

Interventions delivered by classroom assistants

A study of Savage and Carless (2008) explored whether the effects of interventions delivered by classroom assistants (CAs) were still evident at the end of the first phase of schooling, 16 months after the early intervention finished. Children in the study were indistinguishable from national averages at Key Stage 1 on the mathematics test, writing test and reading task performance, but differed on the reading comprehension test and on teacher-assessed attainment. Gains in reading following early phonic reading interventions delivered by CAs were maintained for many children. Savage and Carless conclude:

> In drawing this article together, the present results provide the first evidence of the extent of long-term effectiveness of one form of CA-delivered early reading intervention. Our key finding is that more than half of initially at-risk children who responded to interventions later achieved national average performance on the reading task and the reading comprehension test, whereas less than a quarter of those who could not decode at the end of interventions achieved at the same KS1 level. Success in literacy tasks at the end of KS1 was thus closely associated with the early emergence of decoding skills. We would argue that there is now a clear theoretical and practical need for evidence on various dimensions of CA-delivered interventions in order to meet the needs of those children who did not respond strongly to the intervention, and to provide the additional strategies to allow all treatment responders to reach national average levels of reading comprehension.

> (2008, p.382)

→

Teacher subject knowledge

Hatcher et al. (2006), in a randomised control trial, found that teachers may not possess sufficient and/or accurate knowledge to teach struggling readers. Results indicated a lack of teacher knowledge, specifically highlighting weaknesses in the areas of terminology, phonic knowledge, and phoneme and morpheme awareness, all of which are needed to effectively instruct struggling readers.

Case Study: A support programme at Kingsley

Review the case study below from the Ofsted *Reading by Six* report and note the 'layers of assessment' described, together with the personalised support for each pupil that provides for effective teaching and learning of phonics.

The approach here is described as intensive, methodical and relentless, with no exceptions. If the teaching isn't working for a particular child, the school will seek an alternative way to get through, even buying materials for a single child.

There are layers of assessment. First, all class teachers are responsible for their pupils' progress. Pupils' targets are the teachers' performance management targets. Children are regularly assessed against checklists of letters and sounds. These are supplemented by end of year assessment, when all the year groups are checked against the milestone for the year group. The pupils who have not reached the milestone are identified and listed. Each individual on the list has a 'progression map' and a personalised learning plan or individual education plan. The detail is written into daily plans for support workers.

(Ofsted, 2010, p.27)

Learning Outcomes Review

This chapter has detailed methods of assessment, including the statutory phonics screening check, and provided examples of intervention programmes, together with case studies. The importance of ongoing regular assessment in different ways has been stressed, together with methods of individual assessment where there are particular concerns about a child's progress. One of the keys to successful phonics teaching is to embed assessment into teaching and to track each child's development carefully.

(Continued)

> (Continued)
>
> **Self-assessment questions**
>
> 1. Name some ways in which teachers can clearly note children's progress during lessons.
> 2. Name a method of testing children's ability to blend phonemes.
> 3. Consider how a tracking grid to note children's progress could inform the organisation of teaching.

Further Reading

A clear rationale about the importance of ongoing assessment can be found in:

The Rose Review (2006) Independent Review of the Teaching of Early Reading: Final Report. Nottingham: DfES.

For further guidance on tracking, see:

DCSF (2009a) *Phonics: Assessment and Tracking Guidance* (Ref: 00906-2009PDF-EN-01). London: DCSF.

More ideas on tracking and assessment can be found in Chapter 11 of:

Waugh, D. and Harrison-Palmer, R. (2013) *Teaching Systematic Synthetic Phonics: Audit and Test*. Exeter: Learning Matters.

References

Association of Teachers and Lecturers (2011) *Year One Phonics Screening Check: Response from the Association of Teachers and Lecturers*. Available from: www.atl.org.uk/Images/2011%20%20 Y1_phonics_test_consultation_response.pdf (accessed 5/2/15).

ATL/NAHT/NUT (2012) *Teachers' and Head Teachers' Views of the Year One Phonics Screening Check*. Available from: www.teachers.org.uk/phonics (accessed 5/2/15).

Brooks, G. (2010) *The Government's Proposed Decoding Test for 6-year-olds*. Available from: www. ukla.org/news/professor_greg_brooks_critiques_the_governments_proposed_decoding_test_ for_/ (accessed 5/2/15).

Darnell, C.A., Solity, J.E. and Wall, H. (2017) 'Decoding the phonics screening check', *British Educational Research Journal*, *43* (3), 505–27.

DCSF (2009a) *Phonics: Assessment and Tracking Guidance* (Ref: 00906-2009PDF-EN-01). London: DCSF.

DCSF (2009b) *The National Strategies KS2 Phonics Intervention Programme* (Ref: 01058-2009DOC-EN-01). London: DCSF.

DfE (2011) *Teachers' Standards in England from September 2012*. London: DfE.

DfE (2012) *Year One Phonics Screening Check Framework*. London: DfE. Available from www.gov.uk/government/collections/phonics-screening-check-administration (accessed 22/12/12).

DfE (2013) *The Phonics Screening Check: Responding to the Results*. Available from: www.gov.uk/government/publications/phonics-screening-check-responding-to-the-results (accessed 25/7/13).

DfE (2017) *Phonics screening check and Key Stage 1 assessments in England*. Available from: https://assets.publishing.service.gov.uk/government/uploads/system/uploads/attachment_data/file/654859/Phonics_KS1_SFR_Text_2017_.pdf (accessed 3/5/18).

DfES (2007) *Letters and Sounds: Notes of Guidance for Practitioners and Teachers*. Norwich: DfES.

DfE/NFER (2014) *Phonics Screening Check Evaluation*. Available from: www.gov.uk/government/publications (accessed 5/2/15).

Duff, F.J., Fieldsend, E., Bowyer-Crane, C., Hulme, C., Smith, G., Giffs, S. and Snowling, M.J. (2008) 'Reading with vocabulary intervention: Evaluation of an instruction for children with poor response to reading intervention', *Journal of Research in Reading*, *31* (3): 319–36.

Fuchs, L.S., Fuchs, D. and Compton, D.L. (2004) 'Monitoring early reading development in first grade: Word identification fluency versus nonsense word fluency', *Exceptional Children*, *71*: 7–21.

Gibson, H. and England, J. (2016) 'The inclusion of pseudowords within the year one phonics screening check in English primary schools', *Cambridge Journal of Education*, *46* (4): 491–507.

Hatcher, P.J., Hulme, C., Miles, J.N.V., Carroll, J.M., Hatcher, J., Gibbs, S., Smith, G., Bowyer-Crane, C. and Snowling, M.J. (2006) 'Efficacy of small-group reading intervention for beginning readers with reading delay: A randomised control trial', *Journal of Child Psychology and Psychiatry*, *47*: 820–27.

Johnston, R. and Watson, J. (2005) *The Effects of Synthetic Phonics Teaching on Reading and Spelling Attainment: A Seven Year Longitudinal Study*. Edinburgh: Scottish Executive.

Johnston, R. and Watson, J. (2007) *Teaching Synthetic Phonics*. Exeter: Learning Matters.

Johnston, R.S., McGeown, S. and Watson, J.E. (2012) 'Long-term effects of synthetic versus analytic phonics teaching on the reading and spelling ability of 10 year old boys and girls', *Reading and Writing*, *25* (6): 1365–84.

Jolliffe, W. (2012) *Quick Fix for Phonics*. Witney: Scholastic.

Ofsted (2010) *Reading by Six*. Manchester: Ofsted.

Ofsted (2011) *Removing Barriers to Literacy*. Manchester: Ofsted. Available from http:/dera.ioe.ac.uk/2152/1/Removing%20barriers%20to%20literacy.pdf (accessed 9/5/18).

Ofsted (2014) *Ready to read. How a sample of primary schools in Stoke-on-Trent teach children to read.* Available from: https://www.gov.uk/government/publications/ready-to-read-how-a-sample-of-primary-schools-in-stoke-on-trent-teach-pupils-to-read. (accessed 3/5/18).

Rose, J. (2006) *Independent Review of the Teaching of Early Reading, Final Report, March 2006* (The Rose Review – Ref: 0201-2006DOC-EN). Nottingham: DfES.

Savage, R. and Carless, S. (2008) 'The impact of early reading interventions delivered by classroom assistants on attainment at the end of Year 2', *British Educational Research Journal*, *34* (3): 363–85.

Tal, N.F., and Siegel, L.S. (1996) 'Pseudoword reading errors of poor, dyslexic, and normally achieving readers on multisyllable pseudowords', *Applied Psycholinguists*, 5: 215–32.

University of Oxford (2013) *First Study of Government's Phonics Check Finds it is a Valid but Unnecessary Test.* Available from: www.psy.ox.ac.uk/news/first-study-of-government2019s-phonics-check-finds-it-is-a-valid-but-unnecessary-test+&cd=1&hl=en&ct=clnk&gl=uk (accessed 22/12/14).

Walker, M., Bartlett, S., Betts, H., Sainsbury, M. and Mehta, P. (2013) *Evaluation of the Phonics Screening Check: First Interim Report.* NFER/DfE Publications. Available from: www.education.gov.uk/researchandstatistics/research (accessed 9/5/18).

Wyse, D. and Goswami, U. (2008). 'Synthetic phonics and the teaching of reading', *British Educational Research Journal*, *34* (6): 691–710.

Audit and test

Work through each section below, responding to each question or task. When you have completed each section, you can read the answers at the end of the chapter.

Section 1: Key terminology for a systematic and structured programme

It is important that you understand the terms below before you move on to the next activity. Provide a definition of each and check your definitions against those at the end of the chapter:

- Formative assessment

- Diagnostic assessment

- Tracking pupil progress

- Over-learning

- Pseudo-words

- Word recognition

- Language comprehension

Section 2: The Simple View of Reading

The Simple View of Reading makes it clear that reading necessitates word recognition processes as well as language comprehension processes.

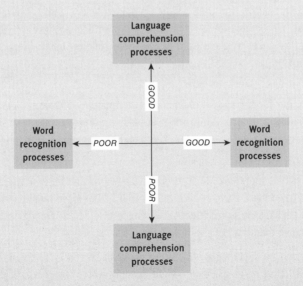

Figure 11.3 The Simple View of Reading

Source: Rose, 2006, p.53.

Read the profiles of each of the four children below and decide in which quadrant each should be placed in the Simple View of Reading above, based on their word recognition and language comprehension abilities. Also, consider what you could do to develop their reading skills further.

Amy does not enjoy listening to stories. She has a limited knowledge of grapheme–phoneme correspondences and finds blending to decode a challenge. She says, 'I don't like books. I can't read them and I get bored when Mr Thomas reads us stories because I get distracted.'

Harry enjoys having books read to him and he is able to talk about the content. He is not yet able to decode words for himself. He says, 'I like listening to stories and looking at books. It is hard to read them myself though.'

Richard is able to read fluently and is keen to answer questions about the content of books. Occasionally, he has difficulty with text that requires specialist knowledge. He says, 'I like reading books by Michael Morpurgo because his characters are very believable. Sometimes his books make me laugh and sometimes they make me sad.'

Harprit is able to decode words on the page but she finds it difficult to make sense of what she has read. She says, 'When we have guided reading, the other children can answer questions about the book but I find this hard.'

Section 3: Assessing and tracking pupils' progress.

The tracking sheet in Figure 11.4 is useful for monitoring children's progress. Children can be assessed on a half-termly basis, using the *Letters and Sounds* progress checks (DCSF, 2009a, Appendix 3, pp.197–207). If they are deemed to be secure in a phase, they are placed in the next phase on the tracking sheet.

Use the assessment information on the three children provided below, and the *Letters and Sounds* guidance on what children should be able to do to be secure in a particular phase (in Figure 11.5), to decide which phase on the tracker sheet to place each of the three children for the second half of the spring term (highlighted column).

Sarah is able to segment and spell most CVC words using Phase 2 and 3 graphemes. When shown a grapheme, she is able to provide the correct phoneme for the majority of Phase 2 and 3 graphemes. Sarah can easily sound out and blend to read CVC words using Phase 2 and 3 graphemes. She is just starting to read some words containing adjacent consonants. She has difficulty with segmenting to spell words that contain adjacent consonants.

Eden is able to use his phonic knowledge to read unfamiliar words and he is now reading both two- and three-syllable words. He has a good grasp of all the GPCs that he has been taught and is able to use them in both his reading and spelling. He is confident with his use of different graphemes for long vowel phonemes and is starting to use them correctly in his spelling.

Mary has developed a good understanding of adjacent consonants and is able to read many words that contain them. She is also starting to use them when spelling words. Mary has a good grasp of all the GPCs taught in Phase 2 and 3.

Are there any children who have not made any progress over the year so far?

Class:

Teacher/Practitioner: 2013–14

Progression			Autumn		Spring		Summer	
Phase 6 – throughout Year 2 *Working on: Recognising phonic irregularities. and becoming more secure with less common grapheme–phoneme correspondences* *Working on: Applying phonic skills and knowledge to recognise and spell an increasing number of complex words. SEE SUPPORT FOR SPELLING*						Michael Abby Heather	Y2	
Phase 5 – throughout Year 1 up to 30 weeks *Working on: Reading phonically decodable two-syllable and three-syllable words.* *Working on: Using alternative ways of pronouncing and spelling the graphemes corresponding to the long vowel phonemes.* *Working on: Spelling complex words using phonically plausible attempts.*				Michael Abby	Michael Abby Heather Craig **Eden** Andrew Steven	Craig Andrew Steven Matthew Anne	Y1	
Phase 4 – (Year R/Year 1) 4–6 weeks *Working on: Segmenting adjacent consonants in words and applying this in spelling.* *Working on: Blending adjacent consonants in words and applying this skill when reading unfamiliar texts.*			Heather Craig Eden Abby Michael Andrew Steven	Heather Craig Eden Andrew Steven Susan Lily	Susan Lily John S Peter **Mary** Matthew Anne	Susan Lily John S Peter Rosie John R	YR/Y1	
	Phase 3 (Year R) up to 12 weeks	*Working on: Reading and spelling a wide range of CVC words using all letters and less frequent consonant digraphs and some long vowel phonemes.* Graphemes: ear, air, ure, er, ar, or, ur, ow, oi, ai, ee, igh, oa, oo *Working on: Reading and spelling CVC words using a wider range of letters, short vowels, some consonant digraphs and double letters.* Consonant digraphs ch, sh, th, ng *Working on: Reading and spelling CVC words using letters and short vowels.* Letter progression Set 7: y, z, zz, qu Set 6: j, v, w, x	John S Peter Mary Lily Matthew Anne Susan Sarah Harry Rosie	John S Peter Mary Matthew Anne Sarah Harry Rosie John R	**Sarah** Harry Rosie John R Rebecca David	Rebecca David Harry		
	Phase 2 – up to 6 weeks *Working on: Using common consonants and vowels. Blending for reading and segmenting for spelling simple CVC words.* *Working on: Knowing that words are constructed from phonemes and that phonemes are represented by graphemes.* Letter progression: Set 5: h, b, f, ff, l, ll, ss Set 4: ck, e, u, r Set 3: g, o, c, k Set 2: i, n, m, d Set 1: s, a, t, p		John R Rebecca David	Rebecca David				
Phase 1 (7 Aspects) – throughout all phases *Working on: Showing awareness of rhyme and alliteration, distinguishing between different sounds in the environment and phonemes, exploring and experimenting with sounds and words and discriminating speech sounds in words. Beginning to orally blend and segment phonemes.*								

(Left margin vertical text: Phase 1 continuous through Phase 2–6. Distinguish between different sounds in the environment and phonemes. Explore and experiment with sounds and words. Show awareness of rhyme and alliteration. Working on: Knowing one grapheme for each of the 43 phonemes.)

Figure 11.4 Phonic progress tracking sheet – Early Years Foundation Stage through Key Stage 1

Children are secure at Phase 3 when they can:

- find from a display all or most Phase 2 and 3 graphemes when given the sound;
- blend and read CVC words consisting of Phase 2 and 3 graphemes;
- segment and make a phonemically plausible attempt at spelling CVC words using Phase 2 and 3 graphemes.

(DCSF, 2009a, p.15)

Children are secure at Phase 4 when they can:

- give the sound when shown any Phase 2 and Phase 3 graphemes;
- find from a display any Phase 2 and 3 grapheme when given the sound;
- blend and read words containing adjacent consonants;
- segment and spell words containing adjacent consonants.

(DCSF, 2009a, p.15)

Children are secure at Phase 5 when they can:

- give the sound when shown any grapheme that has been taught;
- write the common graphemes for any given sound;
- use phonic skill and knowledge as the prime approach to reading and spelling unfamiliar words, including those that are not completely decodable;
- read and spell phonically decodable two-syllable and three-syllable words.

(DCSF, 2009a, p.16)

Figure 11.5 Assessing when children are secure in phases

Section 4: The Year 1 screening check

Look at each of the following statements about the Year 1 screening check and decide whether they are true or false.

1. The screening check can be done as a group assessment.

2. There is no time limit for the screening check.

3. There is a set week for schools to administer the phonics screening check.

4. Children need to read all of the words correctly to reach the expected standard for the check.

5. A teaching assistant may administer the screening check.

6. The screening check forms part of schools' statutory assessment and reporting arrangements.

7. The screening check can be stopped part way through if it is evident that the child is struggling with it.

8. All children in Year 1 must take the check, regardless of their ability in phonics.

9. If a child is absent when the test is administered, they can't do it at another time.

10. Teachers must tell parents whether or not their child has met the required standard.

11. The check must be administered to children in Year 2 if they did not take the check in Year 1 or if they did not reach the expected standard when they took the test in Year 1.

12. The screening check includes pseudo-words in order to prevent bias to those with a good vocabulary knowledge or visual memory of words.

ANSWERS

Section 1: Key terminology for a systematic and structured programme

You were asked to define each of the key terms below.

Formative assessment

Forms an integral part of teaching and learning. It contributes to learning through providing feedback and should inform future planning and next steps.

Diagnostic assessment

Assesses the nature of difficulties that a child might have.

Tracking pupil progress

Involves using assessments to identify children who may need additional support. It is also used to inform the organisation of phonic work. It is designed to make sure all children make maximum progress.

Pseudo-words

These are nonsense words which are used to assess children's ability to decode.

Word recognition

The ability to read the words on the page.

Language comprehension

The ability to understand oral and written language.

Section 2: The Simple View of Reading

You were asked to decide in which quadrant the four children should be placed in the Simple View of Reading, based on their word recognition and language comprehension abilities. You were also asked to consider what you could do to develop their reading skills further.

Amy: has poor word recognition and poor comprehension skills.

Support needed:

- Phonics and language immersion
- A systematic, synthetic phonics programme
- Experience of nursery rhymes and traditional stories
- Developing speaking and listening skills through, for example, using a range of questioning, checking for understanding, modelling active listening and providing opportunities for group discussion.

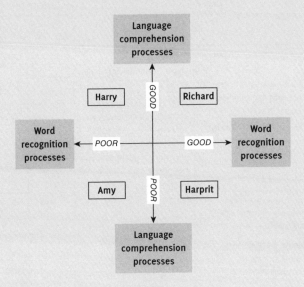

Figure 11.6 Assessment using the Simple View of Reading

Harry: has poor word recognition skills but good comprehension skills.

Support needed:

- More work on letter/sound correspondence
- Help with blending phonemes in order
- Help with segmenting words into separate phonemes
- To be shown that segmenting and blending are reversible.

Richard: has good word recognition skills and good comprehension skills.

Support needed:

- Work on inference and deduction
- Drama: e.g. role-play, hot-seating and conscience alley
- Opportunities to read a wide range of texts
- Reading comprehension activities
- More work on assessing pupils' progress assessment focuses: AF3, AF4, AF5, AF6 and AF7 activities. See the link below for further information
- http://webarchive.nationalarchives.gov.uk/20110202093118/http://nationalstrategies.standards.dcsf. gov.uk/node/20411

Class: Teacher/Practitioner: 2013–14							
Progression		Autumn		Spring		Summer	
Phase 1 continuous through Phase 2–6 *Show awareness of rhyme and alliteration. Distinguish between different sounds in the environment and phonemes. Explore and experiment with sounds and words.*	Phase 6 – throughout Year 2 *Working on: Recognising phonic irregularities. and becoming more secure with less common grapheme–phoneme correspondences* *Working on: Applying phonic skills and knowledge to recognise and spell an increasing number of complex words. SEE SUPPORT FOR SPELLING*	**Phase 1 continuous through Phase 2–6** ***Show awareness of rhyme and alliteration. Distinguish between different sounds in the environment and phonemes. Explore and experiment with sounds and words.***			**Eden** Michael Abby Heather		Y2
	Phase 5 – throughout Year 1 up to 30 weeks *Working on: Reading phonically decodable two-syllable and three-syllable words.* *Working on: Using alternative ways of pronouncing and spelling the graphemes corresponding to the long vowel phonemes.* *Working on: Spelling complex words using phonically plausible attempts.*		Michael Abby	Michael Abby Heather Craig Eden Andrew Steven	**Mary** Craig Andrew Steven Matthew Anne		Y1
	Phase 4 – (Year R/Year 1) 4–6 weeks *Working on: Segmenting adjacent consonants in words and applying this in spelling.* *Working on: Blending adjacent consonants in words and applying this skill when reading unfamiliar texts.*	Heather Craig Eden Abby Michael Andrew Steven	Heather Craig Eden Andrew Steven Susan Lily	Susan Lily John S Peter Mary Matthew Anne	Sarah Susan Lily John S Peter Rosie John R	YR/Y1	
	Phase 3 (Year R) up to 12 weeks *Working on: Knowing one grapheme for each of the 43 phonemes* *Working on: Reading and spelling a wide range of CVC words using all letters and less frequent consonant digraphs and some long vowel phonemes.* Graphemes: ear, air, ure, er, ar, or, ur, ow, oi, ai, ee, igh, oa, oo *Working on: Reading and spelling CVC words using a wider range of letters, short vowels, some consonant digraphs and double letters.* Consonant digraphs ch, sh, th, ng *Working on: Reading and spelling CVC words using letters and short vowels.* Letter progression Set 7: y, z, zz, qu Set 6: j, v, w, x	John S Peter Mary Lily Matthew Anne Susan Sarah Harry Rosie	John S Peter Mary Matthew Anne Sarah Harry Rosie John R	Sarah Harry Rosie John R Rebecca David	Rebecca David Harry		

	Phase 2 – up to 6 weeks *Working on: Using common consonants and vowels. Blending for reading and segmenting for spelling simple CVC words.* *Working on: Knowing that words are constructed from phonemes and that phonemes are represented by graphemes.* Letter progression: Set 5: h, b, f, ff, l, ll, ss Set 4: ck, e, u, r Set 3: g, o, c, k Set 2: i, n, m, d Set 1: s, a, t, p	John R Rebecca David	Rebecca David				
	Phase 1 (7 Aspects) – throughout all phases *Working on: Showing awareness of rhyme and alliteration, distinguishing between different sounds in the environment and phonemes, exploring and experimenting with sounds and words and discriminating speech sounds in words. Beginning to orally blend and segment phonemes.*						

Figure 11.7 Phonic progress tracking sheet – Early Years Foundation Stage through Key Stage 1, with entries

Harprit: has good word recognition skills but poor comprehension skills.

Support needed:

- Work on reading retrieval/comprehension skills
- More experience of reading comprehension activities
- More work on assessing pupils' progress assessment focus AF2 activities. See the link below for further information

http://webarchive.nationalarchives.gov.uk/20110202093118/http://nationalstrategies.standards.dcsf.gov.uk/node/20411

Section 3: Assessing and tracking pupils' progress.

You were asked to use the information provided on three children and the *Letters and Sounds* guidance of expectations of what to look for at each phase to decide where they should be placed on the tracking sheet for the second half of the spring term. Please see the tracking sheet with the three children added below.

You were also asked whether any children had not made any progress over the year so far. Harry has remained in Phase 3 throughout the year.

Section 4: The Year 1 screening check

You were asked to look at the statements about the Y1 screening check and decide whether they are true or false.

1.	The screening check can be done as a group assessment	False: the check has to be carried out on an individual basis
2.	There is no time limit for the screening check	True: however it is expected that the check should take between four and nine minutes for each child. It is important for children to be allowed enough time to respond to each word
3.	There is a set week for schools to administer the phonics screening check	True: the check can be administered on any day during the given week in June
4.	Children need to read all of the words correctly to reach the expected standard for the check	False: each year the school will be sent the threshold mark with the screening check scoring guidance. This will state the number of words the child will need to have read correctly to reach the expected standard
5.	A teaching assistant may administer the screening check	False: the check must be administered by a teacher as it requires professional judgement about which responses are correct. The teacher should be known to the child but should not be a parent or relative
6.	The screening check forms part of schools' statutory assessment and reporting arrangements	True: all maintained schools are required to administer the check along with academies (including free schools), where it is a requirement of their funding agreement. Independent schools are not formally required to participate
7.	The screening check can be stopped part way through if it is evident that the child is struggling with it	True: a teacher may decide to stop the check if the child is getting distressed. If the child is showing signs of fatigue, the teacher may decide to give them a short rest break before continuing
8.	All children in Year 1 must take the check, regardless of their ability in phonics	False: a headteacher may decide that a child should not participate in the check but they should be reconsidered for the check the following year. The headteacher is required to explain their decision to the child's parents
9.	If a child is absent when the test is administered, they can't do it at another time	False: the school can administer the phonics screening check up until the Friday of the following week
10.	Teachers must tell parents whether or not their child has met the required standard	True: this must be done by the end of the summer term at the latest
11.	The check must be administered to children in Year 2 if they did not take the check in Year 1 or if they did not reach the expected standard when they took the test in Year 1	True: if a child has not reached the expected standard in Year 2, they will not need to retake the check in Year 3. Schools will be expected to provide a programme of support for these children
12.	The screening check includes pseudo-words in order to prevent bias to those with a good vocabulary knowledge or visual memory of words	True: these words will be new to all children and, as such, reading them will depend on their ability to use phonics decoding rather than any other strategies

What to do next?

Reinforce your knowledge and understanding of tracking and assessment by doing the following:

1. Observe a teacher carrying out assessments of children's phonic knowledge as part of their tracking of pupils' progress.

2. Carry out an assessment appropriate to the phonics programme used in your school to identify a child's strengths and areas for development.

12. Teaching phonics in Key Stage 2

Learning Outcomes

By the end of this chapter you should have developed:

- strategies for supporting those children who require additional support at Key Stage 2, using methods and resources which address pupils' learning needs but are also suitable for their maturity levels;
- strategies for extending the phonic knowledge and understanding of those children who are successful readers;
- ways of teaching and learning about some less familiar grapheme–phoneme correspondences.

Teachers' Standards

3. Demonstrate good subject and curriculum knowledge:

- if teaching early reading, demonstrate a clear understanding of systematic synthetic phonics.

4. Plan and teach well structured lessons:

- impart knowledge and develop understanding through effective use of lesson time.

5. Adapt teaching to respond to the strengths and needs of all pupils:

- know when and how to differentiate appropriately, using approaches which enable pupils to be taught effectively.

6. Make accurate and productive use of assessment:

- know and understand how to assess the relevant subject and curriculum areas, including statutory assessment requirements;
- make use of formative and summative assessment to secure pupils' progress;
- use relevant data to monitor progress, set targets, and plan subsequent lessons;
- give pupils regular feedback, both orally and through accurate marking, and encourage pupils to respond to the feedback.

Introduction

The national expectation is that 85 per cent of children will be secure at Phase 5 *of Letters and Sounds* (DfES, 2007) by the end of Year 1. This will equate to similar stages in other systematic synthetic phonics programmes such as Jolly Phonics and Read Write Inc. (see Chapter 13). But what happens to the children who still have not reached this level when they enter Key Stage 2? This chapter looks at strategies which can be deployed to support such children. As the 2013 National Curriculum states:

> *It is essential that pupils whose decoding skills are poor are taught through a rigorous and systematic phonics programme so that they catch up rapidly with their peers in terms of their decoding and spelling. However, as far as possible, these pupils should follow the upper key stage 2 programme of study in terms of listening to books and other writing that they have not come across before, hearing and learning new vocabulary and grammatical structures, and having a chance to talk about all of these.*

> (DfE, p.41, Y5–6)

However, phonics teaching at Key Stage 2 (KS2) is not simply remedial for those who have not mastered the basics, but also an opportunity to explore grapheme–phoneme correspondences (GPCs) and to learn more about our language. Teaching and learning of phonics at KS2 focuses on spelling and supporting not only children's reading but also their writing. As Rose (2006) maintains, at KS2 the focus shifts from learning to read to reading to learn. In this chapter we will explore strategies to develop further the phonic knowledge and understanding of all KS2 pupils.

By the time they reach KS2, children should be proficient in making GPCs. However, some will continue to need support and guidance. For some this will be due to learning difficulties, while for others a lack of enthusiasm for reading may be preventing them from making progress. It is essential that children are not simply given more of the same teaching and learning they received in Key Stage 1 (KS1). Even though their reading skills may not have reached the level expected for their age group, their maturity levels will have advanced and they may find the kinds of texts which were used in KS1 dull and immature. For this reason, it is important that we provide engaging and interesting reading activities which will both interest children and help them to develop their phonemic awareness.

For most children, the GPCs from KS1 will have been mastered, but as we have seen in earlier chapters, English contains many GPCs which occur infrequently but need to be understood if we are to read at a higher level. Children can learn many of these through investigations and activities reinforced by direct teaching.

In Chapter 11 we saw the importance of effective assessment and intervention. For KS2 pupils, we might:

- use a range of assessment resources to check children's knowledge and understanding;

- identify their needs and select the appropriate phase from a systematic phonics programme;

- teach using regular, short, focused sessions (see teaching sequence for *Support for Spelling* later in this chapter);

- where specific problems exist, plan for further interventions.

Research Focus: What problems might exist?

The *KS2 Phonics Intervention Programme* (National Strategies, 2009) maintained that some children at KS2 might experience difficulty in reading and/or writing because they have missed or misunderstood a crucial phase of systematic phonics teaching. In their day-to-day learning some children may:

- experience difficulties with blending for reading and segmenting for spelling;
- show confusion with certain graphemes and related phonemes;
- have difficulty segmenting longer words containing adjacent consonants;
- demonstrate a general insecurity with long vowel phonemes (for example, children generally know the most common representation of a phoneme, such as /ai/ in *train*, but require more explanation of and practice in the alternative spellings for any particular phoneme: 2009, p.1).

Layton et al. (1997, p.55) looked at the strategies that struggling readers might deploy as well as those which they were unable to deploy:

- Using whole-word strategies rather than segmenting new words, with the result that inappropriate word choices are made.
- Reluctance to attempt new words because phonic strategies are insecure.
- Selection from a limited range of vocabulary when writing to avoid spelling errors.
- Bizarre spelling errors, which may include letter–sound correspondences in the wrong order or have sounds omitted.

$\longrightarrow$

- Over-generalisation of spelling patterns to inappropriate words, e.g. *tuff* for *tough*.
- Use of sound–symbol correspondences in parts of words which are impossible or very rare in English, e.g. ending words with *j* (*baj* for *badge*), *v* (*hav* for *have*).

The confusion over spelling patterns and sound–symbol correspondences may seem understandable, given the complexities of the English alphabetic system described earlier (see especially Chapter 3). However, Brien maintains that we perceive that there are lots of words we cannot spell 'when, actually, this isn't the case at all. There are really a great number of words which have a problem area but the rest is [sic] accessible to phonic methods' (2012, p.74). The extent to which different texts become accessible once we can master monosyllabic words is highlighted by Solity and Vousden, whose research on so-called 'real books' (those which are not part of a reading scheme) and actual reading schemes led them to conclude:

> It appears that a large proportion of written English is highly regular, and that a small number of core skills will enable children to read the majority of monosyllabic words that they will encounter. When sight vocabulary and phonic skills are combined, children can read 90% of the monosyllabic words they would encounter in adult texts and 88% of monosyllabic words in children's texts, irrespective of whether they occur in a reading scheme or real books. Thus, children will have opportunities to practise their skills as often within real books as within a reading scheme.
>
> (2009, p.503)

Wonder-McDowell concluded from her research into differentiation and intervention that

> student fluency development was best supported when we provided instruction of phonics elements in isolation, provided immediate practice in reading words and phrases with the target sound/spellings, and then provided numerous pieces of decodable text that contained the practiced [sic] words and phrases.
>
> (2008, p.52)

We might conclude, then, that while there are certainly challenges for children who struggle with reading at KS2, some of their difficulties revolve around a perception that the task is actually more difficult than it really is. Children may also find reading unappealing because the texts they are given, though they match their reading abilities, do not interest or excite them. As we will see later in this chapter, imaginative teachers take care to find texts that engage children and help them to develop both their skills in and attitudes to reading.

Activity

Backward readers

Read the text below and then consider questions that follow.

I evah devil raen mahruD rof a raey. tI si a yrev yldneirf ytic dna eht elpoep ekam 'srengierof' ekil flesym yrev emoclew.

yllanigirO, I emoc morf retsacnoD dna I devil ni a gib tip egalliv. yllarutaN, I ma a retsacnoD srevoR retroppus, tub I osla troppus dnalrednuS and kroY. erA ouy gnitteg eht gnah fo siht won? s'tI ton yrev ysae, si ti? fI uoy kniht s'ti drah ot daer, uoy dluohs yrt gnitirw siht yaw!

1. How did you feel as you tried to decode the text?
2. How long did it take you to realise that all the words were written backwards?
3. Was it easy to get meaning from the text?
4. Which strategies did you use? Did you sound words from beginning to end (or is it end to beginning in this case)? Did you make mistakes and have to re-read some words? Were you able to spot some high-frequency words and read them on sight?

Now consider how struggling readers at KS2 might feel when presented with text which they find challenging. You can probably see that they not only need strategies for reading, but also need to see that if they develop these strategies, reading is a potentially very enjoyable activity. In the case study below, you can see an example of a trainee teacher attempting to stimulate children's interest in reading while getting them to look closely at GPCs in words.

Case Study: Developing understanding of consonant digraphs

Rebecca, a trainee on a school-based training course, was working in a small village school with a mixed-age class of Year 3–4 children. She noticed that several of the children, including some who were generally quite fluent readers, frequently made mistakes because they guessed at words or looked only at the initial graphemes before guessing. After discussions with the class teacher, Rebecca planned a shared reading activity using a story opening which she wrote herself. The first three sentences were:

It was dank in the woods. All around her, Kate could here the owls hoofing and the small animals looming for places to hide in the long, damp glass. Suddenly, there was a lout

→

cranking sound and Kate looked up at a huge oat tree to see one of its bunches falling towards him.

Working with a group of ten children whom she had identified as needing to pay more attention to close reading of words and sounding right through words, she told the children that she had been writing a story for them, but had done it in a hurry and thought she might have made some mistakes.

Rebecca read the story opening to the children while they followed on the board, but what she read was:

It was dark in the woods. All around her, Kate could hear the owls hooting and the small animals looking for places to hide in the long, damp grass. Suddenly, there was a loud cracking sound and Kate looked up at a huge oak tree to see one of its branches falling towards her.

Some children spotted some of the mistakes quickly and were eager to point them out, but Rebecca asked them to wait until she had finished. She then gave the children copies of the story opening and asked them to highlight the mistakes as she re-read the passage. She found that children spotted the mistakes in shorter words more easily than in words like *bunches* (branches) and *cranking* (cracking). Three did not spot that *lout* should have been read as *loud*, which she attributed partly to their accents.

Kate developed further activities for the groups involving sentences and individual words which she would read and ask children to spot errors in. She also, at the children's request, continued to write the story and read it to the class each time she completed another chapter!

Support for spelling

There are many resources available for developing children's spelling and their phonological awareness and understanding of GPCs. However, one that is used widely, *Support for Spelling* (DCSF, 2009), offers a programme which develops from the widely-used *Letters and Sounds* programme and can, therefore, be used to exemplify strategies for KS2. We have described below the suggested teaching sequence for lessons using *Support for Spelling*. Notice how this builds upon the teaching sequence described in Chapter 10 for *Letters and Sounds*.

Teaching sequence for *Support for Spelling*

Step 1: Revisit, Explain, Use – building on what children already know.

Step 2: Teach, Model and Define – looking at spelling patterns or rules and modelling their use.

Step 3: Practise, Explore, Investigate – group work and investigations, as well as homework and extension work for more able children. Opportunities to practise new learning in a range of ways.

Step 4: Apply, Assess and Reflect – children use words they have learned about in their writing, and teachers review their progress and help children to reflect upon what they have learned and still need to learn.

This teaching sequence is designed to work as part of five short starter sessions (approximately 15 minutes) over a two-week period. There should be flexibility so that the needs and ability of the children will determine the number of sessions spent on each specific spelling focus.

The guidance for *Support for Spelling* states:

> *Learning to spell is a cumulative process; the materials gradually build the children's spelling vocabulary by introducing new words and giving continual practice of words already introduced. During each half-term, ten sessions should be used for teaching the specific spelling objective and five sessions should be used for the direct teaching of spelling strategies, proofreading, high-frequency words, specific cross-curricular words and personal spelling targets.*
>
> *(DCSF, 2009, p.9)*

The teaching sequence is described below with examples for a lesson on the long vowel digraph /*ay*/ to illustrate how this might work in practice. For detailed information on long vowel sounds, please see Chapter 5.

Revisit, explain, use

This part of the lesson, which should build on what the children already know, should be lively and oral with some quick-write activities, perhaps using mini whiteboards.

Children should use words orally and in context, to ensure that they gain a clear understanding of what they are learning.

Begin by looking at words that children are familiar with which include the *ay* sound, for example *day, way, say, pray.* Ask children to suggest others. They can write some suggestions on whiteboards and then share these with partners and then the class. Some will probably write words which have different graphemes for the *ay* phoneme.

Teach, model, define

In this part of the lesson a range of direct teaching activities are used, including the teacher modelling and involving the children in new learning.

The words suggested by the children could be written on the board or on pieces of card which can be put onto the board with adhesive putty or magnetic holders. Each can be read aloud by the teacher and then by the children and segmented into individual sounds. The graphemic representation for the /ay/ sound in each can be highlighted and the words sorted into groups, for example *day*, *say*, *way*; *take*, *mate*, *same*; *rain*, *paint*, *fail*.

Practise, explore, investigate

In this section of the lesson children can work independently, in pairs or in small groups, to practise and consolidate new learning.

Children could look at different texts and find as many words which include the /ay/ sound as possible. These could be highlighted or copied onto paper and then sorted into groups according to the graphemic representation used. Alternatively, some children might be given sets of /ay/ words to sort into groups. The challenge for the activities could be to find out which graphemic representation of the /ay/ sound is most common. Extension activities can be devised for some children, including trying to find other ways of representing the /ay/ sound and, perhaps, researching the origins of words with less common representations (e.g. *ballet*, *café*, *weigh*, *grey*). In Chapter 5 you will find an example of a chart which shows how different representations of the same phoneme can be presented. Such charts can be created for all children and can be an invaluable aid to making spelling choices.

Apply, assess, reflect

In the final part of the lesson, children reflect on what they have learned and achieved. In order to check and assess their learning they might write sentences including /ay/ words; pairs of rhyming words with the /ay/ sound; or even short poems with /ay/ rhymes. Alternatively, the teacher could dictate a short passage containing several words with the /ay/ phoneme for children to write. This can then be checked to ascertain children's levels of knowledge and understanding and to help prepare for future lessons.

Activity

Consider how you could use the teaching sequence described above to teach other aspects of phonics to children in KS2. Then read the case study below and consider how Ian's lessons could be taught using the sequence.

Case Study: Developing understanding of grapheme-phoneme correspondences

Ian, a third-year undergraduate, found that many children in his Year 5 class in an inner-city school continued to experience problems relating many commonly used graphemes to phonemes. In his class of 19 boys and only seven girls, all of the girls and around half of the boys were working at the level expected of their age group. The boys in particular, and two of the girls, were clearly very interested in football and many had stickers and cards with famous players on them.

Ian decided to focus on football in a series of lessons aimed not only at those who struggled with GPCs, but also at the other children. He began by looking at the names of the teams in the Premier League with them. Children used phoneme frames to divide the names into graphemes and phonemes, for example:

Ch	e	l	s	ea	
B	our	ne	m	ou	th

He was pleasantly surprised to discover that most clubs' names were phonically regular, and the children worked well in pairs to create phoneme frames for all 20 clubs. He then asked those children who were struggling with GPCs to look at the names of teams in the other three leagues and try to match them with a Premier League team. They could do this by finding ones with the same initial phonemes (e.g. Sheffield and Shrewsbury, Norwich and Northampton), the same final phonemes (e.g. Everton and Charlton) or some other criterion related to GPCs (e.g. final two, three or even four phonemes: Manchester and Leicester; first three phonemes the same: Portsmouth and Port Vale). For those children who were already confident about GPCs, Ian provided newspapers with team sheets for each team, and asked them to find the names of players with unusual GPCs. This was especially interesting when looking at those players from abroad where GPCs may be unusual in English and names may be pronounced in unexpected ways: Schmeichel pronounced *shmikle*; Jesus pronounced *yayzuse*; Matic pronounced *matitch*. This led to discussions about how our language has developed and been influenced by other languages, and about the way in which many English names have unusual or unexpected pronunciations.

Ian found that all of the children were fully engaged in the activity, and many came to school the next day with lists of players and teams they had produced with their parents and siblings. Most importantly, the children had developed their knowledge and understanding of GPCs.

> ## Activity
>
> Consider how other activities could be devised to develop GPCs related to children's interests. You will find some suggestions below.

Suggestions for activities

Football snap

Put team names in a hat or bowl, then ask children to draw one out in turn and place face up on the table. When children place a team whose name includes the same phoneme as another on the table, they call 'Snap' and have to explain which phoneme is the same. This can be played so that only phonemes with the same graphemes may count (e.g. Chelsea and Norwich), or for more advanced players, phonemes could be the same but represented by different graphemes too (e.g. Reading and West Brom.). This game could be adapted to use names of TV programmes and personalities, singers and so on.

Alliteration

Challenge children to see how many words they can make which begin with the same grapheme/phoneme/group of letters. Alliterative phrases and sentences could focus on different themes based upon children's interests. For football, they might create alliterative headlines for sports pages (you could find some examples to show to them). For example:

Super Southampton smash sorry Stoke;

Champions Chelsea cheered;

Devastating Doncaster drub dreadful Derby.

Investigating names

Children's first names also provide a rich resource for exploring less common GPCs. Often, children may appear to share the same first names but spellings may differ (e.g. Catherine, Catharine, Katherine, Katharine, Kathryn; Shaun and Sean; Rachel and Rachael; Mohammed and Mohamed). Ask children to use dictionaries to find alliterative adjectives for their names and those of their friends. They can go on to produce alliterative sentences or poems about people in the class (emphasise that only kind things may be said!).

Surnames can also provide a rich source for investigations, especially into their countries of origin and consequent reasons for pronunciation. One of the authors' names is actually pronounced in different ways in different parts of Britain, so that Waugh, which David pronounces *war*, becomes *woff* in north-east England and *woch* (to rhyme with *loch*) in parts of Scotland, while some people tend to rhyme it with *laugh* in other areas!

Explore deliberate misspellings of brands

Many products and services have names which are spelled phonetically but not in the way we might expect (e.g. Weetabix, Kleenex, Kwikfit etc.). Give children examples using photographs and packaging and ask them to use phoneme frames to map the alternative spellings, for example:

B	ea	t	le	s	
B	e	t	a	b	uy

Explore word origins

Given that children will now be meeting many of the 300+ GPCs which tend not to be taught in systematic schemes, now is an opportunity to explore some of the words that have entered English from any languages that children study in modern foreign language (MFL) lessons (e.g. *chute*, *chef*, *café*, *croissant* from French).

Word investigations

Ask children to investigate some of the more unusual GPCs and try to find other words with the same (e.g. *sugar* and *sure*; *who* and *whole*; *pneumatic* and *pneumonia*). The more able children can use dictionaries that include pronunciation guidance and etymological information to find material for a display on some of the less common GPCs.

Exploring menus

Many children will have either visited restaurants or looked at take-away menus. Where these are for cuisines from abroad (Indian, Italian, Chinese etc.), there are opportunities for children to look at GPCs which we now need to know but which, perhaps 50 years ago, were almost unknown in this country (e.g. *ciabatta*, *jahlfrezi*, *chow mein*). Ask children to look at menus and identify some dishes which have unfamiliar GPCs and to find out from the Internet how their names are pronounced.

Exploring nonsense words

Poems and stories can provide a rich source of invented or 'nonsense' words: words which won't appear in dictionaries (although some do eventually). These texts provide opportunities for children to debate the words' possible meanings, as well as working out how to pronounce them. Poems such as Lewis Carroll's (1871) *The Jabberwocky* ('Twas brillig, and the slithy toves did gyre and gimble in the wabe') and stories like Roald Dahl's *The BFG* (1984) which includes such words as *wopsey*, *whiffling*, *glamourly*, *uckyslush* and *bundongle* are an ideal starting point.

Writing for younger children

Ask KS2 children to produce stories or pieces of information for children in KS1 and discuss with them the importance of making their writing easily decodable for their target audience. Encourage them to draft, edit and revise to ensure not only accurate spellings, but also appropriate choices of vocabulary. They could be asked to review their own and each other's writing to highlight words which younger children might find 'tricky'. This activity could be modelled by the teacher with a passage that includes some words which might be replaced by more easily decodable synonyms.

Exploring rhymes

Besides being enjoyable and interesting to read, which should always be a high priority when sharing literature with children, poems with rhymes offer an excellent resource for exploring variations in GPCs. Look, for example, at the opening lines of Hilaire Belloc's (1907) 'Matilda', a cautionary tale that has been popular with children for more than a hundred years:

> *Matilda told such Dreadful Lies,*
>
> *It made one Gasp and Stretch one's Eyes;*
>
> *Her Aunt, who, from her Earliest Youth,*
>
> *Had kept a Strict Regard for Truth,*
>
> *Attempted to Believe Matilda:*
>
> *The effort very nearly killed her,*
>
> *And would have done so, had not She*
>
> *Discovered this Infirmity.*
>
> *For once, towards the Close of Day,*
>
> *Matilda, growing tired of play,*
>
> *And finding she was left alone,*
>
> *Went tiptoe to the Telephone*

And summoned the Immediate Aid

Of London's Noble Fire-Brigade.

As a shared reading activity, you might look at this section of the poem with your class, but this should only be after they have heard the poem in its entirety and discussed it. It is important that you do not reduce literature to being merely a vehicle for analysing language. Ask children to look at the rhyming couplets and the spellings of the rhymes. They will see that the following rhymes have different graphemic representations of phonemes: *lies* and *eyes, youth* and *truth, Matilda* and *killed her, she* and *infirmity,* and *aid* and *brigade.* A range of investigations could follow, including:

- finding as many other words as possible which rhyme with each word and have the same graphemic representations;

- finding further rhymes for the words with different spellings (e.g for *aid* and *brigade* they might find *played* and *weighed*);

- using a range of texts to research which are the most frequent representations of each rhyme (e.g. they would probably find far more examples *–ies* representing the *ise* sound than *eyes,* and may also find that *–ise* and *–ize* are more frequent than *–ies*).

Creating a bank of rhyming words

Children are often asked to write poetry in school, but sometimes struggle because they cannot think of suitable rhymes. Follow up the activity above by asking them to create a bank of rhyming words related to a topic about which they will be writing poems in a future lesson.

Research Focus: Real reading

For children at KS2, it is vital that they see reading as a life skill and a source of pleasure if they are to develop as independent readers who are willing and eager to develop their skills. Rose (2006) strongly emphasised the importance of a rich language environment and the value of children's reading experiences at home. However, Clark and Rumbold bemoan the fact that this element of The Rose Review was neglected by the media:

Although this review recommended that children are taught synthetic phonics at the first instance, it also placed phonics teaching firmly within a language-rich framework that

→

fosters positive attitudes towards reading and a love of books. Unfortunately, this context was lost in the subsequent press coverage.

(Clark and Rumbold, 2006, p.5)

Nevertheless, while a mastery of phonics is essential to children's literacy development, there is considerable research to suggest the importance of setting instruction within the context of a wealth of literature. Clark et al. looked at children's attitudes to reading and found that

[r]eading any type of material outside of class at least once a month was also associated with greater reading attainment. Those who read the more traditional materials, such as fiction, poems and non-fiction, as well as eBooks and comics are more likely to read above the level expected for their age compared with those who read text messages, websites and the like.

(2011, p.7)

In a study of 14 schools across the USA with high proportions of children living in poverty, Taylor et al. (2000) found that those which were most effective used small group instruction, scaffolding by teachers, and emphasised application in real reading when teaching phonics. These schools also worked with parents, and encouraged independent reading.

Krashen, a strong advocate of the value of reading for pleasure, maintained that

[w]hen children read for pleasure, when they get 'hooked on books', they acquire, involuntarily and without conscious effort, nearly all of the so-called 'language skills' many people are so concerned about: they will become adequate readers, acquire a large vocabulary,... and become good (but not necessarily perfect) spellers.

Although free voluntary reading alone will not ensure attainment of the highest levels of literacy, it will at least ensure an acceptable level. Without it, I suspect that children simply do not have a chance.

(1993, p.85)

In a study on intervention (Early Reading Research intervention – ERR) Shapiro and Solity (2008) included asking teachers to read large books to whole classes at least three times a day for four minutes. This 'shared reading' (see National Strategies, 2009) involved both the teacher reading to and with the children and enabled teachers to demonstrate ways of using phonological, phonic and sight vocabulary skills to read a range of texts. The teachers were advised to

teach reading through real books rather than through reading schemes. This is because real books represent the written structures they will encounter as their reading improves and children will see new words in as many different contexts as possible.

(2008, p.602)

⟶

Pressley sums up neatly the importance of texts when stating: 'When the classroom is flooded with literature and there is much interaction about great stories, there are many opportunities for incidental learning of vocabulary' (2001, p.31). Unfortunately, Ofsted (DfE, 2012) reported that 'Between 2000 and 2009, on average across OECD countries the percentage of children who report reading for enjoyment daily dropped by five percentage points (OECD, 2010)' and found that this was supported by evidence from PIRLS 2006 (Twist et al, 2007) which found declining attitudes towards reading amongst children.

It is clear that teachers have a considerable responsibility to ensure that children not only develop an ability to read, but also become readers who use their skills to read and enjoy a range of texts.

Learning Outcomes Review

Through reading this chapter you should have considered strategies for supporting those children who require additional support at Key Stage 2, using methods and resources which address pupils' learning needs but are also suitable for their maturity levels. Strategies for extending the phonic knowledge and understanding of those children who are successful readers have been explored. You will have discovered ways of teaching and learning about some less familiar grapheme-phoneme correspondences.

Self-assessment questions

Can you define each of the following terms which have been used in this chapter?

1. Adjacent consonants.
2. Monosyllabic words.
3. Etymology.

Further Reading

For all aspects of language almost anything by David Crystal will be informative and engaging. Fascinating chapters on language structure are to be found in:

Crystal, D. (2005) *How Language Works*. London: Penguin.

To explore reading comprehension, see:

Tennent, W. (2014) *Understanding Reading Comprehension Processes and Practices*. London: SAGE.

For chapters on a range of literacy issues related to Key Stage 2, see:

Waugh, D. and Neaum, S. (eds) (2013) *Beyond Early Reading*. Northwich: Critical Publishing.

Waugh, D., Neaum, S. and Bushnell, A. (eds) (2013) *Beyond Early Writing*. Northwich: Critical Publishing.

For a readable and interesting guide to different aspects of knowledge about language and, in particular, for areas to consider when studying words, see:

Wilson, A. (1999) *Language Knowledge for Primary Teachers: A Guide to Textual, Grammatical and Lexical Study*. London: David Fulton, especially Chapter 8.

References

Belloc, H. (1907) *Cautionary Tales for Children*. London: Eveleigh Nash.

Brien, J. (2012) *Teaching Primary English*. London: SAGE.

Carroll, L. (1871) *Through the Looking-Glass, and What Alice Found There*. London: Macmillan.

Clark, C. and Rumbold, K. (2006) *Reading for Pleasure: A Research Overview*. London: National Literacy Trust.

Clark, C., Woodley, J. and Lewis, F. (2011) *The Gift of Reading in 2011: Children and Young People's Access to Books and Attitudes Towards Reading*. London: National Literacy Trust.

Dahl, R. (1984) *The BFG*. London: Puffin.

DCSF (2009) *Support for Spelling*. Norwich: DCSF.

DfE (2012) *Research Evidence on Reading for Pleasure: Education Standards Research Team*. London: DfE.

DfE (2013) *The National Curriculum in England, Key Stages 1 and 2 Framework Document*. London: DfE.

DfES (2007) *Letters and Sounds: Notes of Guidance for Practitioners and Teachers*. Norwich: DfES.

Krashen, S. (1993) *The Power of Reading*. Englewood, CO: Libraries Unlimited.

Layton, L., Deeny, K. and Upton, G. (1997) *Sound Practice: Phonological Awareness in the Classroom*. London: Fulton.

National Strategies (2009) *KS2 Phonics Intervention Programme*. London: DCSF.

Ofsted (2004) *Reading for Purpose and Pleasure: An Evaluation of the Teaching of Reading in Primary Schools* (Ref: HMI 2393). London: Ofsted.

Pressley, M. (2001) *Effective Beginning Reading Instruction*. Executive summary and paper commissioned by the National Reading Conference. Chicago, IL: National Reading Conference.

Rose, J. (2006) *Independent Review of the Teaching of Early Reading, Final Report, March 2006* (The Rose Review – Ref: 0201-2006DOC-EN). Nottingham: DfES.

Shapiro, L. and Solity, J. (2008) 'Delivering phonological and phonics training within whole-class teaching', *British Journal of Educational Psychology*, 78: 597–620.

Solity, J. and Vousden, J. (2009) 'Real books vs reading schemes: A new perspective from instructional psychology', *Educational Psychology*, 29 (4): 469–511.

Taylor, B.M., Pearson, P.D., Clark, K. and Walpole, S. (2000) 'Effective schools and accomplished teachers: Lessons about primary-grade reading instruction in low-income schools', *Elementary School Journal*, 101: 121–65.

Twist, L., Schagen, I. and Hodgson, C. (2007). *Readers and Reading: The National Report for England 2006* (PIRLS: Progress in International Reading Literacy Study). Slough: NFER.

Wonder-McDowell, C. (2008) *The Hidden Peril of Differentiation: Fragmented Instruction.* Doctoral Dissertation Award, Utah State University.

Audit and test

Work through each section below, responding to each question or task. When you have completed each section, you can read the answers at the end of the chapter.

Section 1: Key terminology for phonics at KS2

It is important that you understand the terms below before you move on to the next activity. Provide a definition of each and check your definitions against those at the end of the chapter:

Etymology

Grapheme–phoneme correspondence

Adjacent consonants

Monosyllabic words

Free morpheme

Bound morpheme

Prefix

Suffix

Section 2: Exploring morphemes (see also Chapter 6)

Look at the word *friend*. Add a suffix and you can change *friend* to *friendly*, *friends*, *friendless* or *friendliness*. Add a prefix to *friend* and you can make *befriend* or even, from Facebook, *unfriend*! By adding prefixes and suffixes you could make: *befriends*, *befriended*, *unfriendly* and *unfriendliness*.

Look at the words below and see how many words you can create using them as root words and adding affixes (prefixes and or suffixes)

help

like

play

Section 3: Meanings of morphemes

Look at the list of prefixes below and the words next to them and provide a definition for each prefix:

un-   unusual

bi-   bicycle

re-   reuse

anti-   antifreeze

sub-   subway

Notice how the spellings of prefixes tend to be phonically regular. How can learning about prefixes help children with reading and spelling?

NB Many teachers don't tend to segment or use sound buttons on morphemes, as this shifts focus from meaning to decoding.

Section 4: Segmenting words into morphemes (see also Chapter 6)

Look at the words below and segment them into morphemes, for example:

Delighted – de/light/ed

Morphemes which can stand alone as words are called free morphemes. Those which cannot stand alone as words are called bound morphemes. For each word, identify the free and the bound morphemes. For example:

de/light/ed – de and –ed are bound morphemes; light is a free morpheme.

exported

prepacked

defused

Section 5: Modifying words (see also Chapter 6)

Look at the word list of spellings which Year 5 and Year 6 should be able to spell, according to the National Curriculum, and ensure that you feel confident that you can spell them all.

How many words can **NOT** be modified using affixes? For example, *accommodate* can be made into *accommodates, accommodated, accommodation* and *accommodating; achieve* can be made into *achieves, achievable, achieving, unachievable, underachiever* etc.

Now try to provide **ONE** modification for each of the words.

You don't need to write down all the possible modified words for each word, but it may be useful to do this if you are teaching Years 5–6 and want to prepare for spelling lessons.

accommodate	criticise	individual	relevant
accompany	curiosity	interfere	restaurant
according	definite	interrupt	rhyme
achieve	desperate	language	rhythm
aggressive	determined	leisure	sacrifice
amateur	develop	lightning	secretary
ancient	dictionary	marvellous	shoulder
apparent	disastrous	mischievous	signature
appreciate	embarrass	muscle	sincerely
attached	environment	necessary	soldier

available	equipped	neighbour	stomach
average	especially	nuisance	sufficient
awkward	exaggerate	occupy	suggest
bargain	excellent	occur	symbol
bruise	existence	opportunity	system
category	explanation	parliament	temperature
cemetery	familiar	persuade	thorough
committee	foreign	physical	twelfth
communicate	forty	prejudice	variety
community	frequently	privilege	vegetable
competition	government	profession	vehicle
conscience	guarantee	programme	yacht
conscious	harass	pronunciation	
controversy	hindrance	queue	
convenience	identity	recognise	
correspond	immediate	recommend	

Look at the words again and identify the those which include 'tricky' bits which you may need to help children focus upon when they learn them.

Section 6: Poetry and exploring rhyming words

Look at the limerick below. Your task is to write a final line, but first look at the rhyming couplets: *York* and *talk*, and *speak* and *week*.

There was a young lady from York,

Who seemed to do nothing but talk.

When she started to speak,

It seemed like a week,

1. Find rhymes for *York* and *talk* and make two lists: one under *York*, to include words which rhyme with *York* and have similar spellings (e.g. pork), and one under *talk*, with words which rhyme and have similar spellings. Add other lists for other words which rhyme but have a different spelling of the rhyme.

2. Once you have made your lists and checked any unfamiliar words in a dictionary, complete the limerick.

3. What do your lists tell you about possible spellings of words which rhyme with *York* and *talk*. Are there other spellings for the rhyme?

4. Next look at *speak* and *week*. Make lists of rhymes under headings *speak* and *week*.

a. How many words can you write under each in two minutes?

b. What do your lists tell you about possible spellings of words which rhyme with *speak* and *week?*

c. Are there other spellings for the *–eek/eak* rhyme?

Section 7: Exploring activities for KS2

Children at KS2 may still need to develop their phonological awareness, but may be put off doing so if the activities and materials they are given are felt to be beneath their maturity level. It is therefore important to devise activities which engage and interest them while helping them to learn. Look at the list of football teams below and consider how you might use them to develop activities to foster phonological awareness.

Manchester United   Chelsea   Rochdale   Doncaster Rovers   Sunderland   Liverpool   Blackpool   West Ham

ANSWERS

Section 1: Key terminology for phonics at KS2

Etymology

The origins of the formation of a word and its meaning.

Grapheme–phoneme correspondence

The relationship between letters and sounds. The graphemes (letters and combinations of letters such as digraphs and trigraphs) are the written representation on the phonemes (sounds) in words.

Adjacent consonants

Consonants which appear next to each other in a word and can be blended together, e.g. bl in blip, cr in crack (note that the ck in crack is a digraph, as the consonants come together to form a single sound or phoneme).

Monosyllabic words

Words with one syllable – for example, book, dig, run, hot.

Free morpheme

A morpheme which can stand alone as a word – for example, in kicked, kick is a free morpheme, but –ed is a bound morpheme because it cannot stand alone – it needs to be bound to a word to have meaning.

Bound morpheme

A morpheme which cannot stand alone (see free morpheme).

Prefix

A morpheme or affix placed before a word to modify its meaning, e.g. dis- in dislike, de- in defrost.

Suffix

Morpheme or affix added to a word to modify its meaning, e.g. *-ful* in *hopeful*, *-ed* in *jumped*.

Section 2: Exploring morphemes

You were asked to look at the words below and see how many words you can create using them as root words and adding affixes (prefixes and or suffixes).

help could become: *helpful, helpless, helps, helping, helped, helper, unhelpful etc.*

like could become: *likeable, likes, liked, likely, likeness, liking, unlikely, unlikeable, dislike, disliking etc.*

play could become: *playing, played, plays, playful, player, display, replay, unplayable, replaying, replayed, displayed etc.*

Section 3: Meanings of morphemes

You were asked to provide a definition for each prefix.

un-   not

bi-   two

re-   again

anti-   against

sub-   under

Section 4: Segmenting words into morphemes

You were asked to look at the words below and segment them into morphemes.

For each word, you had to identify the free and the bound morphemes.

exported ex/port/ed – *ex-* and *–ed* are bound morphemes; *port* (carry) is a free morpheme.

prepacked: pre/pack/ed – *pre-* and *–ed* are bound morphemes; *pack* is a free morpheme.

defused: de/fuse/ing (the *e* is dropped from *fuse* when *–ing* is added) – *de-* and *–ing* are bound morphemes; *fuse* (blend/join) is a free morpheme.

NB The suffix *–ed* can have different sounds. For example, in *walked* and *danced* it has a t sound; while in *blessed*, *shouted* and *hated* has an ed sound, and in *jogged*, *rained* and *showed* it has a d sound.

Section 5: Modifying words (see also Chapter 6)

You were asked to look at the word list of spellings which Year 5 and Year 6 should be able to spell according to the National Curriculum, and ensure that you feel confident that you can spell them all.

You were then asked how many words can **NOT** be modified using affixes.

Lightning and *especially* are the only words which cannot be modified.

You were then asked to try to provide **one** modification for each of the words.

We have provided the list again below but with each word modified. For many words, there are several possible modifications and your choices do not have to be the same as ours.

accommodates	criticism	individuality	relevant
accompanying	curiosities	interference	restaurant
accordingly	indefinite	interruption	rhyme
achievement	desperately	languages	rhythm
aggressively	determinedly	leisurely	sacrifice

amateurish	developer	lightning	secretary
ancients	dictionaries	marvellously	shouldered
apparently	disastrously	mischievousness	signatures
appreciation	embarrassed	muscular	insincerely
unattached	environmental	unnecessary	soldiers
unavailable	ill-equipped	neighbourly	stomachs
averages	especially	nuisances	sufficiently
awkwardly	exaggeration	occupied	suggestion
bargained	excellently	occurrence	symbolic
bruised	non-existence	opportunities	systematic
categorise	explanations	parliamentary	temperatures
cemeteries	familiarity	persuaded	thoroughly
committees	foreigner	physicality	twelfths
communicate	forties	prejudicial	varieties
community	infrequently	privileged	vegetables
competitions	governmental	unprofession	vehicles
consciences	guaranteed	programmed	yachting
consciously	harassment	mispronunciation	
controversy	hindrances	queued	
convenience	identities	recognisable	
correspondence	immediately	recommendation	

You were asked to look at the words again and identify those which include 'tricky' bits which you may need to help children focus upon when they learn them.

   Some words lose letters when a suffix is added – for example, *hinder* becomes *hindrance*;

   Some change some letters – for example, convenient becomes convenience;

   Some words change the way they are pronounced when a suffix is added – for example *muscle* to *muscular*;

   Some become compound words which sometimes have hyphens, for example *ill-equipped*.

When you teach children about these spelling conventions, use the opportunity to show how they work for other words which they are likely to encounter.

   Some have unusual combinations of letters representing familiar sounds – for example, *yacht, foreigner.*

   Some have double letters which can be missed – for example, *accommodated, recommended, embarrassing.*

   There are silent or not usually pronounced letters in some – for example, *governmental.*

There are many other potential tricky bits in many of the words. When you are planning to teach them to children, it can be a good idea to ask someone to try to spell a selection and to see which bits they find the most challenging.

Section 6: Poetry and exploring rhyming words

There was a young lady from York

Who seemed to do nothing but talk

When she started to speak

It seemed like a week

1. You were asked to find rhymes for *York* and *talk* and make two lists: one under *York*, to include words which rhyme with *York* and have similar spellings (e.g. *pork*), and one under *talk*, with words which rhyme and have similar spellings. You were also asked to add other lists for other words which rhyme but have a different spelling of the rhyme.

    Some suggestions:

York	talk	hawk	torque	baulk
cork	chalk	squawk		caulk
fork	walk			
pork				

2. Once you had made your lists and checked any unfamiliar words in a dictionary, you were asked to complete the limerick.

    A suggestion:

    There was a young lady from York

    Who seemed to do nothing but talk

    When she started to speak

    It seemed like a week

    Of nothing but squawk, squawk and squawk.

3. You were asked what your lists told you about possible spellings of words which rhyme with *York* and *talk*, and if there were other spellings for the rhyme.

    The lists suggest that the most common way of writing the rhyme is *ork*, followed by *alk*. Other possibilities are rare.

4. Next you looked at *speak* and *week* and made lists of rhymes under headings *speak* and *week*.

    a. You were asked to see how many words could you write under each in two minutes.

    b. You were asked what your lists told you about possible spellings of words which rhyme with *speak* and *week*.

    c. You were asked if there were other spellings for the *–eek/eak* rhyme.

Some suggestions:

speak	week	clique	shriek
weak	cheek	boutique	
creak	peek	antique	
freak	seek	unique	
beak	meek	technique	
peak	leek		

Section 7: Exploring activities for KS2

Children at KS2 may still need to develop their phonological awareness, but may be put off doing so if the activities and materials they are given are felt to be beneath their maturity level. It is therefore important to devise activities which engage and interest them while helping them to learn. You were asked to look at the list of football teams below and consider how you might use them to develop activities to foster phonological awareness.

Manchester United   Chelsea   Rochdale   Doncaster Rovers   Sunderland   Liverpool   Blackpool   West Ham

There are many different activities you might develop using football teams or other names which are of particular interest to children. For example:

You could ask children to find football matches by pairing teams which have graphemes in common, for example:

Manchester United v Chelsea

Chelsea v Rochdale

Doncaster Rovers v Sunderland

Liverpool v Blackpool

You could ask them to create matches based only on initial and final sounds, for example:

West Ham v Manchester United

Rochdale v Liverpool

You could ask children to look at league tables to find teams which could play against teams from the group of eight above, using different criteria for pairings.

You could ask children to find names of teams which include:

vowel digraphs (Leeds)

consonant digraphs (Notts County, Hull)

consonant clusters (Fleetwood, Blackburn, Leicester, Bristol City)

trigraphs (Brighton, Bournemouth)

quadgraphs (Middlesbrough)

silent letters (Carlisle, Wycombe)

You could go on to give children common words and ask them to match them with football team cards where they share a sound or grapheme.

What to do next?

Reinforce your knowledge and understanding of decoding by doing as many as possible of the following:

1. Observe phonics lessons at KS2.

2. Build up a bank of resources which will engage children at their maturity level while helping them to develop their phonic knowledge and understanding.

3. Look for poems and songs which can stimulate children's interest in rhyme and vocabulary.

13. Using a range of programmes and resources

Learning Outcomes

By the end of this chapter you will:

- have a basic knowledge of the most frequently used systematic synthetic phonics programmes;
- be aware of the challenges you will face as you work with different systematic synthetic phonics programmes.

Teachers' Standards

3. Demonstrate good subject and curriculum knowledge:

    - if teaching early reading, demonstrate a clear understanding of systematic synthetic phonics.

Criteria for assuring high-quality phonic work (DfE, 2011)

Enable children to start learning phonic knowledge and skills using a systematic, synthetic programme by the age of five, with the expectation that they will be fluent readers having secured word recognition skills by the end of Key Stage 1 (see Note 2).

Note 2: Teachers will make principled, professional judgements about when to start on a systematic, synthetic programme of phonic work but it is reasonable to expect that the great majority of children will be capable of, and benefit from doing so by the age of five. It is equally important for the programme to be designed so that children become fluent readers having secured word recognition skills by the end of Key Stage 1.

Introduction

In Chapter 9 we looked at the rationale and the key ingredients for a systematic structured progression in teaching synthetic phonics. In this chapter, we look at some of the most commonly used systematic synthetic phonics programmes and will focus on three: *Letters and Sounds*, Jolly Phonics and Read Write Inc. Although there are many other phonics programmes, including some which have been created by local authorities and even individual schools, our surveys of trainee teachers and various teacher training providers suggest these three are the most frequently used. We look at some of the general principles behind the programmes and show how they differ from each other.

We begin by looking at typical features of a systematic synthetic phonics programme, as identified by Ofsted's *Reading by Six* report (2010, p.42), which maintained that programmes for phonic work should meet each of the following criteria:

- present high-quality systematic, synthetic phonic work as the prime approach to decoding print, i.e. a phonics 'first and fast' approach;

- enable children to start learning phonic knowledge and skills using a systematic, synthetic programme by the age of five, with the expectation that they will be fluent readers having secure word recognition skills by the end of Key Stage 1;

- be designed for the teaching of discrete, daily sessions progressing from simple to more complex phonic knowledge and skills and covering the major grapheme–phoneme correspondences;

- enable children's progress to be assessed;

- use a multi-sensory approach so that children learn variously from simultaneous visual, auditory and kinaesthetic activities which are designed to secure essential phonic knowledge and skills;

- demonstrate that phonemes should be blended, in order, from left to right, 'all through the word' for reading;

- demonstrate how words can be segmented into their constituent phonemes for spelling and that this is the reverse of blending phonemes to read words;

- ensure that children apply phonic knowledge and skills as their first approach to reading and spelling, even if a word is not completely phonically regular;

- ensure that children are taught high-frequency words that do not conform completely to grapheme–phoneme correspondence rules;

- provide fidelity to the teaching framework for the duration of the programme, to ensure that these irregular words are fully learned;

- ensure that as pupils move through the early stages of acquiring phonics, they are invited to practise by reading texts that are entirely decodable for them, so that they experience success and learn to rely on phonemic strategies.

Research Focus: Commercial phonics programmes

It is difficult to find comparative studies of systematic synthetic phonics programmes, although there are many research papers which compare different approaches to teaching reading and different approaches to teaching phonics (e.g. synthetic v analytic). This may be because the major programmes have been developed quite recently. The commercial programmes, Read Write Inc. and Jolly Phonics, often quote teachers in their publications and publicity but, not surprisingly, the quotes are always very positive about the programmes. The Rose Review also included individual, positive quotes, for example:

> *'I have never seen results like this in 30 years of teaching'. [The teacher] went on to say that, as a result of following the programme, 'I am seeing Primary 3 quality in Primary 1'.*

> (2006, para.213, p.63)

Wyse and Goswami sound a cautious note about such evidence:

> *Such anecdotes share similarities with those supplied by teachers who have received training in various commercial phonics packages: 'THRASS2 is like a new religion! I have seen the light – the answer to how to teach English spelling' (THRASS, 1999); 'Jolly Phonics has given our children the chance to succeed in reading and writing' (Jolly Phonics Case Study, 1999).*

> (2008, p.696)

It might be argued that where teachers subscribe to a programme with enthusiasm and energy, results will improve. However, although there continues to be debate about the efficacy of different approaches (e.g. Wyse and Styles, 2007), there is little that compares individual programmes, apart from Callinan and Van der Zee's (2010) comparative study of two methods of synthetic phonics instruction for learning how to read: Jolly Phonics and THRASS (Davies and Ritchie, 1998).

Rose stated that 'commercially produced phonic programmes provided assessment data that showed very substantial, sometimes spectacular, gains in the performance of beginner readers on their programme' (2006, para.54, p.20). However, since a range of different tests had been used by different programmes to measure the gains, it was impossible to compare them accurately. Rose did, however, maintain that despite claims by producers that there were 'sharp differences' between the programmes, this made 'little difference to the claimed success rates'. He concludes that the elements common to programmes were few, but were 'those that really make a difference to how well beginners are taught and learn to read and write' (2006, para.54, p.20). As we saw in Chapter 9, a key factor in the success of any systematic synthetic phonics approach, identified by Rose, is fidelity to the programme, which

⟶

makes it all the more important that you spend time looking carefully at websites, hand-books and manuals and talking to experienced teachers whenever you encounter and have to work with an unfamiliar programme. The list of criteria above identified by Ofsted (2010), together with the grid produced by the Training and Development Agency (TDA) (DES, 2011a), which appears later in this chapter, can be used to help you to analyse the features of different phonics programmes. The brief descriptions below should only be a starting point for your research.

Read Write Inc.

This is a commercial systematic synthetic phonics programme, designed to be delivered on a daily basis. Teachers and teaching assistants attend training sessions, which provide guidance on how to deliver and assess pupils using the programme. Great emphasis is given to ensuring that the programme is delivered in the same way by all staff to ensure continuity and thorough and rigorous phonics teaching for all pupils.

Each school appoints a Read Write Inc. manager to coordinate the programme. The manager is responsible for resources, timetabling and organisation, further training and supporting and mentoring staff.

Parents are encouraged to support pupils at home in the same way that they are taught at school, and so will usually need guidance to understand the way the programme is delivered. Parents can be informed through information meetings, demonstration sessions, leaflets and homework materials.

Many resources are available to support the programme, including handbooks containing lesson plans and guidance on preferred delivery methods, assessment materials, sound and word cards, reading books, display materials and software to use on computers and interactive whiteboards. A soft toy frog named Fred (see below) is essential to teaching phonemes and decodable words in Read Write Inc.

The five key principles of the programme

There are five key principles that schools are expected to follow:

> Pace: *Sessions should be* 'energetic and rigorous' *(Miskin, 2011, p.12) and there are silent signals for class management, for example showing when it is the teacher or pupils' turn to participate using 'my turn/your turn'. The teacher's time to model is indicated as 'my turn' by touching their own shoulders and the pupils' turn to practise as 'your turn' by pointing to the pupils with both hands.*

Praise – *a lot: A list of sample 'praise phrases' is provided for teachers, including* super, smashing, brilliant sounds, fantastic, fabulous *and* wicked words. *There are also praise actions such as* high fives, fireworks *and* whooshes *(acted out),* Go guys! *(circle thumbs) and* microwaves *(little finger waves). Pupils are also encouraged to invent their own 'praises'.*

Purpose: *The purpose of each activity is made clear to the children, so that they know what they are going to learn and why. Teachers model good partner work with another child or adult.*

Participation: *There is a strong emphasis on all children participating in all of the lesson, and on partner work, with guidance on children teaching each other, partner behaviour, and even on how they should sit together (shoulder to shoulder). Modelling of good practice is central to developing effective partner work and pupils are encouraged by the use of the phrase 'perfect partners'.*

Passion: *The handbook sums this up as follows:*

Be passionate in your teaching. Show the children how much you love teaching the lessons. Exaggerate your modelling of thinking and behaviour. Make your teaching larger than life so children engage in the learning. The greater the passion, the faster they progress!

(Miskin, 2011, p.15)

Getting started

The Read Write Inc. programme is organised into bands. Each band covers a set of phonemes, and pupils move to the next band once they have demonstrated that they can read, spell and confidently use the phonemes from the bands they have already been taught.

Pupils are assessed individually before beginning the programme using the 'Sound and Word Entry Assessment', which indicates the band they should begin studying. Pupils are then organised into groups so that they can be taught at a band appropriate to their needs. It is suggested that these groups should contain no more than 20 pupils. Pupils are then assessed again after four weeks to ensure they are making progress and are indeed in a band group that matches their phonic ability. These groups are not static and, as regular assessment takes place every six to eight weeks, groupings are checked and altered to maintain rapid progress for all pupils. Records of attainment are kept to inform future planning and show individual pupil progression.

Introducing phonemes

Read Write Inc. introduces phonemes, and their corresponding graphemes, sequentially, in three sets of 'speed sounds'. The phonemes introduced in Set 1 are:

m a s d t

i n p g o

c k u b

f e l h sh

r j v y w

th z ch q x ng nk*

*(The nk grapheme is taught as a consonant blend or as adjacent consonants with two sounds in many other programmes.)

Set 2 includes the most common phoneme/grapheme digraphs and trigraphs, such as *ay* (play), *ow* (snow) and *ar* (star).

Set 3 contains more complex phonemes and those with alternative grapheme representations, such as *aw* (straw), *ue* (glue) and *ure* (sure).

Every Read Write Inc. session begins with the teaching of *speed sounds*. Each new speed sound (phoneme) is introduced using a picture card, phoneme card and simple phrase as memory tools. Examples of these phrases are 'may I play' (*ay*), 'blow the snow' (*ow*) and 'start the car' (*ar*). It is expected that new phonemes are taught rapidly, with three or four new ones introduced each week. These are then kept in a pile or a pocket to revisit every session until all pupils in the group can read and spell them confidently. The phonemes/graphemes are displayed in the classroom on 'speed sound charts', which are used for reference and rapid recall.

Fred the Frog

As each new phoneme is introduced, so are a small number of decodable words containing the phoneme. These are known as 'green words' and are displayed on green card. 'Fred the Frog', the soft toy frog, can say these words using 'Fred talk' to encourage the pupils to decode, blend and segment the words.

Non-decodable, or tricky words are also regularly introduced. These are known as 'red words' and are displayed on red card. Pupils are taught that these words cannot be sounded phonetically and that *'you can't Fred a red'*. As each new 'red word' is introduced, it is displayed on a 'red wall' and the words are taught by identifying the tricky bits and by repetition.

Reading books

Once the speed sound teaching has been completed at the beginning of each session, pupils spend time reading books that are matched to the band they are currently working within. Each book contains phonemes and 'red words' that the pupils have learned or are currently learning. All the texts in each band are designed in the same way, so that there is familiarity and continuity every time the pupils encounter a new text. There are fiction and non-fiction texts available. It is not expected that pupils will necessarily read each text in the band if progress is good.

A large proportion of the reading time during the session is used for pre-reading preparation, so that once reading begins pupils have been given the tools they need to read confidently and fluidly. Books from the lower bands of the programme are designed to be read over three sessions, and from the upper bands over five sessions as the texts become longer and more complex.

Pupils read with their partner and a tool is used for pointing, so that the partner who is reading aloud guides the partner who is following the text. All pairs of pupils read at the same time and the teacher visits each pair to guide and monitor.

Each text contains the following activities:

- Speed ounds – quick-fire reading practice of all phonemes children have been taught. Phonemes relevant to the current text are highlighted in bold.

- Green and red words – to identify and practise the specific decodable and non-decodable words; words that will appear in the current text.

- Vocabulary – a simple glossary of words that may be unfamiliar to pupils. These may be related to the subject matter in the text.

- Introduction – information to set the context of the text, often encouraging pupils to think about their own experiences or make predictions before reading the text.

- Reading the text – aloud and using the pointer, both partners will be given time to read and follow the text. 'Red words' are highlighted in red font and pictures are used to support reading.

- Questions about the text – children are encouraged to answer questions to check understanding and encourage thinking around the text. The questions include those that can be answered directly from the text and those that require simple inference and deduction.

- Speed words – quick-fire reading practice of the words from the text that contain phonemes that are relevant to pupil's current learning.

Supporting the programme

The core Read Write Inc. programme is accompanied by complementary programmes such as *Fresh Start* and *Read Write Inc. Spelling* to support those pupils who do not make expected progress. There are opportunities for intervention and one-to-one tuition for those pupils who need additional support, and for those pupils in Key Stage2 who still require dedicated phonics teaching.

There is also a *Get Writing* programme, which can be used with all pupils in conjunction with the core phonics programme. This provides opportunities for children to complete writing and spelling activities, edit text and write independently. The writing activities are linked to the books they are reading within the core programme.

Teachers go on to share a 'simple speed sounds chart' of consonants and vowels, which develops into a 'complex speed sounds chart', which shows a range of spelling alternatives in a similar way to the THRASS grapheme chart (see below).

Jolly Phonics

Jolly Phonics is 'a fun and child centred approach to teaching literacy' (Jolly Learning website). It focuses on 42 letter sounds (compared with 44 for *Letters and Sounds*, Read Write Inc. and THRASS). The letter sounds are split into seven groups, which are learned in order (see below). As with other programmes, this is designed to enable children to begin building words as early as possible.

1. s a t i p n

2. ck e h r m d

3. g o u l f b

4. ai j oa ie ee or

5. z w ng v oo oo

6. y x ch sh th th

7. qu ou oi ue er ar

Jolly Phonics actions

A distinctive feature of Jolly Phonics is the use of actions designed to help children remember the letters. For the first group of letters learned, these are:

> s *Weave hand in an s shape, like a snake, and say 'sssss'.*
>
> a *Wiggle fingers above elbow as if ants crawling on you and say 'a, a, a'.*
>
> t *Turn head from side to side as if watching tennis and say 't, t, t'.*
>
> i *Pretend to be a mouse by wriggling fingers at end of nose and squeak 'i, i,"*
>
> p *Pretend to puff out candles and say 'p, p, p'.*
>
> n *Make a noise, as if you are a plane, hold arms out and say 'nnnnnn'.*

> (Jolly Learning website: http://jollylearning.co.uk/2010/ll/03/jolly-phonics-
> actions/)

Jolly Phonics uses a synthetic phonics approach and identifies five key skills for reading and writing:

1. *Learning the letter sounds:* Children are taught 42 main letter sounds.

2. *Learning letter formation:* Children use multi-sensory methods to learn how to form and write the letters.

3. *Blending:* They blend the sounds together to read and write new words.

4. *Identifying the sounds in words:* They identify sounds in words to help with spelling.

5. *Tricky words:* Tricky words with irregular spellings are learned separately.

Letters and Sounds

Unlike Read Write Inc. and Jolly Phonics, *Letters and Sounds* is not a commercial programme. It was produced by the Primary National Strategy (DfES, 2007) and distributed widely at no cost. Not surprisingly, therefore, many teacher training programmes use it as the basis of their training on systematic synthetic phonics. Although the programme continues to be available online, hard copies are no longer produced.

Discrete teaching

Like other systematic synthetic phonics programmes, *Letters and Sounds* should be taught daily, in discrete sessions. This allows the teaching of phonics to become an important, high-profile part of the school day. It promotes clear focus on the teaching of phonics and gives teachers regular opportunities to deliver high-quality phonics teaching which is not overshadowed by other subject matter.

This dedicated time gives teachers the chance to engage children in a range of activities which will suit different learning styles. It allows time for children to become actively involved in the lesson rather than taking a passive listening role, perhaps participating in games, practising writing words and sentences and so on. This dedicated teaching time also allows for high-quality and informative phonics assessment opportunities which will provide teachers with accurate information for tightly focused planning and target-setting for all pupils.

The need to teach and access phonics will, of course, occur throughout the teaching day, during literacy lessons and other subject areas, whenever children are reading and writing. It is, therefore, important to use the skills and knowledge gained in phonics lessons across all parts of the curriculum.

Matching the needs of all pupils

As you can see in Chapter 9, *Letters and Sounds* comprises six phases. Children are grouped according to the phase that most closely matches their level of attainment. Through continuous assessment and differentiation, pupils are able to progress through these phases at a pace suitable for their individual needs. Children should not move to the next phase until they are able to read and spell high-frequency words, tricky words and decodable words with specific phonemes for the phase they are working within, thus ensuring that the needs of each pupil can be effectively and continually targeted.

Like Read Write Inc. and Jolly Phonics, *Letters and Sounds* provides a clear structure for teaching the knowledge and skills that children need to be able to both read and spell using phonics. *Letters and Sounds: Principles and Practice of High Quality Phonics* (DfES, 2007) provides ideas, activities and guidance for teaching children how to sound and blend phonemes together to read whole words (blending for reading).

Letters and Sounds: Principles and Practice of High Quality Phonics also provides ideas, activities and guidance for teaching children how to break whole words down into separate phonemes to spell words (segmenting for spelling). A wide range of resources has been made available on the Internet to support teaching and learning for all phases of *Letters and Sounds*.

Phonics Bug

Phonics Bug is written by Rhona Johnson and Joyce Watson, the authors of the 2005 Clackmananshire Study (see Introduction), which influenced the Rose Review of reading. The letter order used in Phonics Bug follows that recommended in *Letters and Sounds* (2007), following a sequence that early on makes the reading of a large number of CVC words possible. In Phonics Bug, children proceed from Phase 2 to the end of Phase 3 very rapidly. The skills for these phases are tested in Assessment 4, where the children are asked to read and spell CVC non-words (see Phonics Screening Check, p.152). Phase 3 skills are assessed in Assessment 5, where the ability to read and spell some consonant and vowel digraphs and trigraphs is tested. Phase 4 skills (adjacent consonants) are assessed in Assessment 6, where children are asked to read and spell CCVC, CVCC and CCVCC non-words.

Phonics Bug also provides catch-up activities for slower-learning children, to follow on from these assessments. The programme provides books linked to teaching phases, all of which are available to read online as well as in print. Phonics Bug also has software for the interactive whiteboard as a key teaching method.

You will find web addresses for each programme at the end of this chapter. The case studies below provide examples of trainee teachers' strategies when faced with the challenge of working with a programme they have not met before.

Case Studies

1. New to Read Write Inc.

Amy, a third-year trainee, was preparing to work with a Year 2 class for her final placement. In her first-year placement she had worked with a Reception/Year 1 class using Jolly Phonics. At first she had observed the teacher, but gradually she had taken more responsibility for the class as she had learned the hand signals for different letters. In her final placement, the school used Read Write Inc., a programme Amy knew little about. She had a good knowledge of *Letters and Sounds* from her university course, and was very much aware of the principles of good phonics teaching.

Amy discussed her situation with her tutor, who showed her the teachers' manual for Read Write Inc. and discussed key principles (Fred talk, speed sounds etc.). He then arranged to take Amy and two other students who were also new to Read Write Inc. into a school which had well-established procedures and had used Read Write Inc. for two years. Here, Amy and her friends observed lessons and talked with the teachers and literacy coordinator about the programme and the way in which it was taught. Amy also found the 'complex speed sounds' chart easy to understand, as she had already experienced the THRASS grapheme chart at university.

Amy went into her final placement school for her weekly visit the following week and discussed her experiences and her understanding of Read Write Inc. with the class teacher and the literacy coordinator. It was agreed that she would observe lessons with different groups and would gradually take on some of the teaching of parts of lessons. The school was impressed by Amy's knowledge of the terminology associated with phonics in general and Read Write Inc. in particular, and her ability to enunciate phonemes correctly. It was arranged that Amy would attend the weekly staff meetings, which featured a section on Read Write Inc., so that she could develop her knowledge and understanding of the programme.

2. Familiar with Read Write Inc.

A second-year student, Susan, had a placement in a school that had adopted Read Write Inc. immediately after the Christmas break; the Head and the Literacy Coordinator had visited schools and been impressed by its effectiveness. Staff had been trained and resources purchased.

Susan found that she was allowed to assist with lessons but not take a lead, since the school felt she should not do this as she had not received Read Write Inc. training, although she had gained experience of working with Read Write Inc. while working as a volunteer at the school her daughter attended.

The school, which had previously used *Letters and Sounds* accompanied by hand signals for letters from Jolly Phonics, was in an area of economic and social deprivation, with 60 per cent of its children having English as an additional language (EAL).

$\longrightarrow$

There were some teething problems in implementing the programme as teachers modified their practice and introduced new ways of working to children. Susan's previous experience of *Letters and Sounds* and Read Write Inc. meant that she was able to give some support to her class teacher, on one occasion highlighting a difference between the two programmes which had led to confusion for the children. *Letters and Sounds* introduces the grapheme *ow* as the sound in *now* and *how*, while in Read Write Inc. it is introduced as /oa/ as in *know* and *show*. Susan was also able to assist the teacher in lessons as she got to grips with the new programme. This support was noted with appreciation in her report from the school.

Both case studies illustrate the importance of becoming familiar with phonics programmes quickly and demonstrating to the schools in which you work that you understand the principles of systematic synthetic phonics. Once these have been mastered, it is much easier to adapt to the features of an unfamiliar programme.

Research Focus: Teaching handwriting, reading and spelling skills (THRASS)

As mentioned earlier, a study by Callinan and Van der Zee (2010) compared Jolly Phonics and THRASS. It is interesting to consider THRASS in the context of systematic synthetic phonics, since it can be found widely in some areas of the UK, as well as in many other countries, including Australia and New Zealand. THRASS's information brochure states:

Some teachers ask if THRASS is an 'analytic phonics' or a 'synthetic phonics' approach. Analytic phonics involves whole-to-part teaching, that is, learners analyse lists of 'whole words' (learnt by sight in a 'phonics-free' stage) to look at the parts (usually the 'letter sound/s' at the beginning and end of the words). Synthetic phonics involves children being taught the 'letter sounds' (in a 'word-free' stage) so that they can blend (synthesise) 'letter sounds' to create words (that is, part-to-whole). THRASS uses both approaches (each of the 120 THRASS words/wholes has a bold grapheme/part) but children are required to identify letters by 'name', not 'sound', so that they can more easily 'segment and blend' (analyse and synthesise) the various phonemes of the numerous one-letter, two-letter, three-letter and four-letter spelling-choices. Therefore THRASS differs from the strategies of almost all 'synthetic phonics' programs in that it does not believe in using 'letter sounds' as part of its teaching strategy. We firmly believe that teaching 'letter sounds' is an underlying factor for potential literacy failure in learners of any age, particularly males, because of their learning style.

(THRASS, p.5)

Although THRASS has a systematic element, in that it has ten stages of teaching related to its picture chart, it does not limit the focus to groups of letters and sounds at each stage

→

or phase in the same way as the three systematic synthetic phonics programmes described above. Table 13.1 illustrates the stages and the ages at which they should be taught, although it should be noted that THRASS can be taught to older children and adults too.

Table 13.1 The ten stages of THRASS teaching

Stage number	Age (years)	Stage title	Learning aims
1	3, 4, 5	Picture location	Locate pictures on the chart
2	3, 4, 5	Letter location	Locate and name letters
3	3, 4, 5	Letter formation	Name and form letters
4	3, 4, 5	Grapheme location	Locate and name graphemes
5	3, 4, 5	Keyword location	Locate and name 120 keywords
6	5	Phoneme location	Locate and articulate 44 phonemes
7	5	Keyword synthesis	Blend, read and spell keywords
8	6	Key grapheme recall	Visualise and spell graphemes
9	6	Keyword analysis	Read, spell and analyse 120 keywords
10	7	THRASS 500 Tests	Read and spell THRASS 500

Note: Stages 1 to 9 pertain to the THRASS picture chart.

Source: Callinan and Van der Zee, 2010, p.22.

Despite the staged approach described above, THRASS claims to have a different approach from other programmes:

> THRASS gives learners the whole-picture of English from the beginning, that is, there are 44 phonemes in spoken English but only 26 letters in the alphabet, therefore there are different grapheme choices for the phonemes in words. Learners then work from the 'big picture' to 'smaller pictures'.
>
> (THRASS, p.7)

Over a one-year period from 2006, Callinan and Van der Zee (2010) compared two schools where Jolly Phonics (JP1 and JP2) was taught, with one school at which THRASS was taught in Reception. The limited size of the sample, together with other factors identified by the authors such as timing of lessons, varying roles of teaching assistants and class sizes, led the authors to be cautious in their conclusions. They had anticipated that children who used THRASS would be at an advantage in non-word reading tests (see Chapter 11) and short-term memory performance, but found only that 'by June 2007 the JP school 2 had made greater gains in both word and non-word reading tasks compared to the THRASS school. The JP school 1 did not differ from either school but failed to demonstrate an improvement in non-word reading' (2010, p.26) and concluded that 'Children's improvements in their short-term verbal memory

→

skills could not be linked to the method of instruction they received'. The limitations of this research and its conclusions, and the lack of comparative studies of different systematic synthetic phonics programmes make it all the more important that we look closely at evidence we find in schools when deciding on strategies for teaching phonics.

Discussion

Both as a trainee and as a teacher, you will encounter different phonics programmes and will need to look at them closely to determine how you can use your existing knowledge to teach them, and to ascertain what you will need to learn if you are to teach them in the most effective way. As we have seen, schools often change the programmes they use and some retain elements of ones previously used, despite recommendations to show fidelity to single programmes. In our experience, THRASS charts are one of the resources which many schools continue to use, even after installing one of the systematic synthetic phonics programmes described in this chapter. In view of this, you may wish to find out more about THRASS both from schools which use it and from the THRASS website.

Activity

Analysing phonics programmes

Use Table 13.2 to analyse the phonics programmes you encounter. Produced by the TDA, the table shows the typical features of a systematic synthetic phonics programme. You can use it both to examine the structure of a programme and to *assess* your own knowledge and understanding.

When reviewing the phonics programme, make a note in the right-hand column of how each feature is introduced and taught. Also note any questions this raises for you or issues you want to explore further.

Table 13.2 Typical features of systematic synthetic phonics programmes

Typical features	Name of programme, review, questions etc.
Grapheme-phoneme correspondences (GPCs) introduced at the rate of about 3–5 a week, starting with single letters and a sound for each, then going on to the sounds represented by digraphs (e.g. sh and oo) and larger grapheme units (e.g. air, igh, eigh)	
Blending of phonemes for reading, starting after the first few GPCs have been taught and then working with more GPCs as they are taught	
Segmenting of phonemes for spelling, again starting after the first few GPCs have been taught and then working with more GPCs as they are taught	

Typical features	Name of programme, review, questions etc.
Introduction of the most common spellings for sounds first and then introduce alternative sounds for spellings and alternative spellings for sounds	
Introduction of strategies for reading and spelling common high-frequency words containing unusual GPCs	
Provision of opportunities for the application of word reading skills in reading books which are closely matched to children's developing skills (level-appropriate decodable texts) to support children in using their phonemic strategies as a first approach to reading and spelling and to experiencing success	

Source: DES, 2011a, pp.10–11.

Activity

Making effective use of systematic synthetic phonics programmes

Reflect on your ability to do each of the items below. Consider what additional knowledge, understanding and experiences you require to enable you to be confident in your ability to make effective use of systematic synthetic phonics programmes:

1. Support children in learning phonic knowledge and skills using a systematic synthetic programme, with the expectation that they will be fluent readers having secured word recognition skills by the end of Key Stage 1.
2. Plan for and teach discrete, daily sessions of phonics, progressing from simple to more complex phonic knowledge and skills and covering the major grapheme–phoneme correspondences.
3. Assess children's progress in phonic knowledge and skill.
4. Use a multi-sensory approach so that children learn variously from simultaneous visual, auditory and kinaesthetic activities which are designed to secure essential phonic knowledge and the skills of blending and segmenting.
5. Teach how phonemes can be blended, in order, from left to right, 'all through the word' for reading.
6. Teach how to segment words into their constituent phonemes for spelling and that this is the reverse of blending phonemes to read words.
7. Teach children to apply phonic knowledge and skills as their first approach to reading and spelling even if a word is not completely phonically regular.

(Continued)

(Continued)

8. Teach high-frequency words that do not conform completely to grapheme–phoneme correspondence rules.
9. Teach to the systematic teaching framework of the programmes they are working with.
10. When children are in the early stages of learning phonics, use decodable texts of the appropriate level where children can apply and practise the phonic knowledge and skills they have learned and can experience success by relying on phonemic blending. They should not be expected to use strategies such as whole-word recognition and/or cues from context, grammar or pictures.

(DES, 2011b, p.3)

As you have seen in previous chapters, and underlying all of the items listed above, it is vital that the correct enunciation of phonemes is used throughout the teaching of systematic synthetic phonics. All of the programmes described in this chapter emphasise correct enunciation. Sonic Phonics and some online resources are useful tools for hearing correct enunciation. It is also important to consider differences in accent and dialect, as these affect the way some phonemes are sounded (see Chapters 2 and 3).

On first encountering a phonics programme, the vast array of phonics terminology can be daunting. It can be a difficult task for a trainee or new teacher who is not a literacy or phonics specialist to understand the meaning of and difference between, say, a phoneme and grapheme, digraph and split digraph and so on. Teachers' manuals usually explain terminology and often provide simple definitions. For example, *Letters and Sounds: Principles and Practice of High Quality Phonics* (DfES, 2007) clearly explains relevant terminology and provides a useful guide to those teaching *Letters and Sounds*. Almost all of the terminology found here also appears in other major programmes. However, there are features unique to some programmes which you will need to focus upon should you find that you need to work with an unfamiliar programme. Some of these features relate to the order in which letters are taught, while others concern terminology particular to a programme, such as 'Fred sounds' and 'speed sounds' in Read Write Inc. Yet other features involve pedagogical styles, including using actions for letters in Jolly Phonics or methods of organising partner work in Read Write Inc.

Tightly structured lesson planning

For all systematic synthetic phonics programmes, lessons are designed to be pacey, lively and interactive and should involve multi-sensory activity. You will need to ensure that your lessons are structured appropriately for the programme with which you work. For example,

Letters and Sounds is structured around four elements: revisit and review, teach, practise, and apply. This promotes a fast-paced, well-organised session, during which children are given the opportunity to practise skills and knowledge already gained and to learn new information. See Chapters 7, 9 and 10 for ideas.

What is especially important is that you develop a sound understanding of systematic synthetic phonics early in your course and take every opportunity to observe experienced teachers teaching phonics. This, allied to reading about systematic synthetic phonics, developing your subject knowledge and following up lectures and workshops, will ensure that you are well-equipped to apply your knowledge and understanding when you meet unfamiliar programmes.

Learning Outcomes Review

Through reading this chapter and engaging with the activities, you should have gained a basic knowledge of the most frequently used systematic synthetic phonics programmes and be aware of the challenges you will face as you work with different systematic synthetic phonics programmes.

Self-assessment questions

Look at the Activity above, 'Making effective use of systematic synthetic phonics programmes', and for each point consider what newly qualified teachers need to be able to do to in their teaching of reading and writing.

Further Reading

For a guide to *Letters and Sounds* and useful information on systematic synthetic phonics in general, see:

DfES (2007) *Letters and Sounds: Principles and Practice of High Quality Phonics: Notes of Guidance for Practitioners and Teachers.* London: DfES.

For guidance on the principles and practice for Read Write Inc., see www.ruthmiskinliteracy. com and:

R. Miskin (2011) *Read Write Inc.: Phonics Handbook.* Oxford: Oxford University Press.

For guidance on the principles and practice for Jolly Phonics, see:

www.jollylearning.co.uk/overview-about-jolly-phonics/ (accessed 3/2/15).

For details of Phonics Bug, see:

www.pearsonphonics.co.uk/PhonicsBug/OnlineReadingWorld/OnlineWorld.aspx (accessed 3/2/15).

For information on Sounds-Write, see:

www.sounds-write.co.uk/ (accessed 3/2/15).

For guidance on the principles and practice for THRASS, see:

Davies, A. and Ritchie, D. (1998) *THRASS: Teacher's Manual.* Chester: THRASS.

For Sonic Phonics product information, see:

www.talkingproducts.com/sonic-phonics.html (accessed 24/12/14).

References

Callinan, C. and Van der Zee, E. (2010) 'A comparative study of two methods of synthetic phonics instruction for learning how to read: Jolly Phonics and THRASS', *The Psychology of Education Review, 34* (1).

Davies, A. and Ritchie, D. (1998) *THRASS: Teachers Manual.* Chester: THRASS.

DES (2011a) *'Systematic synthetic phonics in initial teaching training: Guidance and support materials'*, notes issued to ITT providers by the Training and Development Agency (TDA), London.

DES (2011b) *Introducing Systematic Synthetic Phonics: Notes from DES.* London: DES.

DfE (2011) *Teachers' Standards in England from September 2012.* London: DfE.

DfES (2007) *Letters and Sounds: Principles and Practice of High Quality Phonics.* London: DfES.

Jolly Learning (1992) *Jolly Phonics.* Available at www.jollylearning.co.uk/overview-about-jollyphonics/ (accessed 3/2/15).

Miskin, R. (2011) *Read Write Inc.: Phonics Handbook.* Oxford: Oxford University Press.

Ofsted (2010) *Reading by Six.* Manchester: Ofsted.

Rose, J. (2006) *Independent Review of the Teaching of Early Reading, Final Report, March 2006* (The Rose Review – Ref: 0201-2006DOC-EN). Nottingham: DfES.

Teaching Handwriting Reading and Spelling Skills (THRASS) (no date) THRASS for Teaching English as a First or Other Language: Information Brochure for Pre-schools, Schools, Colleges and Universities. Osborne Park: THRASS (Australia).

Wyse, D. and Goswami, U. (2008) 'Synthetic phonics and the teaching of reading', *British Educational Research Journal, 34* (6): 691–710.

Wyse, D. and Styles, M. (2007) 'Synthetic phonics and the teaching of reading: The debate surrounding England's "Rose Report"', *Literacy, 41* (1).

Audit and test

Work through each section below, responding to each question or task. When you have completed each section, you can read the answers at the end of the chapter.

Section 1: Key terminology for using a range of programmes and resources

It is important that you understand the terms below before you move on to the next activity. Provide a definition of each and check your definitions against those at the end of the chapter:

Phonics first and fast

Discrete daily sessions

Fidelity to the teaching framework

Decodable texts

Phases

Core criteria

You also need to know something about each of the major phonics programmes used in schools In England. Find out as much as you can about each and note some key features. Weblinks have been provided to help you.

Read Write Inc.

https://ruthmiskin.com/en/programmes/phonics/

- Jolly Phonics http://jollylearning.co.uk/overview-about-jolly-phonics/
- *Letters and Sounds* https://www.gov.uk/government/uploads/system/uploads/attachment_data/file/190599/Letters_and_Sounds_-_DFES-00281-2007.pdf
- Phonics Bughttps://www.pearsonschoolsandfecolleges.co.uk/Primary/Literacy/AllLiteracyresources/PhonicsBug/phonics-bug.aspx
- Sounds-Write http://www.sounds-write.co.uk/
- Floppy's Phonics http://www.oup.com/oxed/primary/oxfordreadingtree/resources/floppysphonics/soundsandletters/

Section 2: Criteria for successful systematic synthetic phonics programmes

What do you consider are the key features of successful phonics programmes?

Look at Ofsted's (2010) *Reading by Six* report to find out the inspectorate's views (see answers section for extract and the end of the chapter for a weblink).

Before you look at the answers, think about the following:

- word recognition
- assessment

- progression
- teaching methods
- high-frequency words.

Section 3: Programme quiz

Which programme is being described?

1. There are actions for each phoneme.

2. It has a chart of speed sounds.

3. There are six phases, the first of which only involves oral work.

4. It is based upon *Letters and Sounds* and has a range of books, some of which can be used interactively for teaching.

5. It uses an alphabetic code chart.

6. There is a mnemonic to go with each grapheme–phoneme correspondence – for example, *Maisie's Mountain* and *poo at the zoo, cup of tea for ea, what can you see? for ee.*

7. The first five letter sound correspondences are s a t i p.

8. The first eight letter sound correspondences are s a t p i n m d.

9. The first eight letter sound correspondences are m a s d t.

10. This programme claims to teach everything children need for the DfE's Year 1 Phonics Screening Check.

In the answers section you will find charts showing the sequence of grapheme–phoneme correspondences for each of Jolly Phonics, *Letters and Sounds* and Read Write Inc.

Section 4: What to look for when you meet a new programme

Now think about what you would need to find out if you found you were going to work in a school with a phonics programme you had not met before. Make a list of things to ask.

ANSWERS

Section 1: Key terminology for using a range of programmes and resources

Phonics first and fast

Children learn to apply phonic knowledge and skills as their first approach to reading and

Spelling. They do this as part of a systematic programme which is time-limited – for example, *Letters and Sounds'* six phases should normally be completed within Key Stage 1.

Discrete daily sessions

Daily sessions which focus on phonics give teachers regular opportunities to deliver high-quality phonics teaching which is not overshadowed by other subject matter.

Fidelity to the teaching framework

Fidelity to a framework or structure that ensures that all of the 40+ phonemes and their alternative spellings and pronunciations are taught and applied in reading and writing. The *Core Criteria* (DfE, 2011) do not state that this should necessarily be restricted to a specific programme.

Decodable texts

Texts which have a high proportion of words which can be decoded (read) using phonic strategies.

Phases

These are stages in a systematic programme through which children progress. For example, *Letters and Sounds* has six phases.

Core criteria

These are set out in the DfE website and provide clearly defined key features of an effective, systematic synthetic phonics programme.

Section 2: Criteria for successful systematic synthetic phonics programmes

Ofsted's *Reading by Six* report (2010, p.42), which maintained that programmes for phonic work should meet each of the following criteria:

- present high-quality systematic, synthetic phonic work as the prime approach to decoding print, i.e. a phonics 'first and fast' approach;
- enable children to start learning phonic knowledge and skills using a systematic synthetic programme by the age of five, with the expectation that they will be fluent readers having secure word recognition skills by the end of Key Stage 1;
- be designed for the teaching of discrete, daily sessions progressing from simple to more complex phonic knowledge and skills and covering the major grapheme–phoneme correspondences;

- enable children's progress to be assessed;
- use a multi-sensory approach so that children learn variously from simultaneous visual, auditory and kinaesthetic activities which are designed to secure essential phonic knowledge and skills;
- demonstrate that phonemes should be blended, in order, from left to right, 'all through the word' for reading;
- demonstrate how words can be segmented into their constituent phonemes for spelling and that this is the reverse of blending phonemes to read words;
- ensure children apply phonic knowledge and skills as their first approach to reading and spelling, even if a word is not completely phonically regular;
- ensure that children are taught high-frequency words that do not conform completely to grapheme–phoneme correspondence rules;
- provide fidelity to the teaching framework for the duration of the programme, to ensure that these irregular words are fully learned;
- ensure that, as pupils move through the early stages of acquiring phonics, they are invited to practise by reading texts which are entirely decodable for them, so that they experience success and learn to rely on phonemic strategies.

Section 3: Programme quiz

You were asked which programme was being described.

1. There are actions for each phoneme. (Jolly Phonics)

2. It has a chart of speed sounds. (Read Write Inc.)

3. There are six phases, the first of which only involves oral work. (*Letters and Sounds*)

4. It is based upon *Letters and Sounds* and has a range of books, some of which can be used interactively for teaching. (Phonics Bug)

5. It uses an alphabetic code chart. (Floppy's Phonics)

6. There is a mnemonic to go with each grapheme–phoneme correspondence, for example *Maisie's Mountain* and *poo at the zoo, cup of tea for ea, what can you see? for ee.* (Read Write Inc.)

7. The first five letter sound correspondences are s a t i p. (Jolly Phonics and *Letters and Sounds*)

8. The first eight letter sound correspondences are s a t p i n m d. (*Letters and Sounds*)

9. The five letter sound correspondences are m a s d t. (Read Write Inc.)

10. This programme claims to teach everything children need for the DfE's Year 1 Phonics Screening Check. (Sounds-Write)

Below you will find charts showing the sequence of grapheme–phoneme correspondences for each of Jolly Phonics, *Letters and Sounds*, and Read Write Inc.

Jolly Phonics	Week
s a t i p	1
n c/k e h r	2
m d g o u	3
l f b ai j	4
oa ie ee or z w	5
ng v oo **oo** y <u>x</u>	6
ch sh th **th** <u>qu</u> ou	7
oi <u>ue</u> er ar	8

Letters and Sounds	
s a t p	Phase 2
i n m d	(Reception)
g o c k	
ck e u r	
h b f, ff l, ll ss	
j v w x	Phase 3
y z, zz qu	(Reception)
ch, sh, th/th, ng, ai, ee, igh, oa, oo/oo, ar, or, ur, ow, oi, ear, air, ure, er*	
zh	Phase 5 (Y1)

* 'er' represents a schwa (uh) sound, as in mother

Read Write Inc	Group
m a s d t	1
i n p g o	2
c k u b	3
f e l h sh r	4
j v y w	5
th z ch <u>qu</u> x ng <u>nk</u>	6
ay ee igh ow oo oo ar or air ir ou oy	7
ire ear ure	8

NB The letters underlined are not single phonemes: nk (ngk), qu (cw), x (cs), ue (yoo)

Section 4: What to look for when you meet a new programme

Among the things you might wish to find out are:

The order of grapheme–phoneme correspondences in the programme.

How grapheme–phoneme correspondences are taught.

Are there associated decodable texts?

Is training available?

Are there in-built assessments?

What resources and teaching aids are available?

Are electronic resources available?

Is it possible to observe someone teaching using the programme?

What to do next?

Reinforce your knowledge of different programmes by:

1. Observing lessons in schools.

2. Looking at resources for different programmes.

3. Discussing different programmes with teachers.

4. Looking at websites for different programmes.

14. Using technology to support the teaching of phonics

Learning Outcomes

By the end of this chapter you should:

- know about a range of electronic devices and other technology platforms that may be used to teach phonics effectively;
- begin to understand the benefits and limitations of using technology in teaching phonics;
- know a range of resources, including apps, software, online resources and other media, to enhance and support teaching and learning phonics.

Teachers' Standards

2. Promote good progress and outcomes by pupils:
    - demonstrate knowledge and understanding of how pupils learn and how this impacts on teaching.
3. Demonstrate good subject and curriculum knowledge:
    - if teaching early reading, demonstrate a clear understanding of systematic synthetic phonics.
4. Plan and teach well-structured lessons:
    - impart knowledge and develop understanding through effective use of lesson time.
5. Adapt teaching to respond to the strengths and needs of all pupils:
    - know when and how to differentiate appropriately, using approaches which enable pupils to be taught effectively.

Criteria for assuring high-quality phonic work (DfE, 2011)

Use a multi-sensory approach so that children learn variously from simultaneous visual, auditory and kinaesthetic activities which are designed to secure essential phonic knowledge and skills (see note 5)

Note 5: Multi-sensory activities should be interesting and engaging but firmly focused on intensifying the learning associated with its phonic goal [sic]. They should avoid taking children down a circuitous route only tenuously linked to the goal. This means avoiding over-elaborate activities that are difficult to manage and take too long to complete, thus distracting the children from concentrating on the learning goal.

Introduction

Pupils are increasingly accessing smartphones, tablets and other electronic devices in the home. The National Literacy Trust (2018) found that one in eight (13.1 per cent) disadvantaged children in the UK say that they don't have a book of their own and almost all families (97 per cent) with a child under the age of five own touch-screens. Children are being introduced to electronic devices by their parents at an increasingly young age (Chiong and Shuler, 2010). It is clear that an increasing number of children have access to smartphones, tablets and iPads than have access to physical books and that most children are becoming adept at using the technology that is widely available.

As O'Reilly (2018) notes:

> *technology is a powerful tool with which to engage children across disciplines and, in the modern classroom, can incorporate many devices stretching far beyond the computer or the interactive whiteboard.*

(in Bushnell et al., 2018)

Teachers are able make use of these technologies in the teaching and learning environment. Software and websites might be used to demonstrate the correct enunciation of phonemes, games downloaded to a tablet can offer the opportunity to match the correct GPCs and ebooks may provide the chance to practise blending and segmenting. There are opportuntities for schools to use these technologies to make links between the classroom and home, with many schools using online platforms and social media to communicate with parents and through the sharing of information about the technology they use in the teaching of phonics. However, schools are being challenged in the integration of technology in the classroom. It is argued that this technology needs to be used in a careful way, to ensure the effective learning and development of phonics and early literacy (Northrop and Killeen, 2013). Safe use of technology and online resources should be considered carefully, in line with the school's safeguarding policy. Research shows that the learning effects of devices in schools tend to be disjointed (Shuler, 2012) and, as technologies evolve quickly, it is difficult to decide how best to integrate them into the classroom (Cheung and Slavin, 2012).

This chapter will look at some of the reasons why using a range of technology is so appropriate for teaching phonics, and when it may not be. It will explore a range of practical strategies for use in the classroom, some of which might be extended to the home, where children can work with parents or carers to reinforce their learning in school. There will also be a focus on the careful selection of apps and software that support and enhance the phonics curriculum.

What kind of technology is available?

There is an overwhelming choice of technologies available to support the teaching of phonics and so only a small snapshot of what is available can been considered in this chapter. There are also rapid advances in technology, with frequent upgrades and new technologies available on a daily basis. With this in mind, we will explore generic types of technologies, with reference to some specific examples that are currently available. We will consider later in the chapter how teachers might use these technologies to support their teaching of phonics, and how they might choose effective technology that contains appropriate phonics content, from such a broad range of choice.

Large devices

Tools such as interactive whiteboards and smart tables are common used in primary classrooms. They may be used to teach a whole class or larger groups. Their size makes them accessible, and good for teacher modelling and instruction, and their interactivity means that children can be involved in their learning.

Small devices

Laptops, tablets, *Kindles* and other hand-held devices are commonly used for the supported teaching of groups or individuals. This allows teachers to focus more closely on each child, and to ensure appropriate learning takes place for each individual, based on their needs and ability. Add-on technology, such as *Osmo* (a package that offers additional hardware such as a readable whiteboard, number and digit tiles, and coding tools), can transform devices into learning tools and increase the potential for intertaction.

Software

Many schools have access to software that can be used in the teaching of phonics. These often require a subscription. *Espresso* (Discovery Education) is one example of a learning platform that has content that matches the *Letters and Sounds* (DfES, 2007) phonics phases. Many of the published schemes, such as Read Write Inc., some of which were explored in Chapter 13, have developed software to accompany their other teaching resources. Lots of schools use software to plan for their teaching of phonics, and for assessment and record keeping.

Online resources

There are many educational websites that provide games and activities to practise phonics objectives, such as phonicsplay.co.uk. These vary greatly in quality and should be considered carefully before being used with children. Audio-visual platforms and social media channels, such as YouTube, can be used to access songs, rhymes and stories.

Apps

Apps for tablets and other hand-held devices can be useful tools in supporting the teaching of phonics. Israelson (2015) considered the different types of apps available and which types work well for specific phonics and literacy learning goals. Identifying these characteristics can simplify the process of finding suitable apps. A description of each type of app follows:

- **E-book apps.** Some are electronic versions of print texts, such as Dr Seuss's *The Cat in the Hat.* Others are written in digital form only. These apps vary greatly in design and quality.

- **Audio-recording apps.** Apps that afford recording of audio present many unique learning opportunities to develop several early literacy skills. Teachers and children might record the enunciation of phonemes, to hear the differences in accent and to demonstrate the preferred pronunciation.

- **E-versions of traditional tools.** These apps recreate traditional early primary teaching tools in digital form, such as whiteboards and collaborative drawing tools.

- **Rhyming or phonics games.** These apps practise rhyming words or phonics with a gaming element. For example, *Pirate Phonics* offers games to learn and practise phonemes and graphemes using a touch-screen.

- **Alphabet apps.** These apps practise naming or writing letters of the alphabet, such as *ABC Kids.*

- **Handwriting apps.** These apps allow the user to practise forming letters and words, such as *Pocket Phonics.*

- **Sight-word apps.** These apps, which often include a game element and an audio feature, vary in the sight words included. It is worth considering which of these apps contain words from the common exception words lists for each year group in the *National Curriculum: English Programmes of Study* (DfE, 2013).

- **Word-family apps.** These apps engage the children in practising rhyming patterns, words with similar GPCs and onset and rime.

- **Multi-modal composing apps.** These apps are designed to afford digital writing, allowing the user to compose multi-modal texts that may include words, images, audio, video and/or animation. These offer children opportunities for creative expression using multi-modal features that are not possible in traditional print media.

Activity

Choose three of the technologies above that you are unfamiliar with and find out more about them. Consider how you might integrate these into your teaching of phonics.

Case Study: Enhancing the teaching of phonics

Higgins et al. (2012) suggest that teachers should understand which technologies can be used for what specific educational purposes, and then decide how they can be used and embedded across a range of educational contexts. With this in mind, Wingate Primary School, County Durham, uses technology in a variety of ways to support the teaching and learning of phonics in Early Years Foundation Stage (EYFS) and Key Stage 1. The school ensures that a broad range of technology is used to enhance and support the teaching of phonics, alongside teaching through other methods.

The practitioners in the school have developed their own set of PowerPoint presentations linked to each phase of *Letters and Sounds* (DfES, 2007), tailored to their needs in teaching and to the learning needs of their children.

Whole-class and large-group teaching is supported by the use of an interactive whiteboard and the *Espresso* learning platform. Animation and video clips are used to enunciate and teach phonemes and graphemes, and to model blending and segmenting. Activities – for example, sorting, matching and finding games – are used to apply phonics knowledge. The platform can be modified to vary the complexity of content, offering one or more phonemes at a time.

Small group and individual learning, both supported and independent, is often based on laptops and tablets using phonics apps and other software. Children will apply their phonics knowledge by playing games and completing tasks through a variety of phonics-based online activities and apps, such as *Pirate Phonics* and the large selection of games available at phonicsplay.co.uk. Where applicable, children use smaller devices to follow intervention programmes, such as *Lexia*, and these are facilitated and monitored by an adult to ensure appropriate progress is made. When working independently, children often use headphones to allow for greater opportunity to focus and progress independently.

Entertainment versus education

Choosing appropriate technologies can be challenging. We must consider whether our objective is to stimulate and motivate children with exciting graphics, enhanced content, challenges and rewards, or to support the teaching of phonics with appropriate subject content tightly matched to learning objectives. It may be that our aim is to provide technologies that support our teaching of phonics that meet both of these criteria.

There is an overwhelming selection of digital material available; however, standards differ hugely. Apps, software and online platforms may be chosen for a variety of reasons: because they are reasonably priced or free; are visually appealing and 'fun'. These technologies may offer very little effective phonic subject content or might even provide information that is misleading or inaccurate (Israelson, 2015). It is important for teachers to consider the region or accent that phonics apps, software and online platforms are designed to target; there are a large number of American products on the market that offer alternative phoneme pronunciations to those commonly used in classrooms in the UK.

Research shows that children can be distracted by some of the additional content of apps, software and online platforms, such as animations, sound effects and other enhancement tools (Northrop and Killeen, 2013). Most digital platforms that have phonics-based games and activities use enhanced content that is not related to phonics. It is suggested that this may hinder rather than support some children in their learning.

Activity

Consider an app, software product or online platform that you have used, or observed being used, in the classroom:

- make note of the phonics content that is taught and review its suitability;
- consider whether there is any misleading or inaccurate content;
- identify any enhanced content that might be distracting or a hindrance for some learners.

Research Focus: The *App Map*

The *App Map* is a research-based tool for the systematic evaluation of apps for early literacy learning (Israelson, 2015). It helps teachers in finding high-quality apps to support the teaching of phonics and other early literacy objectives. Through her research, Israelson found that many teachers who had a good understanding of best practices in developing early literacy ignored that knowledge when selecting apps. Often, teachers prioritised characteristics such as price or appealing graphics over phonics or literacy content. There are few strategies and frameworks in place to guide teachers in their selection of apps, software and online platforms. Israelson developed a framework, as seen in Figure 14.1 below, to support teachers in their choice of suitable apps. Apps can be considered against a variety of criteria to help teachers make judgements about their suitability.

Activity

Find out more about the *App Map* tool and follow the framework to select a suitable phonics-related app.

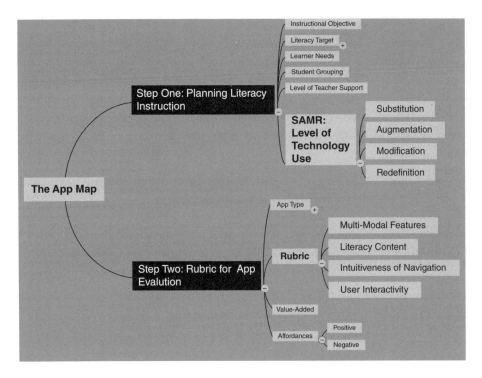

Figure 14.1 The App Map Framework, Israelson (2015)

How to use technology effectively

Although including technology in the teaching of phonics can increase engagement and motivation, researchers agree that technology should not replace the teaching of phonics by other means, but that it should enrich and complement it. Northrop and Killeen (2013) point out that the use of technology does not automatically lead to an increase in children's achievement. Even if a child is proficient in using technology, and capable of successfully accessing apps and software, it does not necessarily mean that they understand the phonics content, or will make progress in their learning of phonics.

Higgins et al. (2012) suggest that:

> *Digital technologies are now embedded in our society. Focus has shifted from whether or not to use them in teaching and learning, to understanding which technologies can be used for what specific educational purposes and then to investigate how best they can be used and embedded across the range of educational contexts in schools.*

(p.3)

Educators need to make decisions about the most suitable technology to support the teaching of phonics and when it is most appropriate to use it. Teachers should be clear in their rationale for including technology in the teaching of phonics, and should consider whether the technology in question will help learners work efficiently and practitioners to teach effectively. The role of technology in the teaching and learning of phonics should be identified, and it needs to be considered if the technology in question is to allow learners to access phonics subject content efficiently. Teachers might consider whether using technology adds value to their phonics teaching.

Northrop and Killeen (2013) suggest a possible framework for successfully integrating apps, software and online platforms into phonics teaching and learning:

- explicitly teach the phonics content before introducing the chosen digital format – using apps, software and online platforms should not replace direct and systematic teaching of phonics;

- use the apps, software and online platforms for guided and independent practice – first with teacher guidance, then independently or with peers;

- check the children's understanding of both how to use the chosen tool and their understanding of the phonics content;

- familiarise yourself with the technology and be aware of the limitations.

It may be possible that using technology is not as successful in supporting the teaching of phonics in comparison to other curriculum areas. Higgins et al. (2012), when completing a meta-analysis of research about the impact of digital technology on learning, found that gains in attainment in mathematics and science tend to be greater in comparison to those in literacy, and in literacy the impacts tends to be greater in writing compared with phonics, reading and spelling. Higgins et al. (2012) recommend that:

> technology is best used as a supplement to normal teaching rather than as a replacement for it. This suggests some caution in the way in which technology is adopted or embedded in schools.

(p.4)

Case Study: Using technology to support phonics with young learners

Busy Bears Children's Day Nursery, Durham, engages children in indoor and outdoor play-based activities, through which phonics is taught as an integrated element of the curriculum. Phonics is taught through the Literacy and Language and Communications areas

→

of learning development in the EYFS framework (DfE, 2017). The focus for those children in the nursery who are 40 to 60 months is on Phase 1 of *Letters and Sounds* (DfES, 2007) and a variety of activities, including those using technology, are offered through free play and adult-led group time. Belo et al. (2016), when considering a range of research literature, concluded that using technology contributes to children's early literacy development, provided that it is used in an adequate way. The practitioners in the nursery ensure that a broad range of technology is used to enhance and support the teaching of phonics, not to simply replace it. Often technology is used to support children in becoming secure and confident in the Phase 1 objectives. Cviko et al. (2012) noted that studies of technology-rich learning environments in early education have promising results with regard to early literacy skills attainment.

The nursery uses a smart table – a large, portable tablet that can be configured for use when standing or sitting. Android apps are downloaded to the smart table and, for safeguarding, wifi is disabled and password protected when the device is being used by the children. Activities include tracing graphemes, simple interactive jigsaws for segmenting and blending, listening to phonemes and identifying GPCs. The apps that are chosen are engaging and relevant, with simple content suitable for young learners.

Practitioners use the smart table for adult-led activities, where specific phonics learning objectives are taught and assessed, and the skills children need to engage with to use the device and the apps can be modelled. The activities and choice of tasks are chosen carefully, and are linked to the nursery's Learning and Development plans – individual, tailored plans that are provided for each child.

Children are also encouraged to use the tablet during 'free access' time to develop their learning. These are child-led sessions, where children independently use apps and software to practice skills they have tried previously during adult-led sessions. These sessions are time-limited and monitored by practitioners to ensure appropriate use.

Smaller tablets and *Kindles* are used for group time, where supported learning takes place. Again, the apps and games are chosen carefully to enhance phonics teaching. Activities during these sessions might include identifying initial letters in common words, matching graphemes with pictures and using the letters in their names.

The nursery uses a range of online platforms to support its teaching. For safeguarding, at least two practitioners access the websites to check suitability before using them with the children. Songs and stories are shared through video and audio platforms such as YouTube and simple online games and activities are played through websites such as BBC Learning.

The nursery uses technology to plan for phonics, and to assess and record the children's progress. Reporting to parents includes the use of an online platform, where practitioners can share comments, photographs and videos of the children engaged in the teaching and learning of phonics.

Group and individual learning

Whole-class teaching

Large devices, such as interactive whiteboards and smart tables, are frequently used to teach a whole class or larger groups of children. The interactive nature of these tools allows the teacher to both teach and model, and to invite children to take part in the activity. Teachers can access purchased software such as *Espresso*, websites such as phonicsplay.co.uk or audio-visual platforms such as YouTube to revisit, teach, apply and practise phonics objectives. As we have already discussed, research shows that when teaching phonics these technologies should be used to support and enhance teaching, and that phonics might be more effectively taught by other means. Effective teachers of phonics are able to choose when the use of technology is most efficient (Belo et al., 2016).

Group teaching

Children may be taught in groups, to learn new objectives or to apply and practise objectives that have already been taught. Smart tables or sets of hand-held devices, such as tablets, are commonly used. This allows teachers to focus more closely on each child, and to ensure appropriate learning takes place for each individual based on their needs and ability. These supported learning sessions might be adult-led, allowing for teaching and modelling, and for the monitoring and assessment of progress. It provides an opportunity to not only teach phonics objectives, but also to ensure children know how to use the chosen technology effectively. Higgins et al. (2012) suggest that collaborative use of technology (in pairs or small groups) is usually more effective than individual use, though some pupils, especially younger children, may need guidance in how to effectively and responsibly work with peers.

Individual and independent learning

Children might use tablets and other small devices to work independently on activities that allow them to practise skills and consolidate their learning in phonics. This allows teachers to provide specific activities matched to the needs of each individual, the opportunity to allow progress at the child's own pace and to develop confidence and independence in the child's own learning. Appropriate guidance and modelling beforehand, and careful monitoring, would be required in order to use the technology most effectively.

Children with additional needs

Higgins et al. (2012) have noted that technology can be particularly practical for lower-attaining pupils in providing intensive support to enable them to catch up with their peers. It can be used to allow children to access phonics in a multi-sensory way, and can provide children with alternatives to reading, writing and recording. Many phonics schemes, of which some are explored in Chapter 13, provide intervention materials; technology might be used to complement these. Phonics intervention should be considered as a planned, short-term catch-up schedule – to allow pupils to rapidly learn specified objectives that they are not yet confident in – rather than consistent provision. Higgins et al. (2012) concluded that:

When providing intervention teaching for those children who do not achieve in phonics at an expected rate, research has shown that technology can be as powerful as a short but focused intervention to improve learning, particularly when there is regular and frequent use (about three times a week) over the course of about a term. However, it has been noted that sustained use over a longer period is usually less effective at improving this kind of boost to attainment.

(p.4)

Research Focus: Technology and gender

Research carried out by the British Educational Communications and Technology Agency (BECTA, 2008, p.3) demonstrated how boys and girls differ in the way they use technology. Key findings included:

- *The use of technology in education improves the motivation and attainment of both girls and boys, though the increases are more marked for boys than girls.*
- *Girls use technology more for schoolwork, whereas boys use it more for leisure purposes. A large proportion of this difference can be accounted for by boys' greater use of computer/console games.*
- *Whereas boys are interested in technology for its own sake, girls see technology as a means of pursuing their interests and furthering their learning.*

The integration of technology in supporting the teaching of phonics can greatly benefit both genders, and, as O'Reilly (2018) suggests,

its use can motivate and raise attainment in pupils, especially boys, and if teachers implement it in a variety of creative ways across disciplines, this may also encourage girls to appreciate a wider spectrum of the applications of technology.

(O'Neill in Bushnell et al, 2018, p.153)

The Programme for International Student Assessment (PISA) report found that boys in England perform less well in reading than girls (OECD, 2016), so the resources available for reading and phonics in the classroom should be given careful consideration. It is likely that offering a range of technologies to support the teaching of phonics will be beneficial for all.

> ## Activity
>
> In the light of the above research focus, choose a particular type of technology platform – perhaps a device, online game or app. Consider how you might use it to support your teaching of a new phoneme. How would you tailor your teaching, and the way you use your chosen technology platform, to meet the needs of all learners, thinking specifically about both boys and girls?

Teacher knowledge and understanding

As we have seen, there is an overwhelming choice of technologies available – only a small snapshot of what is available has been considered in this chapter. Teachers may have a limited understanding about which apps, software and online platforms are suitable to support the teaching of phonics, and may find it difficult to make an informed choice about technologies that are effective and appropriate. Rapid advances in technology can add to the challenge; there are frequent upgrades and new technologies available on a daily basis.

It can be challenging for teachers to use technology in the classroom because it is a complex task to be able to use it to its full potential. Aspects such as the design characteristics of the tool, the content of the software and apps and the complexity of the device may impact on a teacher's understanding and willingness to use available technologies (Belo et al., 2016). Research indicates that teacher competence is a key factor in the integration of technology into teaching. Israelson (2015) suggests that:

> *As literacy texts and related tasks become increasingly transformed by digital technologies and spaces, teachers must understand the new complexities in using digital tools.*

(p.340)

Continued professional development (CPD) is crucial in training educators to use technology most effectively. Teachers should familiarise themselves with some of the appropriate technology that is available. They should access the technology to gain an understanding of the phonics content, and of the skills needed to successfully engage with the chosen platform. Safeguarding issues should be considered, and content should be scrutinised to ensure its suitability. Sharing ideas with colleagues and working together to evaluate the suitability of devices and platforms may be beneficial. Specific and focused training may also be appropriate. Higgins et al. (2012), when completing a meta-analysis of research about the impact of digital technology on learning, concluded that:

At least a full day's training or on-going professional inquiry-based approaches to support the introduction of new technology appear the most successful. The implication is that such support should go beyond the teaching of skills in technology and focus on the successful pedagogical use of technology to support teaching and learning aims.

(p.4)

As well as teachers being trained in the skills of using the technology itself, it is crucial that teachers also learn how to get the best out of different technologies in terms of phonic subject content and how best to promote learning in phonics. Belo et al. (2016) have identified that teachers who are competent in using technology in early phonics and literacy have sufficient knowledge to select effective apps, software and online platforms, determine whether these add value to their teaching and effectively integrate them into their teaching.

Activity

Write a brief action plan, identifying an aspect of using technology that you would like to learn more about, or an aspect about which you feel you would like to improve your knowledge, understanding and skills. Indicate how you might engage in CPD related to your chosen aspect. Specify how you would then use this aspect of technology in the classroom in a phonics context.

The practical suggestions in this chapter will, we hope, provide you with ideas for integrating technology into your phonics teaching. We hope you will have considered your own knowledge about the wide variety of technologies that are available, and how you might select those that are effective and appropriate in both engaging and motivating children and in supporting the teaching and learning of phonics. Using technology to enhance the teaching of phonics rather than to replace it is a key consideration.

Learning Outcomes Review

You should now know about a range of electronic devices and other technology platforms that may be used to teach phonics effectively. You will be able to explore a range of resources, including apps, software, online resources and other media, to enhance

(Continued)

> (Continued)
>
> and support the teaching and learning of phonics. You should be beginning to understand the benefits and limitations of using technology, and be able to make judgements about the suitability of different technologies in supporting the teaching of phonics.

Further Reading

For practical guidance on teaching phonics, look at:

Gill, A. and Waugh, D. (2017) *Phonics: Getting it Right in a Week*. Northwich: Critical Publishing.

For a theoretical perspective on the impact of digital technologies on teaching, look at:

Higgins, S., Xiao, Z. and Katsipataki, M. (2012) *The Impact of Digital Technology on Learning: A Summary for the Education Endowment Foundation*. Education Endowment Foundation (EEF). Available at: https://educationendowmentfoundation.org.uk/public/files/Publications/The_Impact_of_Digital_Technologies_on_Learning_(2012).pdf (accessed 7/18).

For information about a useful digital toolkit, see:

Education Endowment Foundation (EEF) (2018) Digital technology | Toolkit Strand (online). Available at: https://educationendowmentfoundation.org.uk/evidence-summaries/teaching-learning-toolkit/digital-technology/ (accessed 14/6/18).

For information about the App Map, a tool used to select effective apps to support the teaching of phonics, see:

Israelson, M. (2015) 'The App Map: A tool for systematic evaluation of apps for early literacy learning', *The Reading Teacher*, 69 (3): 339–49.

References

BECTA: Leading Next Generation Learning (2008) *How do Boys and Girls Differ in their Use of IT?* Research report. Becta. Available at: http://dera.ioe.ac.uk/8318/1/gender_IT_briefing.pdf (accessed 7/18).

Belo, N., McKenny, S. and Bradley, B. (2016) 'Teacher knowledge for using technology to foster early literacy: A literature review', *Computers in Human Behavior*, 60: 372–83.

Cheung, A. and Slavin, R. (2012) 'How features of educational technology application affect student reading outcomes: A meta-analysis', *Educational Research Review*, 7: 198–15.

Chiong, C. and Shuler, C. (2010) *Learning: Is There and App for That? Investigations of Young Children's Usage and Learning with Mobile Devices and Apps*. New York: The Joan Ganz Cooney Center at Sesame Workshop.

Cviko, A., McKenny, S. and Voogt, J. (2012) 'Teachers enacting a technology-rich curriculum for emergent literacy', *Educational Technology Research and Development*, 60: 31–54.

DfE (2011) *Teachers' Standards in England from September 2012*. London: DfE.

DfE (2013) *National Curriculum: English Programmes of Study*. London: DfE.

DfE (2017) *Statutory Framework for the Early Years Foundation Stage*. London: DfE.

DfES (2007) *Letters and Sounds: Principles and Practice of High Quality Phonics*. London: DfES.

Higgins, S., Xiao, Z. and Katsipataki, M. (2012) *The Impact of Digital Technology on Learning: A Summary for the Education Endowment Foundation*. Education Endowment Foundation (EEF). Available at: https://educationendowmentfoundation.org.uk/public/files/Publications/The_Impact_of_Digital_Technologies_on_Learning_(2012).pdf (accessed 7/18).

Israelson, M. (2015) 'The App Map: A tool for systematic evaluation of apps for early literacy learning', *The Reading Teacher*, 69 (3): 339–49.

Larabee, K., Burns, M. and McComas, J. (2014) 'Effects of an iPad-supported phonics intervention on decoding performance and time on-task', *Journal of Behavior Education*, 23: 449–69.

National Literacy Trust (2018) *What is Literacy?* National Literacy Trust (online). Available at: https://literacytrust.org.uk/information/what-is-literacy/ (accessed 14/6/18).

Northrop, L. and Killeen, E. (2013) 'A framework for using iPads to build early literacy skills', *The Reading Teacher*, 66 (7): 531–7.

O'Callaghan, P., McIvor, A., McVeigh, C. and Rushe, T. (2016) 'A randomised controlled trial of an early-intervention, computer-based literacy program to boost phonological skills in 4 to 6 year old children', *British Journal of Educational Psychology*, 86: 546–58.

OECD (2016) *PISA 2015 Results (Volume I): Excellence and Equity in Education*. PISA: OECD, Paris. http://dx.doi.org/10.1787/9789264266490-en.

Ofsted (2010) *Reading by Six*. London: Paul Chapman.

O'Reilly, F. (2018) 'Using technology to engage reluctant readers and aid writing', in A. Bushnell, R. Smith and D. Waugh, *Modelling Exciting Writing*. London: SAGE.

Rose, J. (2006) *Independent Review of the Teaching of Early Reading, Final Report, March 2006* (The Rose Review – Ref: 0201-2006DOC-EN). Nottingham: DfES.

Shuler, C. (2012) *iLearnII: An Analysis of the Educational Category of the iTunes App Store*. New York: The Joan Ganz Cooney Center at Sesame Workshop.

Conclusion

Reading this book will not make you a good teacher of reading: that's in your own hands. What we hope we have achieved is to have made you think about the factors that contribute to successful teaching of reading.

Part of the pleasure of writing three editions of this book has been taking opportunities to observe outstanding teaching and learning in schools, where qualified teachers' and trainee teachers' enthusiasm and ability to engage and excite children can be inspirational. We've seen lessons in which laughter accompanied learning. We've seen lessons in which children dressed up and dramatised their learning. And we've seen the sheer delight which accompanies children's first attempts at reading sentences on screen and in books and writing their first words. But we haven't just seen: we've listened too.

We've heard teachers talking enthusiastically about each of the phonics programmes described in the final chapter and the impact they have had on children's learning. We've listened to their concerns about some aspects of teaching and learning phonics too. And we've discussed the challenges faced by trainee teachers as they develop their own knowledge and understanding, as well as their pedagogical skills.

Reading this book will not make you a good teacher of reading, but if you consider carefully the strategies described, the subject knowledge which is explained, and the criteria for successful teaching and learning in the context of the excellent practice you will so often find in schools, we hope this book will contribute to your development as a teacher of reading.

Teaching systematic synthetic phonics in itself will not make you a good teacher of reading, unless this is 'securely embedded within a broad and language-rich curriculum' (Rose, 2006, para.35, p.16). The Rose Review has been perceived by some to be simply about phonics, but it is clear that it is about much more. Indeed, Rose emphasises:

> It is widely agreed that phonic work is an essential part, but not the whole picture, of what it takes to become a fluent reader and skilled writer, well capable of comprehending and composing text. Although this review focuses upon phonic work, it is very important to understand what the rest of the picture looks like and requires. For example, nurturing positive attitudes to literacy and the skills associated with them, across the curriculum, is crucially important as is developing spoken language, building vocabulary, grammar, comprehension and facility with ICT.
>
> (2006, para.37, p.16)

So becoming a good teacher of reading involves more than ensuring that children learn, understand and recall grapheme–phoneme correspondences, can blend and segment, and can read 'tricky' or 'common exception' words: it encompasses much more. Perhaps we should keep in mind the reasons why we want children to be successful in learning phonics: without the basic skills in reading, children can be denied access to a wealth of literature, from stories and poems to information texts, both on paper and on screen. They will be unable to participate in most areas of the curriculum, as well as countless other activities, from finding their way around to social networking. It is vital, then, that as teachers we provide rich-language experiences which enable children to see the point of what they learn in phonics sessions.

Through reading to and with children, discussing texts, dramatising stories, labelling our classrooms, providing opportunities for children's interests to be represented in the texts they read, we can make reading and writing real and exciting for them. We can show them why reading is such an important and pleasurable life skill.

Consider for a moment (and please indulge us here!) Harry Kane. Next time you see a games lesson in school, count how many children are wearing a football shirt with his name on the back. These are children who have seen 'the big picture': a football match in which Kane has played. They will also have seen him score with spectacular shots, penalties and headers, and it is these that they so often try to emulate when they play. But to acquire the ability to execute such skills demands more than simply playing in a game. It requires years of practice to develop techniques: techniques that most players will tell you are best developed when training is enjoyable, engaging and takes place in a positive atmosphere.

Now think about reading. Why would children wish to own and read books? Why would they persevere when meeting challenging vocabulary? What do they need to be able to execute the skills necessary to read a book successfully and for pleasure? The phonics sessions that help them to develop these skills underpin their reading ability and need to be enjoyable, engaging and take place in a positive atmosphere. And they need to be set within the 'big picture' of language and reading comprehension: the ultimate goals of reading teaching.

You have seen in this book the importance of fast-paced, multi-sensory lessons which are interactive and engaging. You have read about the importance of structuring lessons effectively and matching learning to children's needs through careful assessment and planning. You know about the value of careful enunciation of phonemes and practice in blending and segmenting. You know how important sound phonemic awareness is when children spell. It is now up to you to use this knowledge and understanding to create opportunities for the children you teach to develop both their ability to decode and their desire to read for understanding.

Good teachers of reading, or of anything else, constantly seek to improve their practice by observing others, discussing strategies and reading the latest research. They reflect upon their teaching and its impact on their pupils, and refine their future teaching as a result. They involve parents in their children's learning and ensure that they, too, understand what their children are learning and why. Good teachers of reading also share their good practice with others and are happy to discuss what they do with trainees and new teachers. They are an invaluable resource for you to draw upon as you develop your teaching.

We are hugely grateful to the teachers whose lessons we've observed and discussed for their contribution to this book. We are very grateful, too, to the trainee teachers who have shared their experiences and allowed us to use them (with pseudonyms) as case studies. Finally, we are grateful to the children, whose enthusiastic response to their teachers' lessons has ensured that the rationale for systematic synthetic phonics has remained firmly at the forefront of our thinking.

Wendy Jolliffe

David Waugh

Angela Gill

Reference

Rose, J. (2006) *Independent Review of the Teaching of Early Reading, Final Report, March 2006* (The Rose Review – Ref: 0201-2006DOC–EN). Nottingham: DfES.

Glossary

Adjacent consonants Consonants which appear next to each other in a word and can be blended together, e.g. *bl* in *blip*, *cr* in *crack* (note that the *ck* in *crack* is a digraph as the consonants come together to form a single sound or phoneme).

Alliteration A sequence of words beginning with the same sound.

Analytic phonics Children learn to identify (analyse) the common phoneme in sets of words in which each word contains the phoneme that is the focus of the lesson. For instance, they might be asked to listen to the words *big*, *bag* and *bat* and decide in what ways the words sound alike.

Blend A combination of letters where individual letters retain their sounds. The consonants retain their original sounds but are blended together as in *slip*, *cram*, *blink* and *flop*.

Blending To draw individual sounds together to pronounce a word, e.g. /c/l/a/p/ blended together reads *clap*.

Common exception words This is the term used in the 2013 English National Curriculum for common words with unusual grapheme–phoneme correspondences. These are the words that *Letters and Sounds* and other phonics programmes refer to as 'tricky words'. They are common words with phonic irregularities, e.g. *one*, *who*, *should*. See also **Tricky words**.

CVC words Consonant–vowel–consonant words. Children's early reading experiences will include words like *cat*, *dog*, *sit* and *pin*, which have single letters for each sound. Later, CVC words will include those with digraphs such as *ship*, *cheap* and *wish*.

Decodable Words which can be easily decoded using phonic strategies, e.g. *cat*, *dog*, *lamp*.

Decoding The act of translating graphemes into phonemes, i.e. reading.

Digraph Two letters which combine to make a new sound.

Encoding The act of transcribing units of sound or phonemes into graphemes, i.e. spelling.

Etymology The origins of the formation of a word and its meaning.

Grapheme A letter, or combination of letters, that represent a phoneme.

Homographs Words which are spelled the same but pronounced differently according to context, e.g. 'That's a new world *record*?', 'I'll *record The Archers* and listen to it later'.

Homonyms Words which are spelled and pronounced in the same way but have different meanings, e.g. *bear*, 'I can't *bear* it any longer', 'The large *bear* growled'.

Homophones Words which sound the same but have different spellings and meanings, e.g. *sea* and *see*, *their* and *there*.

Initial consonant Consonant letter at the beginning of a word.

Kinaesthetic Some people learn better using some form of physical (kinaesthetic) activity: hence the use of actions to accompany phonemes and graphemes in Jolly Phonics.

Long vowel phonemes The long vowel sounds as in *feel* or *cold*.

Mnemonic A device for remembering something, such as '/ee/ee/ feel the tree'.

Monosyllabic word Word with one syllable, e.g. *big, black, club, drop.*

Morpheme The smallest unit of meaning: e.g. *help* is a single morpheme, but we could add the suffix *–ful* to make *helpful*, and go on to add the prefix *un–* to make *unhelpful*, which has three morphemes.

Multi-sensory Using a broad range of senses (hearing, seeing, feeling, moving).

Orthographic system The spelling system of a language, i.e. the ways in which graphemes and phonemes relate to each other. The English orthographic system is more complex than many languages, since most phonemes can be represented by more than one grapheme.

Orthography Standardised spelling – the sounds of a language represented by written or printed symbols.

Phoneme The smallest single identifiable sound, e.g. the letters *ch* representing one sound.

Phonetics The articulation and acoustic features of speech sounds. It explains the distinction between consonants and vowels and can help listeners identify the phonemic pattern of words.

Prefix Morpheme or affix placed before a word to modify its meaning, e.g. *dis–* in *dislike*, *de–* in *defrost*.

Rhyme Words that sound the same but do not necessarily share the same spelling.

Segmenting Splitting up a word into its individual phonemes in order to spell it, i.e. the word *pat* has three phonemes: /p/a/t/.

Split digraph Two letters, making one sound, e.g. *a-e* as in *cake*.

Suffix Morpheme or affix added to a word to modify its meaning, e.g. *–ful* in *hopeful*, *–ed* in *jumped*.

Syllable A unit of pronunciation having one vowel sound. This can be taught by identifying 'beats' in a word. Putting a hand flat underneath your chin and then saying a word can help, as every time the hand moves it represents another syllable.

Synthetic phonics Synthetic phonics involves separating words into phonemes and then blending the phonemes together to read the word. This compares with analytic phonics in which segments or parts of words are analysed and patterns are compared with other words.

Tricky words When teaching systematic synthetic phonics, we refer to common words with phonic irregularities as 'tricky words', e.g. *once, was, could*. See also **Common exception words**.

Trigraph Three letters which combine to make a new sound.

Model answers to self-assessment questions

Chapter 1

1. Phonological awareness often embraces the term 'phonemic awareness' – why is this and what is the difference between phonological and phonemic awareness?

    'Phonological awareness' refers to the ability to hear and discriminate sounds in language generally, whereas 'phonemic awareness' refers to the ability to perceive and manipulate individual phonemes in spoken words.

2. Name some ways in which adults can improve their ability to segment words into the constituent phonemes.

    Making use of a phoneme chart; ensuring that the words are said clearly and slowly; awareness of consonant blends where consonant letters placed at the beginning and end of words are blended together; focusing on the sounds and not the spelling when counting phonemes or segmenting words into phonemes; referring to the international phonetic alphabet.

3. How can phonological awareness be effectively developed in children?

    The use of activities such as phoneme frames, 'phoneme fingers', phonemes buttons.

4. How can any confusion between letter names and sounds be avoided?

    Emphasise the need to differentiate clearly between letter names and sounds so as to not confuse the two and ensure that letters have a name and a sound.

5. State some reasons for the link between vocabulary and phonological awareness.

    Research suggests that gradually there is a restructuring of phonological representations of words from 'holistic' to 'segmental' representations, or phonemes, which serve to differentiate between word meanings. It is therefore important to develop children's vocabulary alongside their phonics skills.

Chapter 2

1. What do we mean by correct enunciation of phonemes?

    We will help children to blend or synthesis phonemes if we sound the phonemes 'cleanly' without adding additional vowel sounds, e.g. for /s/ we should sound *sss* rather than *suh*.

2. What is a *schwa* sound and why should we try, wherever possible, to avoid using it when pronouncing phonemes?

In English many words include a *schwa* sound, which is an unstressed vowel sound, e.g. doctor, teacher, data. However, this should be avoided when sounding phonemes (see above). This is relatively easy to avoid for phonemes such as /f/ (ffff), /l/ (llll) and /m/ (mmmm), but more difficult for phonemes such as /b/ and /d/. If we sound phonemes adding a *schwa,* children can find it difficult to blend (e.g. *suh-a-tuh* does not form *sat* as easily as *ssss-a-t*). Children's spelling can also become confused with letters used to indicate both consonants and vowels, as in *cl* representing *colour.*

3.   What is a split vowel digraph?

In a digraph, two letters make one sound. Where these two letters are vowels and are separated by a consonant as in *same, fine* and *tube,* we call them a 'split vowel' digraph.

Chapter 3

See Table 3.4, p.55.

The following words might be described as 'tricky' or including 'tricky' parts:

- *water* – because children may have learned the split vowel digraph *a-e* as making an /ae/ sound and could, therefore, misread the words as *waiter*;

- *would* – because the *–ould* letter string is rarely found except in *should* and *could*;

- *bear* – because children initially learn that *ea* makes an /ee/ sound as in *meet*;

- *everyone* – because *one* begins with a /w/ sound which is represented by an *o*;

- *find* – because the *i* is long and children tend to learn the short version first, as in *pin*;

- *magic* – because the *g* is soft and children learn the hard *g* as in *get* first;

- *who* – because the initial /h/ sound is represented by *wh*;

- *two* – because it has an almost unique representation of the /oo/ sound;

- *thought* – one of several words which have *–ough* as a letter string, but this can be pronounced in a variety of ways such as *cough, dough, rough, bough, although, through* and even *hiccough (hiccup)*;

- *want* and *wanted* – because the *a* is pronounced as an /o/ sound; however, many words beginning with *w* and followed by *a* have a similar sound, e.g. *wash, watch, wander* and *wasp*;

- *going* – because children may have learned the vowel digraph *oi* as an /oy/ sound;

- *school* – because the *ch* represents a /k/ sound rather than a *ch* sound as in *chip*;

- *has* – because the *s* has a /z/ sound, although children will meet other words in the most common 100 which have a similar sound, e.g. *his, as, was*;

- *other* – because the *o* has an /u/ sound;

- *where* – because the *wh* has a *w* sound, although this is common to many frequently used words such as *why, what, when* and *which*;

- *know* – because the /n/ sound is represented by *kn.*

Can you define each of the following terms, which feature in this and previous chapters?

1. Grapheme

   A letter, or combination of letters that represent a phoneme.

2. Phoneme

   The smallest single identifiable sound, e.g. the letters *sh* representing one sound.

3. Synthetic phonics

   Synthetic phonics involves separating words into phonemes and then blending the phonemes together to read the word. This compares with analytic phonics in which segments or parts of words are analysed and patterns are compared with other words.

4. Decodable

   Decodable words can be easily decoded using phonic strategies, e.g. *run, blink, frog.*

5. 'Tricky' or common exception word

   When teaching systematic synthetic phonics, we refer to common words with phonic irregularities as 'tricky words', e.g. *once, was, could.*

6. Orthographic system

   The spelling system of a language, i.e. the ways in which graphemes and phonemes relate to each other.

Chapter 4

1. Outline the inter-relationship between segmenting and blending phonemes.

   Segmenting and blending are intimately connected in both reading and spelling, and it is not the case that one relates to reading, the other spelling. To read a word, a child sounds out each phoneme and then blends them into a word and checks the outcome. To spell a word, the child says a word, hears each segment in sequence and blends the segments into the word as they write. The processes are inter-connected and it is crucial when teaching young children that we make this explicit by providing opportunities to both read and write graphemes for the corresponding phonemes during every phonics teaching session.

2. What are some of the difficulties in the English spelling system?

    In comparison with many other languages, English has an opaque spelling system with multiple spellings for the same phoneme and multiple ways to decode letters and letter sequences. Other languages, e.g. Finnish, have a highly regular and transparent spelling system which can be learned in approximately one year.

3. What is the role of decodable texts in the teaching of reading?

    Decodable texts provide vital practice for children in reading known phonemes and blending into words. They contain words that are at an appropriate phonemic level for children to decode.

Chapter 5

1. Explain the difference between the basic and advanced alphabetic code.

    The basic code consists of learning one spelling choice for each of the 40+ sounds. The advanced code involves mastering the multiple spellings for each phoneme.

2. Why do the long vowel phonemes cause difficulties for teaching and learning phonics?

    One of the main reasons why long vowel phonemes are complex is that there is a range of alternative spellings for each phoneme.

3. Name ways in which this difficulty can be supported.

    This can be done through: incorporating actions in teaching; including mnemonics, songs/raps and rhymes; building a chart as you teach each grapheme–phoneme correspondence to show the phonemes and their alternative spellings; and using visual prompts for each grapheme–phoneme correspondence.

Chapter 6

1. Morpheme

    The smallest unit of meaning, e.g. *help* is a single morpheme, but we could add the suffix *–ful* to make *helpful*, and go on to add the prefix *un–* to make *unhelpful*, which has three morphemes.

2. Etymology

    The origins of the formation of a word and its meaning.

3. Homonym

    Words that are spelled and pronounced in the same way but have different meanings, e.g. *bear*: 'I can't *bear* it any longer', 'The large *bear* growled'.

4. Homophone

Words that sound the same but have different spellings and meanings, e.g. *sea* and *see*, *their* and *there*.

5. Prefix

Morpheme or affix placed before a word to modify its meaning, e.g. *dis–* in *dislike, de–* in *defrost*.

6. Suffix

Morpheme or affix added to a word to modify its meaning, e.g. *–ful* in *hopeful, –ed* in *jumped*.

Chapter 7

1. Name some ways in which play can support children's early literacy development.

   Supporting phonological awareness starts with playing with sounds with babies to tune young children into language. As children develop, providing informal activities linked to print, in the indoor and the outdoor classroom, helps children link sounds to letters. Providing a language-rich environment with the interaction of responsive adults will support literacy development.

2. How can practitioners make meaningful links between home and school to support literacy development?

   Practitioners should aim to tune in to genuine home literacy practices, without making any cultural or middle-class assumptions, and encourage activities which are brought from nursery to home, e.g. by incorporating media texts.

3. How can resources support fun engaging ways of teaching phonics to young children?

   The following provide enjoyable and engaging ways to support phonics teaching: using rhymes and songs; using puppets; providing individual whiteboards for application of grapheme–phoneme correspondences taught in writing and reading; using magnetic letters and magnetic whiteboards for kinaesthetic activities, physically manipulating letters to create words.

Chapter 8

1. Multi-sensory

   Using a broad range of senses (hearing, seeing, feeling, moving).

2. Kinaesthetic

   Using some form of physical (kinaesthetic) activity to accompany learning, such as the actions to accompany phonemes and graphemes in Jolly Phonics.

Chapter 9

1. Refer to the first case study, 'Systematic and structured phonics teaching'; which of the programmes reflect the criteria for systematic synthetic programmes (DfE, 2011)?

    Programmes 2 and 5 reflect the criteria for systematic synthetic programmes.

2. What grapheme–phoneme correspondences (GPCs) are commonly taught first?

    The commonly taught GPCs are certain consonants and short vowels (commonly *s*, *a*, *t*, *p*, *i*, *n*) that enable the blending of these into CVC words from the outset.

3. Why are some high-frequency words taught alongside a systematic teaching of GPCs?

    A small number of high-frequency words that children will encounter in most texts are complex to decode and are introduced and taught commonly at a rate of three to five per week.

4. What GPCs are commonly taught in the later stages?

    Long vowel phonemes and alternative pronunciations and spellings for graphemes are taught in later stages.

Chapter 10

1. Name the four elements that should be contained in a structured phonics lesson, as highlighted in *Letters and Sounds*.

    The four elements of a well-structured phonics session are: revisit and review, teach, practise and apply.

2. How can each lesson incorporate applications in reading and writing of phonics skills?

    Ensure that every lesson includes opportunities to read and write sentences containing key phonemes and words from the teaching element of the session. This may also involve playing games or reading and writing sentences containing key phonemes and words taught.

3. What kind of activities will support multi-sensory teaching?

    Ensure that each lesson incorporates hearing, saying, reading and writing grapheme–phoneme correspondences.

4. How can differentiation be successfully achieved?

    The most effective way of differentiating phonics teaching is through grouping children by ability and regularly regrouping based on ongoing assessment.

Chapter 11

1. Name some ways in which teachers can clearly note children's progress during lessons.

    Providing regular opportunities for children to demonstrate their understanding, e.g. by writing letters or words on a whiteboard. In addition, careful analysis of children's independent writing can demonstrate their growing understanding.

2. Name a method of testing children's ability to blend phonemes.

    Asking children to read 'non-words' is useful in testing their knowledge of phonemes taught, making it clear that they are nonsense words.

3. Consider how a tracking grid to note children's progress could inform the organisation of teaching.

    A system of recording children's progress on a grid can inform ability grouping and regrouping. It can also help identify those children in need of additional support or intervention.

Chapter 12

Can you define each of the following terms which have been used in this chapter?

1. Adjacent consonants

    Consonants which appear next to each other in a word and can be blended together, e.g. *bl* in *blip*, *cr* in *crack* (note that the *ck* in *crack* is a digraph as the consonants come together to form a single sound or phoneme).

2. Monosyllabic words

    Words with one syllable, e.g. *big, black, club, drop.*

3. Etymology

    The origins of the formation of a word and its meaning.

Chapter 13

You were asked to reflect on your ability to do each of the items below and to consider what additional knowledge, understanding and experiences you require to enable you to be confident in your ability to make effective use of systematic synthetic phonics programmes. Some suggestions for additional knowledge, understanding and experiences are provided.

1. Support children in learning phonic knowledge and skills using a systematic, synthetic programme, with the expectation that they will be fluent readers having secured word recognition skills by the end of Key Stage 1.

    - Find out more about different systematic synthetic phonics programmes, their teaching sequences and pedagogical styles.

    - Ensure that you can enunciate phonemes correctly.

    - Observe experienced teachers and discuss the way in which they plan, teach and assess.

2. Plan for and teach discrete, daily sessions of phonics, progressing from simple to more complex phonic knowledge and skills and covering the major grapheme–phoneme correspondences.

    - Observe experienced teachers.

    - Look at examples of lesson plans in school and in teachers' handbooks for systematic synthetic phonics programmes.

    - Find out and discuss the progression in the systematic synthetic phonics programmes you will be using.

3. Assess children's progress in phonic knowledge and skill.

    - Discuss with teachers the approaches they use for assessment.

    - Find out about both formal and informal assessments.

    - Find out about national tests, such as screening at Year 1.

4. Use a multi-sensory approach so that children learn variously from simultaneous visual, auditory and kinaesthetic activities which are designed to secure essential phonic knowledge and the skills of blending and segmenting.

    - Observe experienced teachers.

    - Look for ideas in manuals and workbooks from systematic synthetic phonics programmes.

    - Share ideas with colleagues.

    - Find out more about the children with whom you will be working to ensure that you plan to take into account their particular needs.

5. Teach how phonemes can be blended, in order, from left to right, 'all through the word' for reading.

- Observe experienced teachers.
- Practise with colleagues.
- Watch video examples of teachers.

6. Teach how to segment words into their constituent phonemes for spelling and that this is the reverse of blending phonemes to read words.

- Observe experienced teachers.
- Practise with colleagues.
- Watch video examples of teachers.

7. Teach children to apply phonic knowledge and skills as their first approach to reading and spelling even if a word is not completely phonically regular.

- Discuss strategies with experienced teachers.
- Observe experienced teachers.
- Ask if you can work with individuals and small groups of children before working with the whole class so that you can focus on pedagogy before having to focus on class management as well.

8. Teach high-frequency words that do not conform completely to grapheme–phoneme correspondence rules.

- Look at the strategies suggested by the systematic synthetic phonics programmes.
- Look at Chapter 3 of this book for guidance.
- Ensure that you can identify the 'tricky' parts of words – what may seem simple to you may be challenging for a child who is not at the appropriate stage to be able to decode some words.

9. Teach to the systematic teaching framework of the programmes they are working with.

- Discuss with experienced teachers.
- Read teachers' manuals.
- Ensure that you are familiar with the resources for the systematic synthetic phonics programmes.

10. When children are in the early stages of learning phonics, use decodable texts of the appropriate level where children can apply and practise the phonic knowledge and skills they have learned and can experience success by relying on phonemic blending. They should not be expected to use strategies such as whole-word recognition and/or cues from context, grammar or pictures.

- Look at any resources which are provided with the systematic synthetic phonics programmes and make use of these at appropriate stages.

- Consider creating your own texts, but discuss these with colleagues to ensure that they are appropriate.

Look at other examples of decodable texts from reading schemes and consider if any are appropriate for the children with whom you are working.

Index